WITHDRAWN

THE
EDUCATION
OF A
NAVY

THE EDUCATION OF A NAVY

The development of British naval strategic thought, 1867-1914

D. M. SCHURMAN

THE UNIVERSITY OF CHICAGO PRESS

Library of Congress Catalog Card Number: 65-24982

THE UNIVERSITY OF CHICAGO PRESS, CHICAGO
The University of Toronto Press, Toronto 5, Canada
© 1965 by D. M. Schurman
All rights reserved
Published 1965
Printed in Great Britain

PREFACE

The Royal Military College of Canada offers a full academic course in naval history to its Cadets. For the past eight years, I have taught that course. As a result, my interest has been aroused in the origins of naval history as a specialized, sophisticated, academic discipline. Over the years, the Gentlemen Cadets have stimulated and sustained that interest. This book is the result.

However, it has not been my intention to write a text book for undergraduates. It is, of course, addressed to naval historians. But it is to be hoped that it will also interest people concerned with the formulation and exposition of military policy. The following pages do not detail exact parallels between the past and the present, but they do reveal important similarities. The historians described in this book were interpreting the naval age of sail to the naval age of steam. They addressed sailors and strategists pre-occupied with keeping abreast of the latest developments in military hardware in a revolutionary age. The historians did not always, or even generally, convince their machine-minded contemporaries of the value of historical perspective and traditions in the process of formulating military policy; but in retrospect it does not appear that the historians were the impractical people. Certainly, the parallels between that age of technological change and our own strike one forcibly.

It has also been my intention to arouse the particular interest of those sailor-scholars of whom Sir Herbert Richmond was such an outstanding example in his own time. I have had the good fortune to meet with some men of this type in both the Royal and the Royal Canadian Navies. Although they necessarily only comprise a small proportion of their service, their value to their country is out of all proportion to their numbers. It is my hope that some budding Richmond will find this book useful.

To write the history of naval historians may be an inbred occupa-

PREFACE

tion, but it has been a revealing one. It has shown me that military and naval historians have no cause to be ashamed of their craft, and good reason to look back with pride on their predecessors, all of whom were able, and some of whom were great historians.

Finally, it is important that historians in general should try to understand the age of steam, and the way people reacted to it. To appreciate the over-all mentality of the naval age of steam, it is as useful to know about Mahan and Corbett as it is to possess knowledge concerning torpedoes and Dreadnaughts. This book will assist those who wish to establish such a rapport.

My thanks are due to Mr. John Spurr and his staff at the Massey Library, R.M.C. The great resources of the library in naval history material, and the courteous help I have had from the staff, especially from Mr. C. R. Watt, have greatly eased the burden of research.

I have also to acknowledge, with gratitude, the kindness of Mr. Geoffrey Snagge, who made the John Colomb papers available to me, and to Lady Gwendaline Snagge and Mr. John D. M. Snagge, who provided me with both material and reminiscences. The Social Science Research Council provided me with a Grant for Study in England in the Summer of 1957, when much of the material was gathered.

I am grateful to the Public Records Office for access to the Carnarvon Papers; to the National Maritime Museum for access to the Richmond Papers; to the Library of Congress for access to the Mahan Papers. I must also acknowledge my debt to Professor Arthur J. Marder, whose book on Richmond has saved me much manuscript research, and whose published works have laid the groundwork for anyone writing on British naval history between 1880 and 1914.

Parts of the book were read by Mr. A. W. H. Pearsall of the National Maritime Museum, Mr. J. D. P. Martin, the Librarian of Trent University, and Dr. Jay Luvaas of Allegheny College. My colleague, Dr. Richard A. Preston read the whole of the first draft, and gave advice on parts of the second draft. His acute criticisms have saved me from many errors. Mr. W. C. B. Tunstall has read the first draft and suggested changes. He made the Corbett Papers available to me, and discussions with him, and with his wife Elizabeth, have been most helpful.

Most of the typing was done by Miss K. Robb, Secretary to the History Department at R.M.C., assisted by Miss Kathleen Macdonald, and my wife, Janice; to all of whom I extend gratitude.

I wish to thank Surgeon Captain Harvey Little, R.C.N. (Retd), Mr. George E. C. Porter, and my family—for special encouragement in different ways.

Donald M. Schurman

The Royal Military College of Canada

April, 1965

CONTENTS

1. *Influences on Naval Writing*   1
2. *Imperial Naval Strategist:* CAPTAIN SIR JOHN COLOMB   16
3. *Clio and the Admiral:* VICE-ADMIRAL PHILIP COLOMB   36
4. *The American:* ADMIRAL ALFRED MAHAN   60
5. *The Editor:* SIR JOHN LAUGHTON   83
6. *Historian in Uniform:* ADMIRAL SIR HERBERT RICHMOND   116
7. *Civilian Historian:* SIR JULIAN CORBETT   147

   Epilogue   185

   Bibliographical Note   193

   Index   199

for Janice

1

INFLUENCES ON NAVAL WRITING

THIS book is about a small group of men who in something under fifty years changed British naval history from a patriotic antiquarian pastime into a serious academic occupation, with rules, standards, and techniques of its own. Until 1867, naval history, other than a record of battles, could hardly be said to have existed. By 1914 not only was naval history popular with naval romantics and patriotic alarmists but it had also begun to influence the calculations of the naval policy makers, and claimed the serious attention of scholars in the universities. In addition naval historians, publicists, antiquarians and naval writers in general formed their own society for the publication of naval documents. Why and how did this transformation take place, and why did it take place at this particular time?

It occurred because of a change in attitudes in and surrounding the naval service, and because the naval revival was conterminous with the birth of modern history. These features merit some introductory discussion.

Although the first of these naval writers, John Colomb, did begin to write in 1867, the rest of them only began to write books after 1884, and it was only after 1890, when Mahan's first book was published, that a steady growth, both in productivity and in refinement in historical method, occurred. This more intense literary activity was paralleled by, and no doubt responsive to, increased public interest in naval affairs generally. Thus public interest gave rise to increased naval building activity that had its most prominent expression in the Naval Defence Act of 1889.[1] It is, of course,

[1] The details of British naval policy have been competently set out and discussed in detail over the period 1882 to 1914 by Professor Arthur J. Marder in *British Naval Policy* (London, 1941), and *From the Dreadnought to Scapa Flow* (Oxford, 1961). All naval historians of this period are in Professor Marder's debt.

obvious that the resultant increased tempo of ship construction also owed much to fears aroused by foreign building programmes, both over the Atlantic and across the English Channel, but in addition it owed something to the age of radical alteration in basic ship design having come to an end. For almost the whole of the previous fifty years the Admiralty had been preoccupied with problems of ship design, and those who pushed the claims of the machine age slowly towards a position of dominance found their opponents, not amongst great strategic thinkers or historians, for there were none, but rather in the ranks of the older admirals and other officers to whom the sailing navy was, for understandable reasons, a sacred cow.

This internal struggle in the navy between the innovators and the conservative sailors, together with the uncertainties about ship design that fostered it, was used by the politicians of both parties after 1865 to keep naval budgets low. In fact naval expenses did not increase between 1865 and 1885. Generally speaking what reporting on the state of the navy that filtered through to Press and Parliament during these years was either confined to debates on the relative usefulness of various warship designs, or emerged as a result of the convenient habit of judging the efficiency of the Royal Navy on the basis of a straight comparison on paper between the numbers of available continental warships with the numbers of those existing in Great Britain. The comparison was invariably quantitative rather than qualitative. These calculations were hastily concocted for the politicians from time to time and their purpose was to still discussion and silence criticism. Politicians, who wished to maintain party standing by reference to low expenditure, and naval officers, who wished to be regarded as efficient despite the fact that they were starved for funds, each had something to gain from this mode of proceeding.[2]

However, the swift acceleration of the age of imperialism that induced military competition, together with the growing disgruntlement within the service evident after 1880, was bound to produce a reaction. This occurred in the naval scare of 1884, and the revelations made at that time began that era of increased public interest that finally brought about the startling increases that began in 1889. Moreover, the increased demands made on the navy

---

Although parts of this introduction re-treads part of the ground he has traversed this has been done to give the characters in this book a background, and not in an attempt to re-assess either his conclusions or his research.

[2] One example of this, among many, may be found in Sir John H. Briggs's *Naval Administration, 1827–1892* (London, 1897), p. 214–19.

coincided with the end of the design experiment stage to an extent that allowed the naval builders virtually a free hand.[3] The unexpected benefits of that much flogged horse, 'Treasury control', could hardly be better illustrated.

Thus as the imperialists, militarists and shipyard industrialists stood at the threshold of the coming age of feverish naval building they were at last face to face with the problem of what national purpose all the proposed ships were to serve. It is true that the notorious two-power standard served as a rule-of-thumb guide but the navy had become both expensive and newsworthy; and it was bound under these circumstances to engage the public attention in a way that would have been unthinkable in 1880.

With the increase in public interest, naval writers were assured of a market for naval books. Moreover, stability in warship type allowed them to consider strategic problems realistically since they now knew, within limits, the nature of the counters on the board upon which the games of the next war were to be placed. It is significant that John Colomb, the earliest of the writers, was concerned much more with the over-all strategy than he was with tactics, and that when he dealt with the problem of filling ships' bunkers with coal to keep them operational he very seldom attempted to differentiate between ship classes and functions. This was natural because of the state of flux of the ship-design situation at the time his early writings reached their limited public. Later writers, however, could write with actual types and classes of warships firmly in mind, and in the case of historians they could make comparisons with vessels which they regarded as having performed similar functions during the age of sail.

The era of technical change had set up other barriers to the utilization of history in naval debate. In the past the warship had been the sail-decked man-of-war, of which the three-decker was the supreme expression. It is not surprising then that when the three-decker vanished from view, the story of her accomplishments began to appear irrelevant. To the sailor, and probably to the politician as well, the end of the three-decker meant the end of naval history. Viewed from this angle the lack of naval historians before 1885 is not difficult to understand. Thus the need for naval historians and the study of naval history was only gradually appreciated.

During this period ships were developed that progressively

[3] The *Royal Sovereign* class of battleship represented a new high in the development of the battleship type. See O. Parkes, *British Battleships*, (London, 1957), p. 356.

could steam faster, hit harder, hit more accurately, and take more punishment. The value of the new ships was gauged from a limited point of view. It was felt that each new vessel must be more technically advanced than her national predecessor or her foreign competitor. Nevertheless the question of what the new sea monsters really existed for, either in classes or as a total navy, was difficult to answer by this method of proceeding. Under what circumstances would a new war be fought? Who would be the probable enemy? What would be the general tactical pattern for future battles? Finally, and most important, what would be the main strategic features of the next war? Certainly the answers to these vital questions did not all emerge at once or easily, and this lack of fundamental strategic thought was due in large measure to the natural technical preoccupations of the Admiralty in the transition period. Men with minds much more rigidly bound by mathematical data and measurement than are even those of the present day were ignorant of, and when they met it impatient with, the reflective quality behind the historical knowledge that assists accurate strategic planning. Indeed the great characteristic of the majority of those who approached science with professional eyes in the nineteenth century was their preoccupation with means rather than ends. Technical developments were vital to naval growth, yet they were not in themselves sufficient to guarantee real fleet efficiency in the light of national purpose.[4]

That it took some time for the limitations of the purely scientific, or inventive, approach to naval calculation to reveal themselves is not difficult to understand if one concentrates attention on the 1860–85 era. In an age like ours, where science builds on itself so rapidly that no one can claim to keep abreast with more than a few specialist developments in depth, the 'all-round', or general scientist, is either non-existent or else a very rare creature. In the middle of the nineteenth century this was not the case. A person who might be called the universal scientific man, that is one who read and understood most of the important scientific periodicals, books and pamphlets, could and did function in the eighteen-sixties. By 1885 the proliferation of scientific publications was such that real specialization and compartmentalism of scientific thought was forced upon most scientists and technicians. In naval terms this can be best illustrated by the history of the development of naval artillery. During this period iron guns cast in one

[4] These attitudes were invariably displayed in discussions following non-technical papers at the Royal United Service Institution during the period 1870–90.

Influences on Naval Writing

piece, firing solid shot by a constant ignition and powder combination were replaced by a rifled, breach-loading, mechanically sighted, machined-steel gun that fired an explosive armour-piercing projectile. Even the projectile was a complicated mechanism in its own right. The technical specialists necessary to accomplish these changes naturally increased in numbers and they also naturally tended to concentrate more and more on particular technical details. This proliferation of progressively specialized technical experts on the material side of the naval service had its natural counterpart in preoccupation with material at the Admiralty. This tendency was heightened because naval change at this time was a part of the second industrial revolution. The intensity of this involvement can be seen clearly if one reflects that the army, right up until 1914, moved largely by horse and foot power: that is, to use a naval comparison, it still worked in the climate that the navy equated with the age of sail. As we have seen, to the go-ahead navalists, steam had abolished sail and therefore there was no useful place for the naval history of sail in the steam age. All that the past had to offer was the continuity of tradition, and patriotic inspiration that stemmed from the recounting of heroic deeds of the steam navy's sail ancestors. Indeed, one of the navy's difficulties was that it was abreast of modern developments and responsive to industrial progress. Hence a situation had developed where the very success of the naval technology tended to reduce over-all thinking about the purpose of the ships designed. Material change called forth material change and most people naturally accepted this specialization that they did not understand, since it seemed eminently plausible, as it still does today, to say 'naval affairs are scientific—leave them in the hands of the experts'. Yet it can be seen in retrospect that there was a need for other kinds of thinkers and eventually one response to this call occurred in the form of naval history.

It will become apparent in the course of these pages that naval history became both more perceptive and more accurate with the passage of time and the work of the practitioners described. But there can be no doubt that the original impulse that sent these men to history books and archives partly stemmed from a dissatisfaction with the narrowing technical viewpoint within the service.

The naval writers attempted to alter this by turning to the past to find guiding 'principles' or rules to help understand a bewildering present. There were lessons to be learned from the past. What lessons? Obviously, and as has been indicated, it would be hard to convince the naval officers and their political masters of the technological age that the history of wind-propelled ships smashing at one another at point-blank range had anything of a tactical or strategic pattern to offer the shell-firing, screw-propelled navy that would fight at ever opening ranges. Since this kind of description was the most prominent characteristic of what passed for naval history up to that point it became incumbent upon those who would instruct through the use of past example to determine just what was the real history, as opposed to the popular romantic history, of the old navy. Had the navy been the only service in Great Britain in the latter half of the nineteenth century, the rediscovery of naval history in detail might have been long delayed. However, the increased interest in naval affairs already described, together with the interest in naval affairs generated by Admiralty rivalry with the War Office for more money, did stimulate such a search of the past. Once the historians unearthed sufficient factual background they began to show what strategy in the sailing ship era really had been—and to assert that it still applied to sea warfare in the steam age. Again, the new naval history had no traditions and the embryo naval historians and naval writers of the industrial age had to face the fact that history itself was not as yet an accepted academic discipline.

The proliferation of historians, searching farther and farther into the past on increasingly specialized paths of endeavour that is so common today, was not a feature of the academic landscape in the late nineteenth century. History grew up outside the universities and then crashed the conservative academic portals, not the other way around as might at first appear to be most likely. Of the six men discussed in this book only two, Laughton and Corbett, had university degrees (both Cambridge) one in Mathematics and the other in Law. If they had desired to read History, and there is no evidence that they did, they could not have done so because there was no such thing as an Historical Tripos in the Cambridge of their undergraduate days.

The naval historians, then, were not specialist deviationists from an established path of activity. They were very much part of the general birth and development of serious, more scientific, history, and, although it is true that they were undoubtedly called forth by the special contemporary needs of the naval service, they developed and practised their craft along similar lines to those followed by the new general school of historians of which they were a natural part.

If the naval writers were influenced by the concurrent general rise of history to respectability, they were also shaped by their dependence upon the outlets available for the public and semi-private expression of their views. This was particularly the case with the two Colombs and Laughton who first reached a wider public through the Royal Colonial Institute and the Royal United Service Institution.

The Royal Colonial Institute, now the Royal Commonwealth Society, was founded in 1868. It provided, as it still does, a meeting place for men interested in Colonial (now Imperial or Commonwealth) affairs. Englishmen wishing to increase their knowledge of 'Britain overseas' as well as colonists wishing to make English contacts found the Institute useful. Aside from a hard core of armchair imperialists who have always haunted the site, the Institute has been constantly stimulated by a changing stream of visitors from overseas, and the intermittent interest of prominent and intelligent Englishmen. For this changing audience the Institute provided a regular series of lectures and discussions that were subsequently printed in the Institute's *Proceedings*. The nature of the topics, the quality of the papers and the importance of the audience all varied enormously. John Colomb was a frequent speaker at the Institute and for over thirty years he delivered talks on his general theme of Imperial Defence. A good proportion of the audience at the Institute was military. Soldiers were the most numerous of all imperial employees, and if they looked at the Empire from a specialist angle they nevertheless had usually seen more of it, and knew more about it, than any other specialist group. The army members were not generally influential soldiers since, Lord Roberts apart, the road to high rank did not customarily pass through Delhi, Cape Town, Victoria, Wellington or Ottawa. Naval men were more representative though less frequent visitors. That is to say the Institute people were not usually men who could directly influence policy. Nevertheless the R.C.I. was an important launching pad for the navalists, especially as the papers given at meetings were subsequently published. The influence of John Colomb's talks in the seventies, for instance, is to be found in the kind of thought senior men produced in 1900, rather than in its immediate appeal when delivered.[5]

More important was the influence not only on the Colombs but on all nineteenth-century naval writers of the Royal United

[5] The Royal Colonial Institute is discussed in detail in A. Folsom's *The Royal Empire Society* (London, 1933).

Service Institution.[6] At this Institution member officers of both the army and navy met monthly to give papers on various aspects of military life, thought and development. In the eighteen-sixties and -seventies the bulk of these papers were of a technical nature, but papers on tactical and even strategic questions were occasionally given as well. The rostrum was not confined to officers of high rank. Indeed the annual competitive prize essay was often competed for and won by a comparatively junior officer. Also the discussion of this prize essay was thorough and generally occupied two Institute sessions. However, the Institute meetings were often attended by persons of very high rank indeed. At a time when Imperial Defence was receiving much publicity in the Press and Parliament the Commander-in-Chief himself, H.R.H. the Duke of Cambridge, took the chair for one of Captain John Colomb's papers.[7] If the Chairman was not necessarily a supporter of the lecturer's views, his presence was an indication of the topical importance of the subject. Admiral Sir Astley Cooper-Key heard John Knox Laughton lecture at the R.U.S.I.,[8] and a few years later when Key became First Sea Lord he was able and willing to assist Laughton's need for restricted historical documents to study—documents under Admiralty control. These are isolated instances but they do show the importance of the Institute as a means of influencing people in military positions of power. In the same way the Institute was one of the places where differences between the services were aired and, as Admiral Philip Colomb's experience showed, it was often the case that a strong naval paper would provoke an answering one from the soldiers. The Institute, therefore, also made possible some dialogue between the services—even if it was competitive rather than co-operative.

The Institute provided the only important arena where purely military problems could be discussed intellectually and in a moderately open way. For its devotees it was a propaganda machine and a substitute for a war college. Men who could not turn to the universities for help in solving modern problems turned to it for informed discussion. Indeed the R.U.S.I. was, despite a certain ineptness in the comparison, the university of the services. It was due to the Colombs and other like-minded men who fol-

[6] These impressions of *The Royal United Service Institution* are derived from wide reading in the Institution's *Journal* over the period discussed. Hereafter referred to as R.U.S.I.

[7] At a meeting held on 31 May, 1886. See J. C. R. Colomb, 'Imperial Federation—Naval amd Military', *R.U.S.I. Journal* (1886), p. 1.

[8] On 22 July, 1874. See J. K. Laughton, 'The Scientific Study of Naval History', *R.U.S.I. Journal* (1874), pp. 18–20.

lowed them that there was some discussion of what armies and weapons were for, and that time was not all spent discussing how armies and weapons worked.

The R.U.S.I. also had a library that provided the general factual basis on which much of the discussion took place. In the same way that the library of the Royal Colonial Institute was useful for its superb collection of colonial information, so the R.U.S.I. library was useful to the military minded. In addition the R.U.S.I. became, with the passage of time, a recognized repository for the papers of military men.

The naval writers and most especially Laughton were able to gain practice in documentary research through their work for the *Encyclopaedia Britannica* and the *Dictionary of National Biography*. The latter volumes were in preparation in the eighties and nineties. This sent contributors to the manuscript material and official records to obtain precise information on the great sailors selected for inclusion and also brought them into close contact with other historians. Hence established historians such as S. R. Gardiner and J. A. Froude joined the navalists as members of the Navy Records Society when that body was founded. A further effect of these projects was to bring naval writers into contact with editors who wielded influence and had money at their disposal. The most important examples of these scholarly associations were Mahan's contacts with *Scribner's Magazine* in the United States, Laughton's long association with the *Edinburgh Review* and its editor, Henry Reeve, and Corbett's important association with the *Monthly Review* when Henry Newbolt was its editor. The work of the naval writers was accepted at two levels: one involved questions of the day and comments on current naval policy; the other level involved *belles lettres* writing concerned with reviews of current historical works and the furnishing of actual articles on interesting naval history subjects. It would be hard to exaggerate the power of nineteenth-century periodical editors as promoters and selectors of serious thought.

The political background to this era of naval history has been written before, but emphasis must be given to political attitudes to defence spending since these attitudes had a direct bearing on the work of the naval historians. The twenty-five years immediately prior to 1884 were years of careful budgeting, and, whenever possible, years when reductions in military expenditures were attempted. During that time the careful spending habits that found their highest expression in the methods of W. E. Gladstone controlled the extent of service planning. Yet the era after 1884

B

was a time of imperial and consequently military expansion. Thus the expansionist tendencies of the imperialist age came into direct conflict with the accumulated habit of regarding small-budgets as virtuous phenomena in themselves. This rivalry continued right up until 1914, although of course the small-budget men were progressively worsted owing to the forcing pace of the internationally competitive atmosphere. Nevertheless the very fact that these tensions existed allowed naval writers to play a vital and unique role. The saner heads in the light-budget school required that adequate defences be provided for the least possible money. The military planners, on the other hand, either advocated large defence spending generally or, and more frequently, argued the case that best results would flow from the allocation of what limited resources existed to promote the development of a particular service, or even a particular weapon. Yet both points of view had in common the need for a mutually recognizable frame of reference, on which to base their arguments. It was this sort of need that the new school of non-technical military writers during this age attempted to meet, and it was the particular merit of the historians that they could argue the case by using examples not immediately suspect because of their contemporary associations. Although there were those who used history simply as a political weapon to limit or extend military expenditure in particular directions, the situation also gave rise to men, such as those described here, whose viewpoint was determined to a larger degree by the conclusions they drew from historical study.

In the years of naval revival, part of which took place during what is known as the *Pax Britannica*, the British Empire and the Royal Navy dwelt together in close juxtaposition in the popular mind. The twin ideas that grew with the last quarter of the nineteenth century were that the Empire was essential to Britain's greatness, and that the navy was the first line of Imperial Defence. Although the popular mind probably never grasped the extent to which the red duster of the trade fleet heightened the importance of the impression, it remains true that it was largely through Englishmen's awareness of importance of overseas and particularly imperial trade that the navy was shaken out of its narrow specialization and so began to cast its thinking in a strategic thought that was world wide. Without the people who were motivated in this way, the great naval changes that took place would never have achieved the elements of popular support and planned development that they came to acquire.

The two Colombs, Captain John C. R. Colomb and Admiral

Philip H. Colomb, were very similar writers in that they both reacted to what they regarded as a very narrow Admiralty appreciation of the demands of modern war, with an attempt to discover principles on which to formulate strategic policy. Their difference in approach was marked by the fact that Admiral Philip Colomb looked to the naval past for the examples necessary to construct his arguments while John tended to investigate shipping-company statistics, and more modern information, to obtain supporting data. John Colomb was not really interested in history. Nevertheless his lucid and determined challenge to British defence thinking marked the beginning of a policy argument from which the historians eventually sprang.

It is not sufficient, however, to distinguish between the brothers Colomb as between strategist and historian. They were pioneers in the application of serious but non-technical thinking to British military problems, and as such pioneers they were a remarkable couple of men. Neither of them had had the benefit of historical or naval historical training, for reasons already explained. Indeed neither of them had had any formal academic training at all to assist them in the almost professorial task that they undertook. Their purpose and their methods were essentially propagandistic and they exerted a profound influence on British military thought right up until 1945. Their limitations, of both training and temperament, naturally rendered their conclusions less than perfect when judged by the actual test of war. They were not invariably right.[9] Indeed there was a tendency on the part of the Colombs as time went by to feel that their conclusions were almost divinely inspired and that their opponents were men unable or unwilling to digest the truth. This over-developed sense of rectitude was due to defects in the Colomb temperament. It was also due to the fact that although in the lecture hall they generally remained masters of the field, audiences refused to be convinced. Years of encounter with such inertia made the arguments of the brothers progressively more inflexible. This is an important point since it illustrates how the very solidity and originality of the Colombs' work in an English intellectual naval strategic vacuum induced the main defects of rigidity that their thought possessed. As pioneers of British naval thought and history their influence is hard to exaggerate.[10]

[9] For instance the importance and complications of submarine warfare was not seen by them, and they underestimated the need for convoy protection of trade. However, they shared this error with numbers of their countrymen.

[10] For a general discussion of John Colomb's thought and influence on Imperial affairs, political and military, see Howard D'Egville, *Imperial Defence and Closer Union* (London, 1913).

Admiral Philip Colomb's main preoccupation was with the use of history to provide a guide to our technical strategic thought. Thus he became the first serving British naval officer to take history really seriously. As he progressively devoted more of his spare time to its study, and finally in his retirement let historical study absorb him completely, he decisively advanced the idea that such study had a real value for serving naval officers and administrators. He arrested the attention even of those whom he did not convert.

Admiral Herbert Richmond, like Admiral Colomb, became convinced that naval history had a contribution to make to the contemporary development of the Royal Navy. Unlike Admiral Colomb, however, Richmond understood the value of accurate research and the use of primary sources. The sophisticated artistic environment in which he grew up gave him the mental equipment to appreciate the nuances of history, and he held a more catholic approach to the world, both of letters and seafarers, than his predecessors found possible. Also, since he was the youngest of the group, he was able to build on the experience of his predecessors. Much of his productive work took place after the 1914 period. Yet his habits of work and mental outlook were both formed in the days when the Royal Navy was still supreme on the oceans of the world. Also his most important historical work was complete by 1914 even if its publication was delayed by the First World War.[11] His career was an illustration of the difficulty of convincing sailors of the practical value of both historical study and of historically minded officers. His achievement was as brilliant as it was unappreciated.

The work begun by the brothers Colomb was given tremendous impetus by the work of the American, Alfred Thayer Mahan. It was Mahan who popularized naval history in England, not the naval history of battle description but rather naval history considered as sea strategy which, as he showed, exercised a powerful influence on developing history—or international relations. Since his reputation stood very high during the period under discussion, and since he wrote about British sea power in a way that made an unparalleled appeal to Britishers, his work forms an organic part of the developments discussed here.

John Knox Laughton influenced the development of British naval history firstly through the magnitude of his research output. His revelations about the nature and extent of the sources for

[11] Herbert Richmond, *The Navy in the War of 1739–48*, 3 vols. (Cambridge, 1920).

Influences on Naval Writing

British naval history significantly reduced the degree of tolerance in which undocumented speculative history would henceforth be held. By his energy and foresight he provided a vehicle to ensure that documentary publication should remain continuous.

Julian Corbett was a self-taught professional historian. In his time he became the leading strategist and historical chronicler of the Royal Navy. Through the efforts of this man, who was an historian first and a strategist second, the idea became popular that staff officers should have both a knowledge and appreciation of the history of their own service in both the precise and wide strategic senses. His work reveals a combination of strategic appreciation, respect for historical sources and a spectacular ability to trace the wider significance and inter-relationship of historical events. He developed naval history to a stature that earlier writers were unable to approach. His achievement can be measured by the realization that while Mahan's main work is still reverenced as a classic its main interest for scholars is now mainly antiquarian, while Corbett's works despite modern research are still main authorities in their fields after fifty years. Not long ago the *English Historical Review* printed two articles devoted to questioning Corbett's appreciation of a Tudor naval campaign.[12] While the re-assessment work was considerable the extent of the investigations necessary to alter Corbett's conclusions was a tribute to the earlier writer.

Thus it may be seen that each of the six men discussed in this book made some definite contribution to the development of naval history as a more sophisticated discipline. In the course of studying their writings, and to a lesser extent their careers, the emergence of this new occupation may be clearly discerned. Although they were nearly all active at some level as naval publicists, and some account of this is implicit in a description of their lives and work, this feature of naval development has been deliberately played down in these pages. It is not claimed that they were the only writers of prominence in the development of naval history, but only that they were the most important in that each made significant and unique contributions to that development. Devotees of the great compilation of W. L. Clowes,[13] those who see great importance in the work of J. R. Thursfield of *The Times* and Lord Sydenham of Coombe,[14] who were so intimately connected

---

[12] R. B. Wernham, 'Queen Elizabeth and the Portugal Expedition of 1589', *English Historical Review* (1951), pp. 1–26 and 194–218.
[13] Sir William Laird Clowes, *The Royal Navy*, 7 vols. (London, 1897–1903).
[14] The two combined in writing *The Navy and the Nation* (London, 1897).

with early expositions of imperial and naval strategy, and even readers of David Hannay are certain to think the omission of these names unfortunate.[15] Clowes, however, was a compiler and he built heavily on the initial impetus of Laughton. Thursfield was more of a publicist than an historian. Lord Sydenham was essentially a politician. David Hannay, despite all the interesting general information his works provide, disdained to particularize sources and thus made his information too suspect for other historians to use. An even more striking example of one who has been omitted is Admiral Sir Reginald Custance.[16] This able admiral and naval strategist is another example of one who used history to provide him with evidence to back up the latest strategic idea produced by his intelligent and inventive brain. Thus, while Richmond and Corbett are examples of men who built on the foundations laid for them by Mahan, Philip Colomb and Laughton, Custance remained at the same state of mental development that characterized Mahan when he wrote his first Sea Power book. To have described his work would add to our knowledge of naval controversy, but not of the growth of naval history.

If one thinks of naval history as a propagandistic weapon and even more if one looks to decisive results of strategic thought illustrated by proven value in war the developing work done by these 'Pens behind the fleet' does not represent a great success story. These writers did not always succeed in capturing the professional citadels guarded by the practical men, and when on odd occasions they did the results were not always felicitous. If the battle of the Falkland Islands and the quick blockade of the High Seas Fleet in 1914-5 owes something to Sir John Colomb, for instance, so does the fact that ships perambulated the world outside convoys until 1917. Like all men they tended to allow original thought to become hardened gospel—and like all hardened reasoning its effectiveness was proportionately diminished. But this book is not mainly concerned with propaganda, and in it one can trace a definite progress in the use of historical method applied to naval affairs by attempting to ascertain what really happened in the past. These men did not begin by being pioneers and end by becoming definitive writers on their various topics. Their literary lives, however, progressively demonstrate that the

[15] See particularly David Hannay, *A Short History of the Royal Navy, 1217-1815* (London, 1898 and 1909).
[16] Custance wrote, among other things *The Ship of the Line in Battle* (London, 1912); *A Study of War* (London, 1924) and under the pen-name 'Barfleur', *Naval Policy* (London, 1907).

pursuit of the truth is a more complex business than it first seems, and this growing awareness both increased their fact-finding competence and improved their methods of explanation. In this sense the road from John Colomb to Julian Corbett was a fruitful one for these men to follow, and it is here that the significances of their work truly lies. In a sense the book will confirm naval officers' worst fears, for the study reveals that history gained more from the work of these writers than did the navy. It is, however, by no means clear that the responsibility for this can be laid at the door of the pioneer naval historians.

2

IMPERIAL NAVAL STRATEGIST

Captain Sir John Colomb

IN London, in 1867, the year of Canada's Confederation, a small volume was published anonymously by a Captain John Charles Ready Colomb, of the Royal Marines Artillery, dealing with the defence of the Empire, and titled *The Protection of our Commerce and Distribution of our Naval Forces Considered*.[1] At the time the work did not give rise to any great public or official reaction; gradually, however, due partly to a change in public interest and partly to the dogged persistence of the author, the views there set down came to dominate British thinking about what eventually came to be known as Imperial Defence. With variations produced by the impact of changing environment, and his own mental development, Colomb continued to expand and urge these views until his death in 1909.

John Colomb was the second son of General George Thomas Colomb, and was born in the Isle of Man on May Day, 1838. He was educated privately and then, deciding to follow a military career, he joined the Royal Marines at the age of 16. After attending the Royal Naval College, Portsmouth, for a year Colomb became a Lieutenant in the Royal Marine Artillery. His subsequent carees in the R.M.A. was honourable but not spectacular. He married in

[1] Colomb's life work is set out in Howard D'Egville's *Imperial Defence and Closer Union* (London, 1913). This is a valuable introductory work, with its selection of evidence determined by its passionate advocacy of Imperial unity. However, since the author wrote his Ph.D. thesis on the subject of *Imperial Defence, 1868–87*, since he has had access to all Colomb's papers and collected pamphlet works, and since he is approaching Colomb's work from a particular point of view, he has felt free to return to the originals when it has seemed appropriate. The pamphlet was published anonymously to protect his military status.

1866 and shortly afterwards he resigned from the service. Equipped with private means he was able to devote himself to writing about politics and the support of public causes without financial worries. He inherited the beautiful estate called Dromquinna in County Kerry, Ireland, and as such a proprietor took his share in Irish local government.[2]

When Colomb's first pamphlet was published he was a relatively unknown figure. His brother, Philip,[3] then a Captain in the Royal Navy, was well known in his service as a technical inventor, since the navy had officially adopted his visual light communication method henceforward known as Colomb's Flashing Signals. John Colomb, however, was forced to wait many years for the official recognition of his ideas. As a result of years of careful training in an ancient corps, Colomb became convinced that his country did not appreciate, or employ, its trained soldiers. Undoubtedly it was while he was forced painfully to reflect upon his own retirement, that he began to question the strategic thought that lay behind personnel economics in the Royal Marines. This led him to think more deeply about military problems in general. In particular he began to think in broad terms about the disposition and use of available British manpower.[4] As he developed his ideas he was irresistibly drawn to the study of the defence of the Empire as a whole. Although, in retrospect, his kind of thinking can be seen to have been timely, the contemporary 'climate of opinion' was not conducive to the ready acceptance of what he had to say.

The cast of British thinking about the possibility of serious warlike activity was dominated, in the eighteen-sixties, by conceptions that gave land forces priority over naval forces. As so often with military developments this tendency was fostered more by a general fear mentality than by a real appreciation of known or traditional military principles as they applied to Great Britain's special position and needs. If this kind of reaction was not entirely rational it was, nevertheless, the product of special events and forces that are historically understandable. The decade of the eighteen-fifties had seen confidence in defence matters undermined by the undistinguished way the Crimean War was

[2] See *Memorandum Relative to Sir John Colomb's work, referring especially to the Protection of Commerce in War*, 12. 12. 02. Colomb Papers. The Colomb Papers are in the hands of Colomb's grandson, Geoffrey Snagge, Esq., who has kindly made them available and deposited copies in the Royal Military College of Canada and the National Maritime Museum, Greenwich, England.
[3] See Chapter 3.
[4] J. C. R. Colomb, *The Protection*, etc., p. iv.

executed.[5] Such nervousness was increased by a growing public fear that changing developments in naval warfare had rendered British coasts open to sudden, and probably unpreventable, military invasion from the Continent.[6] When, therefore, Napoleon III began to rattle his sabres towards the end of the decade he produced an invasion 'panic' in England.[7] Patriotically, the Poet Laureate asked his compatriots to rally and 'Form, Riflemen Form'. The Volunteers thus came into existence and they formed in their thousands. The result was that the army was forced to embrace a phenomenal number of patriotic citizens to its bosom, recruitment for the regular forces was made more difficult, funds were diverted from their usual task, and consequently the generals surveyed a collection of men to whom they would have hesitated to entrust the picking up of scrap-paper in Hyde Park. Enthusiasm rather than professionalism was the order of the day. Yet the panic produced still other results. A Royal Commission was set up to report on the Defence of the United Kingdom, and almost at once a Select Committee of the House of Commons investigated the same problem. The Reports of both the Commission and the Committee agreed that Britain's defence problems had acquired new aspects. As a result of their work plans were made to withdraw British troops from abroad in order to concentrate the army in the United Kingdom. Also, by the construction of serious formal coastal fortifications, the United Kingdom was to be transformed into a veritable 'fortress' bristling with guns and defended by enthusiasts.[8] All eyes were on the army and the drawbridges were up. This identification of national safety with the army-centred Fortress England idea received more impetus from the cross-Channel events of 1866, when the well-organized Prussian Army gave the world a glimpse of its military capability on the battlefield of Sadowa.

The navy, which had provided the traditional defence against

[5] Most military authorities agree that the leadership and performance of Britain's Crimean Expeditionary Force was undistinguished, although the naval aspects have not been universally condemned. See Julian S. Corbett, *Some Principles of Maritime Strategy* (London, 1911), p. 292.

[6] This idea received circulation through publication of a letter from the Duke of Wellington to General Sir John Burgoyne. See George Wrottesley, *Life and Correspondence of Sir John Burgoyne*, 2 vols. (London, 1873), Vol. I, pp. 444–51. If considered in its proper context the letter was not alarmist, nevertheless it gave rise to the phrase 'Steam has bridged the Channel' which caught the popular imagination.

[7] W. C. B. Tunstall, 'Imperial Defence, 1815–1870'. *Cambridge History of the British Empire*, Vol. II (Cambridge, 1940), p. 821.

[8] *Ibid.*, p. 824.

invasion, was no longer considered adequate to guarantee that kind of security. This alteration in strategic priority arrangements was the direct result of the growth of invasion-centred military thought. For this the navy was itself somewhat to blame, since neither serving sailors nor their supervisors at the Admiralty stated clearly that the menace could be met by the fleet alone. The fleet was there but its intrepid commanders remained silent in the face of what must seem to later generations, army heretical doctrine. Such reticence prevailed partly because essentially conservative naval personnel did not pioneer new strategic concepts. Similarly they did not remember to apply old strategic doctrine to the new emerging naval conditions.

Indeed naval officers generally did not know what the old strategic doctrine was, and what they remembered of it from Nelsonic times had not been enriched by the necessary constant re-assessment and re-appraisal to keep it up to date. This was understandable. It was natural to forget that the special competence shown in the last great war against Napoleon owed much to the Royal Navy's very considerable warlike experience in the eighteenth century, and the fact that this accumulated experience had progressively improved the strategic knowledge of the service. In the nineteenth century, however, fighting experience was not of the total-war variety, was generally limited in scope and had not been either extensive or as demanding as those of the previous one. Therefore despite the special problem posed by the Crimean War a certain state of somnolence had developed in the field of strategy. Those naval personnel who did think about these things kept their thoughts to themselves, for service people thought naval strategy was something too difficult or too mysterious for amateurs, or people outside the Admiralty, to grasp, and since strategic thought generally only develops as a result of discussion, progress in this field was halted. Even so, more original strategic thought might have been undertaken by a service that was free to contemplate its strategic place in the home defence schemes resulting from the panic mentality of the early eighteen-sixties. The naval service, however, had its attentions distracted by the swift advances then taking place in ship design as the naval revolution carried away Nelson's ships, and, as they thought, the techniques of his age as well. Within the service traditionalists, or 'old sail hands', battled stubbornly to frustrate every change that modern naval architecture proposed, as the Admiralty adapted the scientific discoveries and techniques of the machine age to the development of modern ships. Thus by the eighteen-sixties change was taking place and producing sufficient controversy within the service to absorb what energy naval officers might have had for other kinds of discussion.

In 1860 the Royal Navy countered the new and armoured French steam warship *La Gloire* with HMS *Warrior*. The *Warrior* was iron, both screw- and sail-propelled and she carried sixty guns. She was revolutionary. A mere twelve years later, however, and HMS *Devastation* slid down the ways. *Devastation* was mastless, iron-hulled, armour-plated and screw-driven. She carried four guns in two turrets. Although she was generally disliked in the service, she was stamped none the less with the approval of a special Admiralty *Committee on Designs* as 'the ship of the future'.[9] The pace was fast, and one need not labour the point that during the intervening twelve years the attention of virtually the whole service was centred on technical change, both in ensuring that it came about properly and in digesting the symbolic coal smoke of the result. The navy was not free to quarrel with army-centred strategic doctrine. It fell to John Colomb, not only to state the navy's strategic claims, but also to enunciate the principles of world-wide defence that emphasized the need for co-operation between the armed forces of the Crown. He used the rest of his life attempting to make this need for co-operation axiomatic to the political moulders of high policy.

Colomb's first paper of 1867 contained the kernel of his thought. What separated it at once from the generality of contemporary British military opinion was that it focused attention on ends before means. It was a virtue of his mind not to allow itself to become mesmerized by the development of, and international competition over, weapon types. When he analysed Sadowa, it was not the technical advantages of the Prussians that impressed him, but rather the fact that the battle demonstrated the triumph of a military machine carefully adjusted to satisfy the requirements of the Prussian state's special position in Europe.[10] Thus it was that while his countrymen were intent upon matching gun for gun, Colomb's mind moved naturally to the question 'what for?'. Specifically he wanted to know what Great Britain's special position was and how she should adapt her forces to maintain the position. The answers he produced provided a whole theory of

---

[9] O. Parkes, *British Battleships* (London, 1957), pp. 195–202. 'The "Devastation" class represents in its broad features the first-class fighting ship of the immediate future,' See also T. A. Brassey, *The British Navy*, 5 vols. (London, 1882), Vol. III, p. 526.

[10] J. C. R. Colomb, *The Protection*, etc., p. iv.

defence that lifted the subject out of the small arena of technical debate and small island panic, and set it on a peak that surveyed the world. Colomb asserted that the world-wide greatness of Britain in the nineteenth century stemmed from her paramount position as a trading nation.[11] Militarily speaking, however, the security of that position was dependent upon three things: the security of the homeland, the security of the dependent Empire (countries governed by Britain, with a native population), and the maintenance of safe communications between the homeland and both foreign and colonial trade centres. The author was aware that these facts were apparent to the trading men in the City of London. He also knew that the interdependence of these factors could not be properly recognized in any theory of defence that involved the concentration of attention on the defence of Britain, for this meant the exclusion of the trade of which it was both the seat and the main profiteer. Not for a moment did he underrate the necessity of securing the base of greatness against invasion, but he insisted that the base would swiftly lose that greatness were it shorn of its lines of supply, sustinence and power.[12] Furthermore, because the shipping on which the economic superiority was founded was kept moving by delicately balanced modern financial arrangements, Colomb held that the whole edifice was extremely vulnerable to concentrated intelligent attacks on the water. That is Britain's island prosperity could be shattered swiftly if it was hit hard in the right way.

These were the original ideas that issued from Colomb's mind in 1867, and to them he remained faithful for the rest of his life. They constituted the basis for a theory of Imperial Defence.[13] It is important to emphasize, however, that he seems to have developed these ideas as a result of a contemplation of the mismanagement of the manpower resources that Great Britain had at her disposal. When he referred to what he called 'the national peculiarity', he was talking about the fact that in Britain trained manpower had been, and probably always would be, in short supply.[14] He was not naïve enough to believe that this deficiency could be changed simply by preaching about it in peace-time, but he did think that the politicians ought to be concerned to ensure that the available manpower of the nation should be used as efficiently as possible.

[11] Colomb, *The Protection*, etc.
[12] *Ibid.*, pp. vi, vii.
[13] Tunstall, 'Imperial Defence, 1815–1870', p. 840.
[14] Colomb, *The Protection*, etc., p. vi.

Irresistibly this led him to the unenviable task of attempting to establish standards of priority. As he did so his horizons widened since he became quickly convinced that the whole trading Empire ought to be considered as a connected defensive unit.[15] In time he came to advocate army–navy co-operation with each service performing its proper function;[16] but in his first essay he expected the fleet's military requirements to be performed by the navy's sea-soldiers, the Royal Marines.

His belief in the need for inter-service co-operation for defined ends, however, did not mean that Colomb shirked the task of deciding which of the two services should be the keystone of Britain's defensive system. From the beginning he was convinced that a great maritime trading Empire was most deeply dependent upon the navy for its protection. This conclusion led to his being categorized as a purely naval thinker. Later in the century there grew up what came to be known as the 'Blue Water School' of naval thinkers: propagandists who were committed wholeheartedly to the view that the navy was more important than the army. Yet many of these later thinkers frequently showed a disposition to view national military problems through naval rather than national glasses, and also often considered national defence as simply planning for protection against invasion. Colomb was probably the originator of the Blue Water idea in that he placed the navy first in his thinking about national security, but his spectacles were nation and not navy tinted and he saw a good deal more to defend than just the island kingdom.[17] These refinements are necessary for a proper appreciation of the realism that informed Colomb's thought, as opposed to its exaggerations in other hands. Nevertheless, the very fact that he placed the navy first, no matter what the reason, caused him to be regarded as pro-sailor and anti-soldier—a designation that no naval thinker has ever been entirely able to avoid. But, during the first fifteen years of pleading his cause, he was extremely careful to stress the idea of service partnership rather than naval primacy.

The navy did come first, however. From this basic idea he developed his concept of the value of military communications.

The distribution of the forces for the protection of our commerce is a most important and, at the same time, a most difficult problem to

---

[15] Colomb, *The Protection*, etc., pp. 1, 2.
[16] Tunstall, 'Imperial Defence, 1815–1870', p. 839. The fact that Colomb was no naval fanatic was established by Tunstall.
[17] *Ibid.*

Captain Sir John Colomb

solve. The magnitude of this national requirement is only equalled by the difficulty of meeting it with the means at our disposal. Like everything else upon a gigantic scale, it can only be accomplished by the proper application of general principles. Now, in all naval or military operations there is a golden rule, to neglect which is certain ruin; it is the fundamental law which applies to all warfare, and is simply this—that the success of all operations depends upon the disposition of the forces in such a manner, as will best secure the base of operations, and ensure safety and freedom of communication. Knowing this to be true it remains with us to show how far it can be acted upon, and applied to the object in view.[18]

It is clear that to Colomb the defence of trade meant the defence of sea communications. As he surveyed the world-wide network of British sea lanes he was impressed by the fact that there were certain trading concentration areas more deserving of protection than others. In his initial pamphlet he did not attempt to lay down any fixed priority pattern, although he did make some suggestions.[19] The English Channel was obviously a vital area and was treated most fully. In any war involving a European power, invasion of the homeland must be countered and enemy naval forces must be contained. Also he noted that British trade was most vulnerable as it approached the great bottle-neck of the English Channel. Like the home-defence addicts, whose general thinking he opposed, he was aware that the greatest proportion of sea power must be concentrated in those waters, and in this concentration he placed some faith. However, it was when he looked abroad that his thought out-distanced that of his contemporaries. He was convinced that the protection of trading lines of communication, both in the English Channel and overseas, was necessary to British success in war, and he attempted realistically to fit the strategic conclusions to the new navy in the process of creation by the steam revolution.

The idea that ships operate most effectively to protect trade when based in secure places of refuge, refit and supply was not new in the eighteen-sixties. The whole concept of British sea power from the Dutch to the Napoleonic Wars rested on the possession and exploitation of such overseas posts. Indeed, the growth of the power of Britain at sea bore a striking and traceable relationship to the acquisition of such bases. All during the eighteenth century Britain secured more of these strategic bits of territory, and these numbers were significantly augmented at the

[18] Colomb, *The Protection*, etc., p. 1.
[19] As a general reference for what follows, see *ibid.*, pp. 1–36.

expense of France, Spain and Holland in 1815. Nor had the process of base collecting ceased when Napoleon went to St. Helena. Singapore, Hong Kong and Esquimalt were all post-Napoleonic acquisitions, to mention only three. Colomb's unique contribution was to emphasize that the dependence of the new navy on coal raised the status of overseas bases from important to essential. He foresaw clearly the complete replacement of sail by steam and, more significantly, he saw the implication—that a vessel with her coal bunkers empty was of no value whatever in a time of crisis. Furthermore, he realized that the vulnerability of iron hulls to ocean wear and tear made the provision of strategically placed, well-stocked dry docks overseas much more important to the new ships than it had been to more easily careened wooden warships of the past. Finally, it seemed to him that such bases must be properly defended if they were to be of any real value in time of emergency. This was not a task that could be realistically performed by the navy alone. To be of value, fleet bases must be secure; yet if the navy remained in harbour in order to protect its own bases then its freedom of action would be heavily circumscribed. Such protection should therefore devolve on shore-based artillery and infantry.

Colomb's thought on this subject in 1867, however, was not completely developed. His vision was limited by a desire to find a really useful role for the Marines and his own corps, the Royal Marine Artillery, and he worked out a system of interchangeability with the fleet personnel.[20] He also tended in this argument to rely very heavily on naval coast defence vessels, unconsciously echoing conservative naval opinion about the future function of ironclad warships—for many naval officers saw coast defence as their only useful function.[21] What did emerge clearly, despite this special pleading, was that the navy should not have its operational lines narrowed by being forced to tie sea-going fighting ships to the defence of its own essential supply points. This remained constant in his thought, and it was essentially along these lines as he laid them down in 1867 that Imperial Defence was to develop up to and past the First World War.[22]

It will be immediately apparent, and perhaps puzzling to the

[20] Colomb, *The Protection*, etc., pp. 36–99.
[21] Although the Admiralty Committee on Designs was convinced that the *Devastation* represented the ship of the future, the word 'future' needs emphasis since both *Devastation* and her sister ship *Thunderer* spent their service as coast defence vessels. See Parkes, *British Battleships*, p. 202.
[22] For example the concept was used in D. H. Cole, *Imperial Military Geography*, 11th ed. (London, 1953), pp. 1–5.

student of Imperial Defence to note, that in this discussion of Colomb's initial thought no mention is made of the problem that came to dominate such thinking—the question of what financial or manpower contribution the various parts of Britain overseas should make to this scheme. In only a few years he himself was attempting to formulate rules for such contributions by the colonies, and this imperial political question soon became his main preoccupation. It seems, therefore, worth underlining the purely military and nationalistic outlook of this first essay of John Colomb's. Although he touched on the reality that the Empire was made up of colonies of British settlement (populated by British settlers), in fact when he wrote of a maritime empire he meant a great trading empire. He was addressing himself to an essentially British problem, seeing it in world perspective. The solutions he proposed were British solutions aimed at maintaining British primacy. If in time he came to be an important imperialist, even an Imperial Federationist,[23] it must not be forgotten that his thought was both military and British in its formative period. It is true that his thinking about 'Colonial Defence' helped to produce changes in Empire constitutional developments, and he was no supporter of Englishmen whose views remained parochial in the age of the Empire, but this must not blind one to the fact that he was a Britisher, *not* an Australian or a Canadian. He took his imperial stance in England. For the student of naval history it is further worth noting that while the Admiralty appreciated the naval primacy ideas of his original theory and slowly came to adapt itself to his base-centred concepts, it really never made very serious efforts to understand and play on his ideas of colonial co-operation. This was the general attitude of the professional sailors of the time, who tended to view military problems with non-political eyes.[24] The pragmatic minds of the sailors afforded no assistance to British attempts at cost-sharing with the colonies; neither did they contribute directly to attempts to secure imperial co-operation.[25]

[23] He was certainly a prominent member of the *Imperial Federation League*, and, later in life, claimed that he and Hon. E. Stanhope were the two prime movers of the League movement. See *Colomb Papers* 'Memorandum Relative to Sir John Colomb's work, etc.', 12. 12. 02.

[24] Although the tendency of military men to resent the intrusion of 'political' factors into neat military situations is not the special property of any specific period of historical time.

[25] An exception to this was the negotiations carried on by Rear Admiral Sir George Tryon, who negotiated a Colonial Naval Defence agreement with the several Australian colonies between 1884 and 1887.

C

Paradoxically but understandably, and although Colomb's intention was to create inter-service harmony, the attempt to give primacy to the navy actually helped to open the wound of inter-service strife. To achieve inter-service harmony requires a reasonable desire for co-operation on the part of the soldiers and sailors, and firm political control of military affairs. This situation did not then exist and consequently Colomb was involved in difficulties. The defence of a large number of naval bases from the land was naturally a matter for soldiers. But a scheme that saw the navy favoured over the army was not calculated to appeal to the denizens of the War Office. It did not appeal to them. The hope for army co-operation was rendered even less likely by Colomb's idea that the over-all command of each particular base ought to be vested in one man.[26] Since this command would, in his view, include the ships attached to the base the senior post should go to a sailor, unless of course one thinks that he was seriously considering placing naval vessels under the command of soldiers, or contemplating fleets commanded by Major Generals. Strangely enough Colomb almost always regarded the occupants of the War Office as the greatest obstacles to the fulfilment of his military aims. Although it was true that these men were not easy converts to his ideas, they did do him the honour to take his views seriously enough to debate them, and eventually the schemes that emerged bearing some resemblance to his original ideas were prepared and advocated by soldiers. The Admiralty ignored him.[27]

It is a curious feature of Colomb's early military thought that it should have almost completely neglected India. India was very much in the soldier's, and indeed the national mind when he wrote, and stories of Cawnpore were still standard nannie ammunition for children's story-time; yet Colomb simply made the remark that 'India must stand alone', whatever that meant. How he expected soldiers to think imperially and yet keep India in a separate category is not apparent, and it may be noted that such an ambivalent attitude towards that British military outpost in Asia remained with him even when he began to insist strongly on imperial unity. This attitude is customary with most writers on Imperial Defence, which fact is perhaps a further testimony to his eventual influence.

[26] Colomb, *The Protection*, etc., p. 26.
[27] Colomb's ideas on commerce protection were first brought officially to the notice of the Cabinet by the War Office. See D. M. Schurman, *Imperial Defence, 1868–1887* (Unpublished Doctoral thesis, Cambridge University, 1955) pp. 74–95.

Again, however much Colomb may impress one as a redefiner of naval needs along traditional eighteenth-century lines of thought, it must be emphasized that he was by no means, like his brother Philip, soaked in naval history. He blamed lack of naval gunnery practice on an idea he had that such practice had not existed in Nelson's time when the great tradition was 'grapple and board' the enemy.[28] This was not historically true. Such a desire may well have titillated the mind of every aspiring admiral in the eighteenth century, but it was certainly not the accepted practice in those times. In fact Colomb was far from being a careful student of history, and what ideas he had of that sort were probably produced by his brother.[29]

John Colomb put forward a theory of British defence that looked to the protection of the homeland together with the inviolability of its exterior lines of communication upon which the homeland depended for its economic strength and power. It was a theory based on the primacy of the navy. It recognized the limitations of the national temperament, of the changing technical nature of war, and was capable of refinement to the extent that it allowed for the establishment of reasonably exact priority standards in order to facilitate the financing of imperial bases. It was a military conception and imperial only in the sense that trade was imperial, and that its protection posed an imperial problem.[30] Militarily Colomb's ideas had much to commend them, politically they were and proved to be almost unworkable. This was partly because Colomb underestimated national thinking in the dominions and colonies, and partly to the very logic of his approach. In the first case he was a representative Englishman; in the second he was not.

If John Colomb did not win converts to his ideas easily it was largely because he placed too much faith in the natural efficacy of a too-rigid logical process. He was, after all, not always right. Also there was a Germanic rigidity about his thought that, while it

[28] Colomb, *The Protection*, etc., p. 67.
[29] The question of which brother was the dominant mind is open to debate. It is, however, fairly clear that John Colomb formulated his own strategic ideas. See 'Memorandum Relative to Sir John Colomb's work, etc.', 12. 12. 02. Colomb Papers.
[30] The principle that the extent of base defences should bear a relation to the annual value of passing commerce was used in the Report of the Carnarvon Commission. See *Third Report*, P.R.O. 30/6-126. It was also used by the Deputy Director of Fortifications in 1877-8. See P.R.O. 30/6-115. It was, however, originally suggested in rudimentary form by Sir John Colomb. See *The Protection*, etc., p. 20.

possessed both accuracy and comprehensiveness, did not accord well with the national custom of thinking about war. To begin with defined ends and to proceed to means may appeal to the logician; it has not generally been the British way. In addition it was not necessarily the best way. When faced with inconvenient facts, such as imperial or service traditions and viewpoints, that conflicted with his careful arguments, Colomb did not adapt and modify his proposals, but simply repeated them over again in their original form.

At the same time it is true that British defence planning needed basic concepts to work from. The national propensity to piecemeal adaptation probably ought to have been shocked away by Germany's military success against Austria and France, and the arrival of the technical warfare age. However, complacency born of wealth, insularity and successful democratic methods was not conducive to sudden change. Although eventually Colomb's ideas came to dominate the field of Imperial Defence thinking, he himself must not be given all the credit. Some political changes were necessary before Colomb's ideas became popular. The politicians waited for the strong wind of popular opinion to blow, and until it did they let the military, professionals and amateurs, play with their toys and their piecemeal schemes undisturbed.

Much space has been given to the consideration of the *initial* ideas of a man who had many years of activity before him, and who let few years go by without raising his voice in public on questions that involved the naval primacy. Yet the fact is that although Colomb had much to say and a good deal to contribute to thought on strategic matters as time went by, in 1867 he once and for all made his really original contribution. His subsequent writings remained attached to this original anchorage, and it is revealing that his utterances after 1895 tended more and more to return to that firm base from which he had operated before 1870.

After the initial publication of his views Colomb's career was for a time confined to putting them forward whenever an opportunity presented itself. Outside the columns of the London Press his main outlets were the platforms and journals of the Royal Colonial Institute and the Royal United Service Institution, where he spoke frequently over a quarter of a century. In the period 1884–92 he also spoke from the platforms and wrote in the publications of the Imperial Federation League.[31] In 1886, as a Unionist,[32]

[31] See note 23 above.
[32] He was an Irishman, but his seat was a London one—Bow and Bromley.

he was elected a Member of Parliament and, with the exception of the period 1891-4 when he was out of the House of Commons, regularly rose to embarrass unready War Office and Admiralty spokesmen.[33]

Beginning in 1872 and continuing right through until 1900 Colomb developed the argument that, since the Empire was a commercial unit, the colonies ought to contribute reasonably and proportionately to the whole scheme of Imperial Defence. Sometimes his argument along these lines had reference to maintaining Imperial Bases, by which he meant bases that were as essential to colonial as they were to British trade, and sometimes it referred to colonial monetary contributions to the navy which existed to protect the whole Empire. He began with the idea that careful presentation of 'facts' would convince the practical colonists,[34] and he went so far at one time as to become an Imperial Federationist. Yet, despite the work of the Colonial Conference of 1887 which he did much to promote, he came to realize that colonial governments were not inclined to pay for defences that committed them to British control, especially when they could get the protection free of charge.[35] It is not surprising, therefore, that during the years immediately prior to the South African War, Colomb attempted to convince the British taxpayer of the hollowness of colonial loyalty cries, and strove to persuade the British taxpayer to accept the Imperial Defence burden alone.[36] Colomb never completely understood the colonial mind or position, but by 1900 he did understand that they were generally against making payments for defence forces they could not control.

Another time-consuming occupation of Colomb's was his constant vigilance to prevent the efficiency of the navy being lowered because of the piecemeal planning of over-all defence or because of the domination of army interests. This self-imposed task had three

[33] Colomb was defeated in the election of 1892 and was absent from Parliament for four years. When he returned to the House of Commons it was as the representative of Great Yarmouth, which seat he held until his death.

[34] Captain J. C. R. Colomb, *On Colonial Defence* (Reprint of a paper read before the Royal Colonial Institute at their Annual Meeting on Saturday, 28 June, 1873) (London, 1873), especially p. 23.

35. Canada would assume no responsibility for Imperial Defence, and neither the South African nor the Australian colonies were enthusiastic in their reaction to British suggestions about cost sharing. M. Ollivier, ed. *The Colonial and Imperial Conferences, 1887-1937*, 3 vols. (Ottawa, 1954), Vol. 1, pp. 3-61.

[36] J. C. R. Colomb, 'British Defence: its Popular and its Real Aspects', *The New Century Review* (1897), pp. 315-19.

main facets: to guard against losing sight of national defence aims through the lack of co-operation and communication between the War Office and the Admiralty; to expose the fallacy of every army scheme that operated on the assumption that the navy was defunct; and to check the administrators at the Admiralty for their attempts to work from hand to mouth under the guise of high policy, without themselves either examining or providing the House of Commons with the kind of information on which intelligent debate concerning modern imperial naval defence could take place.

He made a gallant attempt to slay the dragon of departmentalism. It was along the lines suggested by Colomb that a Royal Commission on the Defence of British Possessions and Commerce Abroad (commonly known as the Carnarvon Commission, 1879–82) was appointed. Although this Commission was chaired by an ex-Colonial Secretary[38] and cleared through the Colonial Office, it had at the same time developed according to a plan worked out at the War Office he despised.[39] Furthermore, the War Office plan was based on his original work. The navy was represented on the Commission by an ex-First Sea Lord[40] who did not bother until near the end of the Commission's Sessions to determine exact Admiralty attitudes on the matter. The results were not spectacular. For political reasons the Commission never reported fully to the public, but it did single out the Imperial Base problem for attention and work was begun on those defences. Yet, when it concluded the old departmental barriers were raised again and by the eighteen-nineties the army was again ringing the changes on the invasion menace. By this time, however, due partly to other causes of a different nature and partly to Colomb's own work, the navy was not neglected and army strategic planning was not allowed to go forward uncontested.[41] This was a useful change, but still the rivalry between the specialist services remained unhealthily active and in 1896 Captain John was still

[37] J. C. R. Colomb, 'British Defence, 1800–1900', Royal Colonial Institute *Proceedings* (reprint) (London, 1900). The paper was read on 10 April, 1900 and the remark was made by Edmund Barton of New South Wales.
[38] Henry Howard Molyneux Herbert, Fourth Earl of Carnarvon (1831–90), twice Colonial Secretary (1866–7 and 1874–8) and advocate of Imperial Defence and co-operation.
[39] D. M. Schurman, *Imperial Defence*, p. 210.
[40] Admiral of the Fleet Sir Alexander Milne (1806–96).
[41] The so-called two-power naval standard was both inaugurated and generally accepted then, and from that time the strength of the navy's position, *vis-à-vis* the army, was considerable.

vainly calling for a statement of national defence principles since the naval estimates were once again being considered separately by the House without reference to British over-all defence requirements.[42]

His already mentioned distrust of the soldiers was keen and did not diminish with time. When the Carnarvon Commission was formed he wrote gaily that 'the War Office idol was shaken on its pedestal in Pall Mall'.[43] He was enthusiastic, but quite wrong. Later on, after over a decade of opposing invasion talk, he was stopped by the Speaker in the House of Commons from talking about general defence principles while opposing a vote for army increases, on the grounds that he was out of order.[44] He took his case to the public and wrote that 'the wooden militarism of the Department seems impervious to any rational conception of the grim realities of a situation, which hundreds of army corps and square miles of fortresses could not save'.[45]

It is doubtful whether Colomb ever seriously thought that the navy was not sound in wind and limb and heart; it was only the brain that worried him. In a department where one could count the students of strategy and war function on one hand, the intense desire for the *status quo* was both remarkable and dangerous. His first contribution to the breaking down of this attitude was a paper read to the R.U.S.I. in 1881.[46] In this he advocated the creation of a department of naval intelligence where relevant strategic information could be collected and assessed, so that war plans could be realistically made. The talk contributed to the setting up of the department in 1882, but it was a long time before the Admiralty took its work very seriously. To get results Colomb took pains in the House of Commons to ask the First Lord of the Admiralty the sort of questions that would reveal Admiralty neglect of what he regarded as vital work. It is a fact, however, that as the Admiralty estimates increased in size after 1889, the bureaucrats could afford more and more to ignore the seemingly querulous questions of a man who was concerned with

[42] J. C. R. Colomb, 'Defence of the Empire', speech in the House of Commons on 13 March, 1896. Reprinted from *The Parliamentary Debates* (London, 1896), pp. 3, 4 especially.
[43] Howard D'Egville, *Imperial Defence and Closer Union*, p. 21.
[44] J. C. R. Colomb, 'Military Policy', Speech in the House of Commons on 14 May, 1901. Reprinted from *The Parliamentary Debates* (London, 1901), pp. 7–11.
[45] Sir John Colomb, *British Dangers* (London, 1902), p. 7.
[46] J. C. R. Colomb, 'Naval Intelligence and Protection of Commerce in War', *R.U.S.I. Journal* (1881), pp. 553–78.

policy and principles. A big navy meant big self-satisfaction at the top.

Colomb who saw his own ideas become so much a part of the fabric of the military aspect of the state was granted little recognition during his lifetime. He was knighted,[47] it is true, and Balfour who understood defence requirements and defence debate, gave him his Grand Cross in the Order of St. Michael and St. George in 1904. Yet he never was regarded as a seriously big figure. When in 1879 he asked to be included on the Carnarvon Commission, Carnarvon wrote of him that 'he would add nothing to its weight', that 'he is perpetually striving on this subject in the newspapers' and that 'he probably feels like a small dog whose bone has been taken away by a bigger one'.[48] This assessment was reasonably accurate, if somewhat uncharitable, since his knowledge could surely have benefited the Commission's work. His single-minded pursuit of one line of endeavour made him an excellent public representative in the House of Commons on the one hand and a poor House of Commons man on the other. When he rose to speak towards the end of his career members knew what was coming, even if most of them did not understand or wish to understand what he really had to say. He was reduced at times to replying to questions of 'by what authority do you question us?' with the angry, true, yet somewhat desperate reply 'knowledge of the service and forty years of study'.[49] The greatest humiliation was to have his remarks cut short on the grounds of irrelevance by a militarily illiterate Speaker. The House of Commons does not promote its schoolmasters.[50]

If his rather scholarly personality militated against his own personal advancement he had blind spots in his thought as well. One curious example was his share of the modern disease of over-reliance on statistics. When Colomb produced 'facts' the statistics poured out in a steady stream, and like most of those who are hypnotized by figure-juggling he tended to think the figures would convince by themselves once presented. When he dealt with 'colonials' for instance he always operated from the premise that they should be brought to see the rightness of his 'facts'. He sometimes listened to their point of view, but the schoolmaster's cane was always ready for the naughty ones who remained un-

[47] His K.C.M.G. was awarded in 1888.
[48] Carnarvon to Beach, 12 September, 1879. P.R.O. 30/6–52.
[49] 'Debate on the Navy Estimates.' Reprinted from *The Parliamentary Debates* (London, 1900), p. 22.
[50] See note 44.

convinced when he replied. This rigidity of his thought kept his central idea alive over years of frustration, but it did not convert people who had 'facts' of their own to contend with. Yet the statistical cast of Colomb's thought had its positive side as well. When Imperial Federation was the order of the day it kept him relatively free from that propensity to identify Empire solidarity with the effusiveness that came so naturally to enthusiasts after a good dinner. That he wanted Empire solidarity is clear, but he never expected that it would come all at once, and his statistics allowed him to see that however desirable more Colonial defence might be, a significant increase in it was not a likely contingency. He was not a wishful thinker.

A third and no less powerful defect was his failure to appreciate the realities of party political struggle, and of the conflict in progress between the military and the politicians. After listening to a Colomb paper in 1886 the Duke of Cambridge commented on the fact that finance had not been mentioned.[51] Now if Colomb's ideas were practically taken up this would not necessarily mean more military expenditure and the Duke seems to have missed this point, but similarly Colomb did not seem to realize that the soldiers and sailors felt the great fight to be against political parsimony. If one would win the practical support of men in high places it is of no immediate advantage to tell them that their efforts are all pointed in the wrong direction or to ignore their pressing concerns.

Casting questions of personal success and recognition aside, Colomb's life was extraordinarily fruitful. It was his thought that formed the talking basis of the Carnarvon Commission. As a result of that investigation, plus the awakening of public opinion that Colomb had done much to prepare the ground for, coaling stations for the fleet all over the Empire received attention. In 1886 Lord Randolph Churchill resigned because his Prime Minister was not prepared to let that work be by-passed.[52] By 1900 even Colomb himself was alarmed at the pell-mell way such work was absorbing defence money. Perhaps he lived to think he had created a monster.

Yet it must have caused him some gratification and it certainly

[51] J. C. R. Colomb, 'Imperial Federation—Naval and Military', *R.U.S.I. Journal* (1886). See Discussion, pp. 26–27.

[52] Winston S. Churchill, *Lord Randolph Churchill* (London, 1952), p. 575. Although there were other important factors influencing Churchill's resignation, this one, the actual occasion for it, is seldom accorded much weight. See R. R. James, 'Lord Randolph Resigns', *History To-day*, November and December, 1958; especially pp. 764–7.

underlined his usefulness when Admiral R. Vesey-Hamilton in 1900 stated publicly that,

the influence of sea power on history is now an accepted principle, but that principle, I would remind you, was brought forward by Sir John Colomb as far back as 1873. Speaking for myself, I may say that when I was Commander-in-Chief on our China Station some years ago I based my plans for the defence of our commerce on that station on those lectures of Sir John Colomb's at the United Service Institution, and on the works of his brother Philip, and although Captain Mahan has gained such credit for his book which is so wonderfully well put together, I would point out that he derived the foundation of that work from the Colombs.[53]

It was Colomb who was one of the leaders of the Imperial Federation League's delegation to the Government to suggest calling the Colonial Conference of 1887, the first Conference in a line leading to the Statute of Westminster.[54] By 1895 his insistence on naval primacy was accepted by a large part of the nation which had become very navy conscious—so much so that sometimes the fleet seemed to be run from the editorial desks of British newspapers and periodicals. It is true that the walls which separated the Admiralty and the War Office were never completely levelled before 1914, but the formation of the Committee of Imperial Defence in 1903–4 ensured that at least some of their squabbles would be under the view and control of the politicians. In fact by 1905 the navy was impregnably placed in the national affections and budget and well supported financially. In so far as the illogical development of British and colonial political and military institutions allowed, general defence policy was based on an idea of Imperial Defence remarkably like that put forward by Sir John Colomb in 1867, He was, however, by no means the only thinker who had a hand in producing that result. He was followed by historians.

Sir John Colomb was not a naval historian but he produced the first rational explanation of the naval place in national or even Imperial Defence thinking in the new era of iron ships and steam propulsion. His hard thinking about British strategic problems provided a framework in which historical investigations of the past could be employed fruitfully. It was within this strategic thought framework that his brother, Admiral Colomb, John Knox

[53] J. C. R. Colomb, 'British Defence, 1800–1900', Royal Colonial Institute *Proceedings*, Reprint, 1900. See Discussion, pp. 26–7.
[54] J. E. Tyler, *The Struggle for Imperial Unity* (London, 1938), pp. 204–5.

Laughton and even the great Admiral Mahan wrote their histories and sold them to the public of the United Kingdom. Without Sir John Colomb's ideas, other theories of defence would no doubt have grown up in the machine age and been incorporated in historical examples; what is important is that Sir John's theory carried the day and influenced the writing of every naval historian of note who has written since.

3

CLIO AND THE ADMIRAL

Vice-Admiral Philip Colomb

THE fundamental ideas on which Philip Colomb built his conception of naval function were never very different from those of his brother John. He often referred to their remarkable measure of agreement, and in matters of Empire Defence he acknowledged John's primacy.[1] Like his brother, Philip lived to see his ideas influence the minds of responsible defence planners and yet to see his own personal effectiveness somewhat lessened by a tendency to lecture the uninstructed repetitiously. John's efforts in the House of Commons in the eighteen-nineties were paralleled by Philip's lengthy letters to *The Times*. Indeed, Sir John Fisher referred to him wittily but unkindly in 1893 as 'not a naval authority' and one who 'never comes to the point. He is now called "a column and a half" in view of his lengthy letters.'[2] But Lord Fisher's judgements were not always as sound as they were pungent. While diffusion of talent may be justly ascribed to Admiral Colomb, the talent was unmistakably present. In short he was a man of parts, as both his naval career and his scientific, historical, literary and propagandist work amply reveal. For, unlike his brother, Philip mixed his intellectual activities reasonably successfully with the pursuit of a professional career. It was precisely because he was an intellectual sailor that he may be credited, if not with being the founder of the serious study of naval history, at least with making it slightly respectable.

[1] See Captain P. H. Colomb, 'Great Britain's Maritime Power', *R.U.S.I. Journal* (1878) p. 5.
[2] Quoted in A. J. Marder, *The Anatomy of British Sea Power: A History of Naval Policy in the pre-Dreadnought Era, 1880–1905* (New York, 1940) p. 47, note 6.

Vice-Admiral Philip Colomb

Although he neither commanded fleets nor reached the position of First Sea Lord, nevertheless, Colomb's career was varied, productive and filled with accomplishment. This man whose views came in time to irritate soldiers greatly was born in 1831 the son of a General. He left the military environment of his home and entered the Royal Navy in 1846 at the age of 15. Between that time and 1855 he served on the Irish, the Mediterranean and China stations. He was present at the capture of Rangoon during the Burmese War in 1852. Following his promotion to Lieutenant while serving in the Baltic on HMS *Hastings*, he attended the gunnery school, HMS *Excellent*, passing out in 1857. For the next ten years Colomb was not attached to a floating command. As Flag Lieutenant to the Admiral Superintendent at Devonport he became interested in fleet signalling. The Admiralty soon recognized his knowledge by requiring him to examine and pronounce on various signalling devices, and ended by accepting a system devised by Colomb, henceforth known to the service as 'Colomb's Flashing Signals'. This scheme which adapted the Morse Code to hooters and lamps was officially adopted by the Royal Navy in 1867. It was during this period that he made his first contact with general military thought by contributing and listening to the lectures at the Royal United Service Institution, and he increased his experience through being temporarily attached to the Royal Engineers to advise them on signalling matters.

In the summer of 1868 he took command of the sloop, HMS *Dryad*, and for two years he endured the frustrations and the hazards of attempting to prevent slave movements between Africa and Arabia. The result of this experience was a book, which not only described in detail the nature of the trade with suggestions for its prevention but also contained a shrewd commentary on the probable effects of giving national backing to five or six missionaries who were assaulting a whole black continent.[3] The book was extremely well written and remains a valuable document on its subject.[4] After another period of Admiralty desk work[5] Captain Colomb, as he then was, served as Flag Captain to Vice-Admiral Sir A. Ryder on the China Station (1874-7). In 1881 he

[3] Captain P. H. Colomb, *Slave Catching in the Indian Ocean* (London, 1873).

[4] Note that the merit of this work has also arrested the attention of an eminent British naval historian. See C. C. Lloyd, *The Navy and the Slave Trade* (London, 1949) pp. 251-7.

[5] In 1870 Colomb was advanced to Post Rank and employed at the Admiralty preparing the 'Manual of Fleet Evolutions' which was issued in 1874. This invited unfavourable comment later on, such as that of Sir John Fisher quoted above.

commanded HMS *Thunderer*[6] in the Mediterranean. This appointment was not a plum because the low free-board of the *Thunderer* caused her to be used for harbour defence work. After an interval as Captain of the Steam Reserve at Portsmouth, Colomb went to Portsmouth as Flag Captain to Sir Geoffrey Phipps Hornby in HMS *Duke of Wellington*.[7] He retired from active service in 1886, was promoted Rear-Admiral in 1887 and Vice-Admiral in 1892. During his period of retirement he was employed at the Royal Naval College, Greenwich, as instructor of naval tactics. He died of a heart attack in 1899. Aside from his work on slave catching and his shorter papers and articles at the R.U.S.I., Colomb's most active period of writing occurred after his retirement. A series of articles in the *Illustrated Naval and Military Magazine* were joined together to make the book *Naval Warfare* in 1891.[8] In 1893 he published a collection of his R.U.S.I. papers entitled *Essays on Naval Defence*,[9] and finally in 1898 he published his biography of Admiral Sir Astley Cooper-Key[10] which is probably the best written and, for the time, the most revealing work in existence on a nineteenth-century Admiral. All in all he lived a full life.

Experience, added to a keen natural power of observation and exposition, formed the basis of Colomb's written work. The shape of his thought, however, was largely moulded within the walls of the Royal United Service Institution, where he was both student and teacher for nearly forty years. Therefore, in leaning heavily on this main source it is possible to trace the development of the ideas that flowered during the last fifteen years of his life.

His first lectures to the R.U.S.I. were concerned mainly with technical and scientific development. As might be supposed his first paper, delivered in two parts in May and June, 1863, was on signalling.[11] It may or may not be significant to note that in arguing the value of clear, dependable, simple signals at distance he reinforced his case by suggesting that, had Lord Raglan been

---

[6] A sister ship of HMS *Devastation*, the first mastless, turreted and protected new battleship.
[7] A naval shore establishment.
[8] Admiral P. H. Colomb, *Naval Warfare* (London, 1891). A second edition was published in 1899 which simply applied his principles to the very latest developments in steam warfare. The pagination remained the same. Twenty-one pages of text and fifty-one pages of Appendix were added, the latter dealing with the Spanish American war.
[9] Admiral P. H. Colomb, *Essays on Naval Defence* (London, 1893).
[10] Admiral P. H. Colomb, *Memoirs of Sir Astley Cooper-Key* (London, 1898).
[11] Lt. P. H. Colomb, 'Naval and Military Signals', *R.U.S.I. Journal* (1863) pp. 349-69 and pp. 370-93.

possessed of a proper visual signalling device, the charge of the Light Brigade at Balaclava might never have taken place. Yet this was an isolated case of the use of historical example. In 1866 he read another paper on signalling.[12] This was remarkable for the fact that, since he had some hard things to say about the lack of standardization of ships' lights at sea, the Board of Trade had sent an official down to bridle him. The young lecturer was courteous to a rather urbane bureaucrat and held to his position. This anticipated the future because, although Colomb had a natural respect for authority, he was to be sorely tried by the obtuseness of officialdom all his life.

Another brace of papers appeared in 1871–2.[13] These were still technical and very contemporary. They dealt with ship and fleet warlike evolutions, and reflect the mind of a junior hand at the Admiralty who was at that time engaged in preparing such schemes for his superiors. Since Colomb never commanded a fleet these lectures were remembered years later as being the product of a 'theoretical Admiral'.[14] When Lord Fisher discounted Colomb in 1893, he revealed the disdain felt by the 'practical' sailor for a 'book' sailor. Even so, although Colomb had never commanded a fleet, he had in fact logged plenty of 'seatime'.

The year 1878 saw the R.U.S.I. select Colomb's paper for the Naval Essay Prize.[15] It was a huge rambling affair, sound in heart and limb, but long in wind. Valiantly he grappled with the whole problem of Great Britain's maritime power and its future development. Much of the essay was taken up with putting forward, in slightly different perspective, John Colomb's views on commerce protection and Imperial Defence. In so doing he handsomely acknowledged his indebtedness to, and his agreement with, his brother's thought.[16] This was indicative of the fact that Philip's mental development had now reached a significant stage, for John Colomb's thought, although not based on historical research was in fact traditional in character. Philip Colomb was to carry

[12] Lt. P. H. Colomb, 'Ship Lights at Sea', *R.U.S.I. Journal* (1866) pp. 517–30.
[13] Captain P. H. Colomb, 'The Attack and Defence of Fleets', *R.U.S.I. Journal* (1872) pp. 258–302 and pp. 303–28.
[14] See note 5 above.
[15] Captain P. H. Colomb, 'Great Britain's Maritime Power', *R.U.S.I. Journal* (1878), p. 1 ff.
[16] 'For my conception of the Empire I am entirely indebted to the writings of Captain J. C. R. Colomb, with whose general principles of Imperial Defence I cordially concur.' *Ibid*, p. 5.

historical analogy to much greater lengths in the next decade, and the beginnings of this new approach were visible in the Prize Essay. He began by suggesting that many appeals to the past related to fancied rather than real history. In addition he advanced two propositions: that Britain had traditionally based her type of naval force on her special requirements as a maritime state rather than on simple response to the building activities of other powers; and that Britain's naval role had been traditionally defensive. In both cases he used historical examples to show that his claims were valid. This was not entirely new since, as we shall see, John Knox Laughton had suggested in 1874[17] that naval history comprised something more than the quotation of Nelsonic maxims—but he was only a professor. The originality of Colomb's essay is that it represents the first attempt of a naval officer to base his case partly but firmly on historical evidence. It was the beginning of a new naval idea, even if it did not capture the imagination of all serving officers at once; indeed, most of the Philistines remained unconvinced, as they do to this day.

If this paper was important as a turning point in naval historiography, it had other features as well. It classified the kinds of ship necessary to the Royal Navy, and in so doing gave short shrift to 'coast defence' vessels. Colomb knew something about these ships, having been confined to the short-ranged HMS *Thunderer* in the Mediterranean for a year. The *Thunderer* was a sister ship to the *Devastation*.[18] Probably with good reason, Colomb thought these vessels relatively useless. However, he clearly failed to realize that, though slow and cumbersome, they were built as prototypes for future battleship development.[19] That they turned out to be coast defence ships was due to a certain unwieldiness in performance, and to service and public mistrust of *any* new design after the foundering of HMS *Captain* in 1870.[20] Apparently Colomb thought of

[17] J. K' Laughton, 'The Scientific Study of Naval History', *R.U.S.I. Journal* (1874) p. 509.

[18] HMS *Devastation*. The first turreted, mastless, steam-driven, sea-going ironclad. Launched 1871. Completed 1873. Due to service suspicion she did not undergo her speed trials until 1875. See Chapter 1 above and O. Parkes, *British Battleships*, (London, 1957) pp. 195–202.

[19] The Admiralty *Committee on Designs* saw this in 1871, writing, 'we are unanimously of the opinion that, subject to any improvements which further investigations in the direction to which we have already pointed may render possible, the "Devastation" class represents in its broad features the first-class fighting ship of the immediate future.' See Sir Thomas Brassey, *The British Navy*, 5 vols. (London, 1882–3), Vol. III, p. 526. Yet it would be rash to suggest that this represented general services opinion.

[20] HMS *Captain*, see O. Parkes, *British Battleships*, pp. 137–43.

Vice Admiral Philip Colomb

these ships as being built to Admiralty design for a special purpose when they were actually revolutionary ships of limited capabilities forced by public and service mistrust to work at menial naval tasks.[21]

The third interesting feature of this paper was its shrewd attempt to understand and grapple with the bureaucratic mind, with the politicians and with a rather indolent public. Colomb suggested that in a democracy it was best not to attempt to secure national adhesion to absolute theories of naval force, but rather to have the naval service converted to certain broad principles, principles that could and ought to be realistically pursued under peace-time conditions. What he meant was that constantly to proclaim war requirements in peace-time served only to alarm the fickle politicians without securing realistic preparations for wartime function. Hence he argued that war plans should proceed carefully under peace-time conditions and restrictions with the service not demanding more than it was likely to get, and at the same time making peace-time building and ship dispositions easily translatable to, if not coincident with, war-time necessities. Since in a short fifteen years the navy was to be built up largely on a public alarm mentality that he helped to create, this early note of caution is noteworthy because Colomb was careful to state that naval preparation ought to go forward under conditions of calm reflection, with care taken not to inflame public opinion. This was really responsible thought at a time when new naval ideas were often put forward by amateurs without much reference to practical possibility. It also indicated a degree of faith that the Admiralty was alive to its responsibilities which proved to be rather optimistic.[22] Like so many reformers who attempted moderation, he was to find that other methods are necessary to reorient or change established habits of official thought.

If these three lines of thought seem the most striking in retrospect, they did not dominate the contemporary discussion[23] on the Prize Essay paper. Colomb had also mentioned that intelligent planning rested on a frank reliance on steam power. This

---

[21] *Devastation* and *Thunderer* were unwieldy vessels but the fact that they were relegated to coast defence harbour duties was due as much to service suspicion as to poor performance.

[22] Having worked for a time at the Admiralty and seen the problems of the Naval Revolution from the centre it is probable that at this time he was inclined to be sympathetic to the difficult position of the naval pundits.

[23] The discussions on Colomb's paper were held on 21 and 26 June, 1878, at the R.U.S.I.

D

was prudent, wise and prescient. However, aside from Admiral Hamilton[24] who commented favourably on that part of the paper that dealt with commerce protection and with the need for careful naval financing, and Commander Custance[25] who spoke of the Admiralty's special knowledge concerning the armour and guns controversy, the discussion turned on the old sail–steam argument. The author must have been very unhappy to see his solid points neglected, while the old sail ghost was walked back and forth in inconclusive fashion. That particular spirit was to remain in motion for some years to come. More important, however, was the fact that this reaction illustrated clearly the inability of serving officers to think themselves out of the purely technical consideration of naval problems. Colomb must have been shocked by this rigidity of mind, and the experience must have been a powerful stimulant to his search for striking, convincing evidence to support his points of view; a search that led him slowly but firmly to the historical muse.

The great productive period of Colomb's life, and the real beginnings of his historical work, were coincident with his retirement from active service and his appointment as lecturer on tactics and strategy at the Royal Naval College, Greenwich. There, both the nature of his work and undoubtedly his contact with John Knox Laughton determined the firm commitment he now made to history as a determining guide for the study of modern naval problems. Laughton, who had been teaching history at Greenwich since 1876, retired in 1885 but still continued to frequent and lecture at the College.[26] Further, Laughton was now devoting his full time to writing naval history.

The setting in which the new naval historian emerged had something to do with the type of work he produced. From 1884 to 1892 the Imperial Federation League flourished. One of the main planks of the Leaguers was the necessity of imperial co-operation

---

[24] Sir R. V. Hamilton (1829–1912), Admiral. On Franklin searches; West African Squadron; C-in-C China, 1884; Admiral K.C.B., 1887; prepared report on which Naval Defence Act, 1889 based; First Sea Lord, 1889–91; President, Royal Naval College, 1891; Retired with G.C.B., 1895; wrote *Naval Administration* (London, 1896).

[25] Sir R. N. Custance (1847–1935), Admiral. Assistant Director of Naval Intelligence, 1886–90; Director of Naval Intelligence, 1899–1902; Second-in-Command Channel Fleet, 1907–8; Admiral, 1908; retired 1912, writer on naval history, strategy and tactics who suffered professionally for expressing strong opinions on naval questions.

[26] Despite the fact that Laughton almost immediately became Professor of Modern History at King's College, University of London.

Vice-Admiral Philip Colomb

in defence matters, and much of this discussion was based on Sir John Colomb's ideas on naval defence.[27] The British Government's interest in the subject is indicated by the fact that the Colonial Conference of 1887 was called partly because of the agitation of the Leaguers,[28] and when it met, one half of its time was given to defence discussions in which the question of naval function was widely aired, if not generally understood.[29] At the same time the Government began to accept responsibility for the provision of secure bases and coal stations for the Fleet. Money was voted for this purpose in 1884-5[30] and a permanent committee was set up to deal with the problem in 1885.[31] As we have seen, the issue on which Lord Salisbury accepted Lord Randolph Churchill's resignation was Churchill's refusal to earmark funds for overseas fortifications. As the idea permeated Whitehall that Imperial Defence was important, so also the idea that the navy was not on an entirely satisfactory footing gained credence. Although seemingly unconnected, these events, taken together, marked the end of the era of public complacency towards Admiralty policy. The great public stimulus to those ideas were largely traceable to W. T. Stead's articles in the *Pall Mall Gazette* entitled 'The Truth about the Coaling Stations', and another series under the heading 'What is the Truth about the Navy?'.[32] These articles created the first of the series of naval panics that were to force the pace in naval shipbuilding right up to 1914.

Furthermore, international tensions gradually focused British

---

[27] See Chapter 2 above.

[28] Sir John Colomb led the delegation from the Imperial Federation League on 11 August, 1866, that urged on the Prime Minister and Colonial Secretary the value that would accrue to Empire Defence from a colonial conference which ought to place this subject high on the agenda. Lord Salisbury referred to it as 'a somewhat urgent question'. For an account of the interview see C.O. 323/366-15482.

[29] Because the British Government had not clearly formulated a detailed defence policy that was agreed on by their experts, much time was wasted at this first conference, and colonial delegates were disillusioned. This was especially evident in the debates concerning King George's Sound and its defence. See *Parliamentary Papers*, LVI, 1887, 'Proceedings of the Colonial Conference'.

[30] See 'House of Lords Report', *The Times*, 3 December, 1884. Arguments and adjustments continued over the whole winter of 1884-5.

[31] The Colonial Defence Committee. See N. H. Gibbs, *The Origins of Imperial Defence* (Oxford, 1955.)

[32] See 'What is the Truth about the Navy?', *Pall Mall Gazette*, 15 September, 1884. This was the first article in a series. See also 'The Truth about our Coaling Stations', *Pall Mall Gazette*, 16 October, 1884.

thinking on their world-wide responsibilities. The Russian war scare of 1885, the intense interest displayed in the death of General Gordon, the increasing colonial acquisitive tendencies of other European powers, the sharpening foreign economic competition and the slow hardening of continental regional alliances all combined, in different ways and circumstances, to provoke much nationalistic, not to say jingoistic, sentiment in Britain. The cumulative result of all of these developments was that a public was assured for any writer who chose to alarm his readers, for it is a truism that grandiloquent appeals to nationalism are generally associated with a fear mentality. Therefore, the whole British nation, from the Prime Minister down to the publican strategist, surveyed the national defence scene convinced that all was not as well as it might be, and yet uncertain what the cure should be. In this atmosphere it was only natural that the hitherto barely concealed rivalries between the army and the navy should cease to remain secret. The result was the beginning of appeals to special argument to aid service assaults on the public purse. In this contest it was Admiral Colomb's fate to conscript history on the side of the navy.

Army primacy in British defence thinking had been part of the national pattern for at least thirty years. It has been pointed out that this was due partly to one-sided concepts of national defence and partly to a lethargy on the part of the Senior Service traceable to a preoccupation with technical progress.[33] Therefore, Colomb's attack when it came was aimed both at demolishing the props under the contentions of the soldiers, and at waking up the sailors to the idea that their position was being undermined by their own mental habits. The assumption of this task was not calculated to make the Admiral universally popular.

Admiral Colomb only slowly emerged as a hard-shelled navalist. In 1886 he spoke at the R.U.S.I. in support of his brother, to point up the fact that their conception of Imperial Defence did not assume large-scale outlays for overseas or home fortifications.[34] In that year also Admiral Fremantle[35] read a paper to the R.U.S.I. on naval tactics. Commenting on the paper, Colomb contended

---

[33] See Chapter 1.
[34] Captain J. C. R. Colomb. 'Imperial Federation—Naval and Military', *R.U.S.I. Journal* (1886). Discussion, pp. 865–66.
[35] Sir E. R. Fremantle (1836–1929), Admiral. Writer on naval tactics; Friend of Admiral Colomb; attended R.N.C. Portsmouth (1871–2); to Gold Coast with Wolseley, 1872; Prize Essay, R.U.S.I., 1880; C.-in-C. China, 1892; C.-in-C. Devonport and promoted Admiral 1896; retired, 1901.

that the study of old wars reveals principles that do not change, despite the fact that circumstances vary from age to age; that one must not slavishly adhere to an old line in detail, but should adapt old lessons to new conditions.[36] This was the talk of one who placed some reliance on history.

In 1887 Colomb gave two papers, one on blockade and the other on convoy.[37] His approach in each was historical, involving the study of old wars to arrive at general rules for application in modern naval planning situations. The conclusions he drew were tentative, but in both papers he attempted to show clearly what had been the real practice in the past. For instance, in the case of blockade he drew useful distinctions between 'sealing up' an enemy port, 'masking' a fleet from the commander of an enemy force in port and 'observing' an enemy fleet in port or adjacent to it. In the case of the convoys, he showed as an example that in Napoleonic days they were not, as many supposed, port-to-port groups under escort, but rather that they comprised groups of merchantmen forced by insurance contract to submit to naval authority for such periods as that authority deemed it necessary for their safety. Hence, when Colomb asked the question 'Are convoys possible?' he was not referring to a sea-going, physical possibility but rather to the degree of co-operation that presently existed between the navy and the City brokers, or to what co-operation might develop in time of war. The naval officers present must have pinched themselves to make sure they were really hearing about their new scientific navy. This was a fresh breeze.

In early 1888, Colomb spoke to compliment Admiral Fremantle for using the historical method on a paper concerning speed in naval war,[38] and on another occasion he referred ominously to the War Office and Admiralty neglect of the problem of commerce protection, due to their invasion-centred mentality.[39] March of that year found the Admiral delivering a paper on naval mobilization that was so full of congratulations to the Admiralty that even

[36] Hon. Edmund R. Fremantle, R.A. 'Naval Tactics', *R.U.S.I. Journal* (1886). Notes on Discussion, p. 227.
[37] Admiral P. H. Colomb, *Essays on Naval Defence*. 'Convoys: are they any longer possible?', pp. 230–57 and 'Blockade: under existing conditions of Warfare', pp. 194–229. Both papers read before R.U.S.I. in 1887.
[38] Hon. E. R. Fremantle, R.A. 'Speed as a Factor in Naval Warfare', *R.U.S.I. Journal* (1888). Notes on Discussion, pp. 134–6.
[39] Lt. W. C. Crutchley. 'On the Condition of the Mercantile Marine Personnel and Matériel, with a view to its more complete utilization as a Reserve for the Royal Navy', *R.U.S.I. Journal* (1888). Discussion, pp. 196–8.

his brother John was amazed.[40] No doubt Colomb himself was uncomfortable amongst the angels. On Friday, 18 May, 1888, however, the happy atmosphere was shattered by a tremendous broadside and service rapport was divided and disrupted.

The broadside was in the form of an R.U.S.I. paper entitled 'The Naval Defences of the United Kingdom'.[41] In this paper Colomb finally left behind the safe doctrine of pleasantly divided naval and military responsibility for invasion defence that had been fostered and dominated by fortification experts at the War Office since 1860. He roundly advocated a purely naval conception. Carefully unpacking his historical case book he showed that there were two traditional ways to keep England from invasion: either what he called the Earl St. Vincent method of close blockade of enemy ports;[42] or the defensive waiting with intact fleet method[43] that he associated with the name of Lord Howe. He challenged his audience, or anyone else, to come up with another possibility. He then went on to point out that either system would protect both the homeland and moving commerce in the south-western approaches. What then was the need for extensive, or indeed any, fortifications of English ports and harbours if the naval dispositions were adequate? He reminded his audience that existing and projected fortifications were a result of the deliberations of the Royal Commission on the Defences of the United Kingdom set up in 1859. That body, he claimed, had not arrived at reliable conclusions because the terms of reference of that Commission were not designed to determine whether to fortify, but rather what to fortify. Thus, contended Colomb, the whole basis of subsequent thought on this subject was unsound, and he threw out the sheet anchor of the coming Blue Water school when he said that 'nothing can be done in the way of territorial attack with a disputed command of the sea'. It was a shattering challenge.

The reaction of the immediate audience that night was diverse. All, of course, were stunned by the audacity of the stand taken. Senior naval opinion was not captivated. Both Admirals Sir R. V.

---

[40] Sir John Colomb stated 'We must recollect that the Admiralty are in quite a different position to what they were two or three years ago, before the discussions at this Institution produced the Intelligence Department'. See Admiral P. H. Colomb, 'Naval Mobilization', *R.U.S.I. Journal* (1888). Notes on Discussion, p. 500.

[41] See *R.U.S.I. Journal* (1888) pp. 565–601.

[42] *Ibid.*, pp. 565–73.

[43] It did not appear to Colomb to matter which method proved most adaptable to modern conditions since command of the sea was necessary as a preliminary to either scheme.

Vice-Admiral Philip Colomb 47

Hamilton and Sir George Elliot[44] were opposed to Colomb. Elliot was annoyed because he had been a member of the Royal Commission of 1859, and since Colomb had come close to calling the decision of that Commission insane, Sir George naturally felt that he was being called a lunatic by inference. Admiral Sir Spencer Robinson[45] thought the speaker irresponsible for making a suggestion that paved the way for competitive departmental assaults on the public purse. Captain Bowden-Smith,[46] however, deplored the lack of common conviction amongst naval officers on this question and he welcomed this attempt 'to educate public opinion . . . in this great question of naval defence'. Captain Penrose Fitzgerald[47] was positively delighted to the extent where he indiscreetly but gleefully attacked the First Lord of the Admiralty with the aside 'I may as well be hanged for a sheep as a lamb'. The soldiers present were not at all pleased. Colonel Nugent, of the Fortification Department at the War Office, regarded the paper as an attack on himself and he was probably not too far wrong in that line of reasoning.[48] Yet it was Colonel Brackenbury[49] who went at once to the heart of army feeling when he stated that such a doctrine, once accepted, meant army reductions. This instinctive reaction remained constant for twenty years for it was true that the army could not afford to admit that Colomb was right. Civilian reaction was divided. John Colomb supported his brother. Lord Cowper[50] was certainly representative of the puzzled politicians when he wished that the military men

[44] Sir George Elliot (1812–1901), Admiral. C.-in-C. Portsmouth; published in 1888 *A Treatise on Future Naval Battles and How to Fight Them*.
[45] Admiral Sir R. Spencer Robinson (1809–89), Rear-Admiral and Controller of Navy, 1860; Lord of the Admiralty, 1868–71; Admiral, 1871; writer to *The Times* on matters concerning shipbuilding and Admiralty organization.
[46] Sir Nathaniel Bowden-Smith (1838–1921), Admiral. Rear-Admiral, 1888; commanded *Britannia*, 1883; British representative at International Maritime Conference, 1889; C.-in-C. Australia, 1892–5; C.-in-C. Nore 1899–1900; Admiral, 1899.
[47] C.C. Penrose Fitzgerald (1841–1921), Admiral. R.N. College; Superintendent, Pembroke Dockyard; Second command of China Station, 1898–99; Admiral, 1905; author on naval subjects.
[48] Sir Charles B.P.H. Nugent (1827–99), Colonel R.E. For many years attached to Fortifications Department at War Office and was responsible for many fortifications schemes, some of which were considered by the Carnarvon Commission, 1879–82.
[49] Rt. Hon. Sir Henry Brackenbury (1837–1914), General. Various campaigns; Director of Military Intelligence, 1886–91; Commandant, R.A., 1897; General, 1901; writer on military tactics.
[50] Francis Thomas de Grey Cowper, 7th Earl (1834–1905), Politician. Lord Lieutenant of Ireland, 1880–2.

would make up their minds. It was the old politician's dilemma: what does one do with experts—whip them or worship them?

Things might have quietened down, but a Captain Stone[51] of the Royal Artillery ventured once again to advance the army case.[52] Colomb replied in withering fashion in March, 1889.[53] In his previous paper, when discussing the need for fortifications in the light of purely United Kingdom defence, Colomb had laid himself open to the interpretation that his concept applied only in that special contingency. This time he narrowed his topic to 'The Relations between Local Fortifications and a Moving Navy', so that his argument stood clearly revealed as one designed to destroy, not simply to weaken, the soldier's argument, claiming as he did that all overseas invasions were subject to naval rules. Even more forcefully than in the earlier paper, he rested his case on Britain's traditional customs as revealed by history. In a letter to *The Times* previous to the delivery of this rigid presentation, he had mentioned that he intended to try to force a solution to the forts versus ships controversy by adopting an extreme position and acting as 'devil's advocate'.[54] Consequently, it was not surprising that his three main attackers, General Nicholson,[55] Lord Carnarvon[56] and General Sir Lintorn Simmons,[57] should accuse him of overstating his case. It is probable that Colomb expected to be accused of waving a red flag at an irate army but he must have been pleased to discover that his opponents could not pinpoint just at what point he went too far. Nicholson was worried at the effect of overstatement on public opinion. Lord Carnarvon had never doubted that the navy held the primacy in Imperial Defence but regretted this theoretical attempt to make such primacy absolute.

---

[51] Francis G. Stone (1857–1929), Brigadier-General, R.A. Boer War and World War I; Inspector Artillery, Canada, 1899–1900; Prolific writer on military subjects, especially to *Nineteenth Century and After* and *Fortnightly Review*.

[52] Referred to in Admiral P. H. Colomb 'The Relations between Local Fortifications and a Moving Navy', *R.U.S.I. Journal* (1889) pp. 150–1.

[53] *Ibid.*, *R.U.S.I. Journal* (1889) pp. 149–202.

[54] *Ibid.*, Notes on Discussion, p. 174.

[55] Sir Lothian Nicholson (1827–93), General, R.E. Served with distinction in Indian Mutiny; Inspector-General of Fortifications, 1886–91.

[56] Henry Howard M. Herbert, Fourth Earl of Carnarvon (1831–90), Politician. Colonial Secretary, 1867–8, 1874–8; Chairman of Royal Commission on Defence of British Possessions and Commerce Abroad, 1879–82; Speaker on, and advocate of, Colonial Defence.

[57] Sir John L. A. Simmons (1821–1903), Field-Marshal, R.E. Inspector-General of Fortifications, 1875–80; Member of Royal Commission on Defence of British Possessions and Commerce Abroad, 1879–82; F.M. 1890.

Vice-Admiral Philip Colomb

Carnarvon's views were respected because he had been chairman of 'The Royal Commission Appointed to inquire into the Defence of British Possessions and Commerce Abroad' (1879–82), but since the whole of that body's reports had never been made public by the Government, he was prevented from producing effective documentary support for his views.[58] In fact, the portions of the Report that had been released dealt mainly with apportionment of fortifications and other costs between home and colonial governments. That the impression there given suited the army case admirably he did not seem to understand. Simmons had also been a member of Lord Carnarvon's Commission and he glibly supported the contention that security reasons made the publication of the report inadvisable. He further stated that the conclusions of the Commissioners had been unanimous. This was quite wrong[59] because Admiral Milne,[60] also a Commission member, had submitted a minority report deprecating army domination of the Commission's work.[61] Interesting as this may be to the historian, there was nothing in the statements of these two men about the Carnarvon Commission that either disturbed Colomb's contentions or that was substantial enough for him to attack. Security is always the official shield in defence matters. Although he was incapable of concretely refuting Colomb's case, however, Simmons was an experienced hand at suffering delays and frustrations due to service disagreement and he did state that decisions in such circumstances were properly political. Arguments like the present one, he felt, should be resolved by a Minister of Defence who would co-ordinate army and navy ideas.[62] This was thinking along the lines that finally led to the formation of the Committee of

[58] Only a limited portion of the Carnarvon Commission's Report was made available to the Colonial Conference of 1887. What was made available had been edited by Lord Carnarvon who, during the Commission sittings, had been made to realize the nervousness of politicians about disclosures of military information to the public. What was published appeared as an Appendix to the 'Proceedings of the Colonial Conference of 1887'. *Parliamentary Papers*, LVI, 1887.

[59] See *Third Report of the Royal Commissioners Appointed to inquire into the Defence of British Possessions and Commerce Abroad*, Carnarvon Papers, P.R.O. 30/6-126.

[60] Sir Alexander Milne, Baronet (1806–96), Admiral of the Fleet. Senior Naval Lord of Admiralty, 1866–8, 1872–6; Member of Royal Commission on Defence of British Possessions and Commerce Abroad, 1879–82.

[61] Although the Carnarvon Commissioners were not 'Departmental' much of the groundwork, current information, and the dominant personality (General J. L. A. Simmons) were products of the War Office.

[62] This was sound thought in the light of future developments. It is probable that Simmons was convinced that army officers could more easily move politicians than their more taciturn navy counterparts.

Imperial Defence in 1903–4. Colomb, however, was convinced that purely logical argument would prevail by virtue of its own strength and he rejected the idea that political power was indispensable to resolving the rivalry. He held, one imagines, the naïve view that politicians were merely the registers of public opinion.[63] Lord Salisbury would have smiled at that.

When it came to the question of whether or not historical arguments were reliable for the discussion of modern problems, Colomb received support only from John Knox Laughton. Indeed, he was generally attacked for his use of the historical method. General Nicholson said it was not a valid method and Captain Stone asserted that history was no test in 'scientific' cases.[64] The lecturer was also accused of departing from the 'principles' laid down by his brother years ago. Both brothers denied this. There was, however, some substance in it or at any rate it exposed a chink in the Colomb armour, for the paper had concluded with the words 'It is a mere instinct with me which admits light batteries at the entrances of such (local) ports. I cannot, when I face it, reconcile their existence with my reason.'[65] Both John and Philip contended that they had never advocated *heavy* local defences, though they had advocated some such protection. This was, seemingly, evidence of altered views. The inconsistency rested on the fact that neither of the Colombs ever denied that single or small groups of raiding enemy vessels might evade the Royal Navy and strike some sort of hit-and-run blow at ports or other coastal installations. They maintained also, however, that large-scale army forces, if they were strong enough to effect a serious lodgement on shore, could never evade proper British naval disposition. The line between these two contingencies they left uncomfortably vague and it remained for a later historian to make the concrete distinction between an 'invasion' and a 'raid'.[66] It was between these two concepts that 'no-man's

---

[63] Colomb stated 'But if the Navy and the Army can thus settle what their functions are to be, even the Ministry of Defence, which Sir Lintorn Simmons is so anxious to have, would become not a necessity, for we should have settled all the points which the Minister of Defence could settle, before he was appointed to his post.' Colomb, *op. cit. R.U.S.I. Journal* (1889). Discussion, p. 201.

[64] This argument was the favourite one that had hindered rational over-all appreciation of defence policy ever since 1860. Anything new was 'scientific'. This is not an argument that should present problems for 'Moderns' of the 1960s. For Captain Stone's remarks, see *ibid.* Discussion, p. 174.

[65] *Ibid.*, p. 167.

[66] See Sir Julian S. Corbett, *Some Principles of Maritime Strategy* (London, 1911), p. 287.

land' lay in this great argument and it was at this point that the Colomb brothers were most exposed.

Yet the Admiral remained master of the stage at the R.U.S.I., even if his audience often murmured darkly against him. As early as the first of May, Major G. R. Walker,[67] R.E., advanced on the R.U.S.I. with material to blow Colomb sky high. No doubt he was the army's mouthpiece and in honour of the fireworks Lord Wolseley himself took the chair. Colomb, however, had seen the paper beforehand and he presented the meeting with a prepared (not delivered) paragraph-by-paragraph refutation.[68] Lord Wolseley wisely adjourned the discussion.[69] When it was finally held, the great soldier did not again appear. At the adjourned discussion Walker did not shine and the same old arguments were trotted out on both sides. The lines were drawn.

It would be wrong to leave this controversy with the idea that Colomb was only interested in an academic solution to the inter-service differences raised. He did not deliver these lectures simply to resolve a service difficulty by a display of academics, but for the practical reason that in 1888 there was a reduction of £900,000 in the navy estimates while £3,000,000 were voted for fortifications.[70] If the soldiers were unable to crack the Admiral's case, they were perceptive enough to divine that his motives were not disinterested. As for the Admiralty, that body just did not recognize its friends, for the work of the naval propagandists, of whom Colomb was one, got results. It is worth noting that, as the great debate continued, public money went to the navy as the newly defined two-power standard was supported by a huge building programme. Colomb's efforts and also those of others brought work on overseas forts to a halt. Major G. R. Walker designed a fort that proved to be redundant because of the success of Colomb and his supporters. For as 'a result of this criticism no more permanent defences of land fronts were constructed in any part of the Empire'.[71]

---

[67] Major, G. R. Walker, R.E. At that time employed as a senior officer in the Fortifications Branch at the War Office. Designer of forts.
[68] Major G. R. Walker, 'Fortifications and Fleets' *R.U.S.I. Journal* (1889), pp. 659–81. Colomb's refutation was printed in the *Journal* immediately following Walker's paper. Colomb had at least reached the place where he had influence at the R.U.S.I.!
[69] At the R.U.S.I. on 9 May, 1889. Discussion on Major Walker's paper (see note 63). *R.U.S.I. Journal*, pp. 697–720.
[70] See Colomb, *R.U.S.I. Journal* (1889). Notes on Discussion, p. 201.
[71] W. Baker-Brown, *History of the Corps of Royal Engineers*, Vol. IV (Chatham 1952), p. 230.

Admiral Colomb's great work on naval history was first produced in the form of a series of articles written for the *Illustrated Naval and Military Magazine*[72] and finally produced as a book, *Naval Warfare*, in 1891. It went through two editions and demonstrates both the strength and weaknesses of Colomb's mind.

Naval Warfare was the first reasonably sound, and yet far-reaching, British historical work on naval history. It has been somewhat neglected because it had the misfortune to appear almost at the same time as the powerful American work of Captain A. T. Mahan, under the now famous title of *The Influence of Sea Power Upon History*. Colomb himself, in the preface to his book, spoke of 'an abler pen and a deeper thinker' across the sea. Indeed, at the time he wrote to Mahan the letter here reproduced:[73]

97 St. George's Road, S.W.,
April 26, 1891.

Dear Captain Mahan.

My book on 'Naval Warfare' which was in course of publication when your fine book came out is now complete and will be published in a week of so. I have told the publishers to send you a copy with my compliments.

They are endeavouring to make arrangements with Messrs, Putnam & Sons to publish in your country.

I hope you were satisfied with the reception your book received in this country. I think all our Naval men regarded it as *the* Naval book of the age, and it has had a great effect in getting people to understand what they never understood before. I had the great pleasure and privilege of reviewing you in one or two influential quarters and I hope may have helped to direct attention to the book.

My book comes a long way behind yours in literary worth, for we have all been struck by the beauty of your style as much as by the force of your arguments. I have ventured to say in my preface that my book is in some respects the complement of yours. But written and printed as it was from month to month, and while, indeed, I was very unfit for writing, there are many blemishes.

---

[72] In serial form which undoubtedly contributed to the rambling tendency that contrasted unfavourably with the organized symmetry of Admiral Mahan's book.

[73] Mahan Papers. Library of Congress, Washington, D.C. (The letter was headed, in Mahan's hand, 'Admiral Colomb—a well-known authority on Naval Warfare'.)

But still I think there is a good deal of useful matter in it.

I am afraid we over here think your views are so sound that we only hope your countrymen may not adopt them, unless before you do we may make a league to keep the rest of the world in order between us.

Believe me,

        Yours truly,
        (Signed) P. H. Colomb.

This letter is remarkable for the charity of view of one who had been 'scooped' and for the eye it cast into the future.

From the first, however, the American wore the popularity laurels. This was because Mahan's book was superbly organized, it was somewhat detached in its infrequent references to contemporary problems and it gave the air of being impartial—being written mainly about Britons for Americans. It was also due to Colomb's own outlook. Since Colomb represents a vital link in the chain of naval historians, the strengths and weaknesses of his thought processes revealed in this book are worthy of some examination.

The basic idea on which the whole argument in *Naval Warfare* hung was that sea power could only produce effective national benefits if 'command of the sea' was assured. Colomb claimed that Elizabethan and Early Stuart times showed only examples of 'cross ravaging' by which he meant rather unco-ordinated attacks of raids by opposing sea powers on the forts, land and personnel of the enemy.[74] The Dutch Wars with the sea supremacy of England and Holland staked closely on the outcome changed all that, and hence the decisive sea battle was the event that would award 'command of the sea' to the victor.[75] Once battle had given command of the sea, then commerce, as a result, would be generally protected and plans could be made to preserve its safe movement in detail and safely ravage enemy communications on or near enemy territory.[76] After the Dutch Wars, Colomb felt that the English had this supremacy and only required to defend it. Having made this corner-stone point, he then went on to discuss the requirements and preventative actions involved in an invasion of the British Isles. As we have seen, this question was not new to him and he proceeded to deal with it in detail and he must have hoped with finality. Carefully and methodically he

[74] P. H. Colomb, *Naval Warfare*, pp. 1–2.
[75] *Ibid.*, pp. 24 and 46.
[76] *Ibid.*, p. 81.

discussed every projected invasion of consequence between 1690 and the Trafalgar campaign, and he came to the conclusion that the inviolability of the British Isles was not an accident.[77] The great French mistake, repeated with monotonous regularity, was to imagine that an invasion attempt could be coincident with rather than be the successor of a sea battle. Consequently French planners were nearly always guilty of the basic military error of operating two plans simultaneously without first giving one priority either in execution or preliminary planning.[78] The Earl St. Vincent some ninety odd years before had referred to those without confidence in the navy's protective role as 'the old ladies'.[79] Here at last, were ninety-five pages of chapter and verse to calm all the ladies.

Warming to his task, Colomb then turned to discuss projected land invasion overseas, and for two hundred pages he detailed the failure of such projects in the eighteenth century, in cases where the sea was not commanded, and even where a smaller undefeated protective naval force was in the vicinity of the projected landing.[80] He certainly worked his history hard and undoubtedly his full exemplification bored many a reader. The Admiral, however, was alive to the fact that principles of warfare, like unseen shoals, were only gradually discovered. Aware of his own weakness, as well as that of his reader, he remarked, humorously, after some fifty pages filled with historical example, that 'we may suppose that it [the shoal] is now marked in the historical chart, and that its position is well known'.[81]

In the same careful fashion he used his historical examples to discuss the ships versus forts controversy. Veering slightly from his 1889 position at the R.U.S.I., he now demonstrated that ships were almost certain to come badly out of an engagement with forts.[82] At the same time he maintained that forts were only a delaying mechanism in the face of a determined attack by superior combined naval and land forces, and concluded that one of the

[77] P.H. Colomb, *Naval Warfare*, pp. 107-221.

[78] *Ibid.*, p. 147.

[79] Referring to plans to meet invasion threats by increased manpower, the Earl St. Vincent wrote of 'the item of his estimates of no other use than to calm the fears of old ladies both in and out'. See Admiral Sir William James, *Old Oak* (London, 1950), p. 190.

[80] P. H. Colomb, *Naval Warfare*, pp. 203-430. This was done in meticulous detail, and in the work there is a wealth of material for the practising naval historian.

[81] *Ibid.*, p. 272.

[82] This assumed, however, the absence or defeat of the fort's protecting sea force. But see *Ibid.*, p. 416.

requisites of successful invasion was to land the invaders well clear of the formal reception preparations on shore. Actually this accorded well with the general eighteenth-century view of the purpose for which fortifications existed.

This, in brief, was *Naval Warfare*, a book by an Admiral that treated history as a serious source from which to form principles about the nature and use of sea power. Yet his method was historical rape rather than historical seduction. Colomb unceremoniously dismounted his muse from the scholarly coach where conclusions are seldom absolute, and fiercely demanded that she 'stand and deliver'. For the historian there is something slightly vulgar in this self-confident, masterful sailor pushing and pulling about at history to produce the results he wanted. Yet it is not too difficult to understand his reasoning. Casting about for the clue that made sense of the whole naval revolution he found the answer in history. Here was the safe stick with which to reform the navy and bludgeon the army, and he laid about him with vigour. It must also be borne in mind that his historical examples were not crudely presented and that he was much of the time talking good sound common sense. His chief difficulty was that he laid too heavy a burden upon history, even naval history, without entirely understanding either his own, or the subject's, limitations. The subject's weakness is that history is a record of the past, and although prophets may extract high probability values from a study of that record and call them 'principles', reputable historians are seldom wise to attempt such pronouncements. History and prophecy are not the same thing. If a house has been burgled every night for 364 nights it might not be unwise to speculate that a constable's presence would be useful on the 365th night, but history cannot guarantee that the constable will see action. This simple fact is by no means clear to or even accepted by all academics today and it is small wonder that an amateur coming to the subject rather late in life found it troublesome.

This lack of understanding gave to Colomb's work certain blemishes that neither his accuracy nor his case compilations could eradicate. For instance, take his basic contention that 'command of the sea' was the primary principle in naval war. From a limited, sailor's approach to the history of the Dutch Wars, he deduced 'principles' that he applied rigorously to all subsequent wars. Writing years later another Admiral who was not himself averse to quoting history with the answers already in mind, Sir Reginald Custance put his finger on the trouble when he stated that Colomb never defined 'command of the sea' properly 'but', Custance wrote, 'he confused the relations between the national or political object and the military aim by introducing the term'.[83] Colomb's intense desire to elevate the idea of naval usefulness led him to the position where he virtually declared that naval war was an end in itself and not the means to an end;[84] indeed he blamed the prevalent misunderstanding of the true nature of sea power on the then current failure to comprehend that idea. It was only a brief, shaky step from that contention to the absurdity that the nation existed for the navy.

With the basic contention unstable, it is not surprising to find the detailed examples suffering from the same over-confidence. For instance, when Colomb looked at the problem of island invasion in the Caribbean in the eighteenth century, he selected his evidence from that local area: opposing fleets hovered in proximity, results or lack of them were studied and conclusions reached. The investigator did not feel constrained, however, to ascertain whether the movements described might be the product of, for instance, instructions from home to the local commanders. That is to say his wars were largely fought in convenient sealed-off geographical or command compartments, even as his historical navy operated in a compartment that was sealed off from the political and social life of the State. Similarly Colomb's bludgeoning technique prevented him from thinking his way into an historical period so that he often interpreted facts to suit conclusions at which he had already arrived. Writing of a British squadron being delayed from action by forts at Vigo for eight days in 1718, he remarked on how much more valuable a preponderance of naval force might have been to the Spaniards. Why this *non sequitur*? Spain was not a great naval power and Colomb knew very well that the whole purpose of fortification in the seventeenth and eighteenth centuries was not to win wars but to delay an enemy and that here was a perfectly good example of a fort serving that function admirably. A useful land fort, however, did not suit the Admiral's naval argument, and so he deliberately drew a conclusion that suited his propagandist rather than his academic intention.[85]

Colomb's work suffered from a too smug presumption that

[83] Admiral Sir Reginald Custance. *A Study of War* (London, 1924), p. 102.
[84] Colomb, *Naval Warfare*, p. 80.
[85] *Ibid.*, p. 331. Colomb argued with himself about this, and based his defence on the fact that the delay gained by the Spaniards did not allow the relieving land force to arrive in time to be effective. Not very strong reasoning for one addicted to drawing 'principles'.

history could be exploited for immediate practical results, and the blemishes are visible both in general and in detail. He overplayed his hand. His ideas were in line with the compartmentalized thinking prevalent at the time which strangely enough the Admiral was attempting to destroy. His error was probably a dual one; on the one hand, he dealt with naval warfare as a phenomenon isolated from the organic life and purposes of the State, and on the other he attempted not only to raise the status of the navy to a position of equality with the army, but even to make it supreme. These two tendencies were complementary in his thought, and there is probably much justification for such an approach to strategy on the part of a naval officer-historian who wrote with the successful navy of an island kingdom in mind. The actual result, though, was that he tended to fall into the same specialistic errors that marred the thought of the soldiers whose ideas he was attempting to refute.[86]

It must not be thought that because his work was flawed, it was of no value. The reverse is true. His special use of history made some naval men, and others, look upon the study of naval history as a useful occupation. By presenting such history in a strong light, even if sometimes it was over-illuminated, he made it appear respectable. Along with Mahan and Laughton he had much to do with the great surge of interest in naval history that marked the years 1890 to 1915. He was a pioneer and if he helped to provide an arena for all sorts of crude propagandists he also disclosed a fertile field for his distinguished historian successors to till.

It must further be acknowledged that Admiral Colomb's general treatment of the requirements for, and preventives against, overseas invasion represented a more sound doctrine than anyone else, either pro- or anti-navy people, had been able to develop up to that time. If his argument was weakened by the overstatement of ideas that could never be entirely conclusive, it nevertheless represented a line of thought that was functionally sound and was capable of development and refinement by other scholars who gradually accumulated more historical evidence and technique. He had written the 'New Testament' of the Blue Water School, and naval apologists and those who supported the idea of a naval-centred defence owed him a great debt—even if often they failed to acknowledge it. Lord Fisher and Winston Churchill were by no

---

[86] It is worth noting here that if the soldiers tended to serve their own interests, they did at least grapple with the problem. The navy tended to be disdainful of any 'conference-type' attempts to arrive at strategic over-all policy.

means the only people responsible for what essential naval readiness there existed in 1914. History had a big part in this and Colomb pioneered for its acceptance.

It must be also acknowledged that Colomb was, within the limits sketched, a real historian. It is probable that the piling of example upon example that sometimes seemed to stem from a desire to overwhelm his reader opponents was also traceable to a craftsman's delight in the accumulation of historical material. *Naval Warfare* is shot through with those telling asides that reveal a mind immersed in its subject and with historical processes in general. There can be little doubt that the extravagant use of example was partly the result of a desire to perpetuate intellectual discoveries in print. The work, within its limits, was reliably done.

After his long apprenticeship in naval controversy at the R.U.S.I., and his sharp passage of literary arms with the army people through his lectures in 1887-90 and in *Naval Warfare*, Colomb must have sensed that his real talents lay more in the literary-academic than in the pure propagandist field. He was moving towards the purely academic field. It is not surprising, therefore, that his last significant work was a biography of a sailor for whom he had deep respect. It described the career of Admiral Sir Astley Cooper-Key[87] and was published in 1898. Colomb skilfully used the life and personality of this pro-steam sailor to tell the story of the Royal Navy in transition in the nineteenth century. It was a congenial task to describe the frustrations and eventual success of one who, early in his career, staked his future on being part of the new developing iron navy. Biography had its difficulties as well, however, for when writing of Key's tenure of office as senior Naval Lord at the Admiralty, he was faced with the fact that his reformer somewhat unaccountably proved to be a damp squib in high office and the further fact that the Admiralty authorities censored what revelations Colomb could produce.[88]

The result was a work that demanded a crescendo conclusion both which ended on a muted and unhappy note. Compared with the salty inanities recorded of many another Victorian sailor, it represents accurate and well-written scholarship. His trend towards descriptive rather than combative writing continued as he

[87] Sir Astley Cooper-Key (1821-88), Admiral. Member of Royal Commission on National Defence; First President and founder of R.N. College, Greenwich, 1872-6; Senior Naval Lord of Admiralty, 1879-85.
[88] See P. H. Colomb, *The Memoirs of Sir Astley Cooper Key*, Preface, p. vii.

prepared a biography of Lord Torrington.[89] This work was cut short by Admiral Colomb's death.

The work of Philip Howard Colomb and that of his brother John, on whose foundation he built, advanced the cause of naval history as an academic endeavour, strengthened the position of the Royal Navy in a time of uncertainty and, Lord Fisher's thoughtless disdain notwithstanding, laid the groundwork for the defence of the reforming work at the Admiralty in the next pulsating decade of naval growth.

---

[89] Arthur Herbert, Earl of Torrington (1647–1716), Admiral of the Fleet. Appointed Admiral, Lord of Admiralty, and C.-in-C. Channel Fleet in 1688–9; Action 30 June, 1690; Court martial, December, 1690; acquitted, not employed again.

4

THE AMERICAN

Admiral Alfred Mahan

FROM the time that *The Influence of Sea Power Upon History* was published in 1889 until the death of its author in 1914, Alfred Thayer Mahan was the most influential naval writer alive.[1] Although he was not the first, nor even perhaps the most profound, of the new school of writers who saw in naval history something more significant than the customary mere chronicle of courage in combat afloat,[2] the impact of his work made naval history a subject of serious study not only to naval leaders but also to monarchs, naval publicists, politicians and bureaucrats during the years preceding the catastrophe of 1914. Since his first 'Influence' book was published at a time when naval rivalries were becoming pronounced in Europe, it is difficult to determine the degree to which the book intensified the naval race or conversely the extent of the influence of naval consciousness on the sale of the book.[3] It is safe to say, however, that there was mutual stimulation. It can also be said that by showing the extent of naval influence in European affairs in the eighteenth century, Mahan provided budding naval apologists with an historically-

[1] For authoritative estimates and comment on this point see Arthur J. Marder, *The Anatomy of British Sea Power* (New York, 1940), pp. 45–7 and William E. Livezey, *Mahan on Sea Power* (Norman, Okla., 1947), pp. 51–76.

[2] William James, *Naval History of Great Britain* (1783–1810), 6 vols. was a standard work, and Mahan stated that James 'had not a military idea in his head'. Captain A. T. Mahan, *From Sail to Steam* (New York, 1907), p. 279.

[3] The extent of his influence upon naval rivalries is discussed by most writers and commentators on Mahan. He made the points himself in his Presidential address to the United States Naval Institute in 1892. See A. T. Mahan, 'The Practical Character of the Naval War College', *U.S.N.I. Proceedings* (1893), pp. 156–57.

based pattern of sea power which appeared to reveal immutable rules concerning the role of navies in international affairs that could be neglected only at a nation's peril. Statesmen in Washington, Whitehall and the Wilhelmstrasse kept their blue-pencilled copies to hand ready to quote 'Captain Mahan' with an air of conscious finality to the unwary small-navy man. The big-navy prophets now had a bible. In the universities and the academic periodicals, the arrival of a new and important historian was acknowledged with parallel alacrity.[4] Even the French, wedded to new interpretations of doctrine that had helped to defeat the great Napoleon, recognized his ability.[5]

Mahan's impact then was international. More particularly his influence on both the growth of British naval power and on the beginnings of the new school of British naval history was profound, and in this sense he belongs in the main stream of British naval historians. It is significant, for instance, that the first full-scale and still very valuable biography of Mahan was written by an Englishman, C. Carlisle Taylor, in 1920.[6] Indeed the first American biographer, Captain W. D. Puleston, had as one of his main objects the reclaiming of Mahan for Americans as an American-centred writer.[7] In this task of repatriation Puleston was successful if one values Mahan chiefly in terms of his prophetic or propagandist activity. After all Mahan was for most of his life a serving officer in the United States Navy. His patriotism is beyond question. Further, a high proportion of his time was spent in either instructing American sailors in the nature of sea power, or in lecturing his fellow nationals on the proper use of sea power for the purpose of advancing the interests of his own country.

American needs called forth his genius and retained his attention. For years he was an influential Presidential and State Department adviser; and it was probably the neglect of his advice by the American administration in 1914 that hastened his death.[8] In so far as he was a propagandist and a government servant,

---

[4] For example by Sir John Knox Laughton in the *Edinburgh Review*. Mahan was given honorary degrees by both Oxford and Cambridge.

[5] Margaret Tuttle Sprout, 'Mahan: Evangelist of Sea Power' in *Makers of Modern Strategy*, ed. Edward Mead Earle (Princeton, 1952), pp. 441–2.

[6] Charles Carlisle Taylor, *The Life of Admiral Mahan* (London, 1920).

[7] W. D. Puleston, *Mahan* (London, 1939), p. 13.

[8] Although Mahan's outspoken support for Great Britain in 1914 caused President Wilson to forbid him to write, the historian had a disciple in the Department of the Navy—Franklin Delano Roosevelt. See W. L. Neumann, 'Franklin Delano Roosevelt: A Disciple of Admiral Mahan', *U.S.N.I. Proceedings* (1952), pp. 713–9.

therefore, there can be no doubt about Mahan's American orientation. Viewed as an historian, however, he must be looked at somewhat differently. Aside from his own native inventive genius much of his early inspiration seems to have come from the pages of the *Journal* of the R.U.S.I. upon which the brothers Colomb and Professor Laughton had stamped their opinions indelibly.[9] Also the historical subjects he chose to write on concerned British sea power. The three 'Influence' works[10] and his *The Life of Nelson*[11] were all centred on the Royal Navy and these books represented his most solid work as an historian. His *The Life of Admiral Farragut*[12] and *The Gulf and Inland Waters*,[13] his two major historical works on American naval history, are somewhat less impressive. *The Gulf* was written before 1885 and before he had begun to formulate his theory of sea power. *The Life of Admiral Farragut* was written while work was in train for the second of the 'Influence' books and he himself regarded this 'short' book as an 'interruption' in the more important task that he had set himself.[14] Mahan's admiration for the British nation and especially its navy had no real bearing on the fact that his work was largely done in British history. It was simply that the area in which he practised his craft and the purpose for which he exercised it were different. In studying to determine naval 'influence' in the recent past, Mahan found that the Royal Navy provided the best continuous examples for his theme so that as an historian he worked in that field. The lessons he drew for contemporaries were resolutely applied to his native land. Nevertheless, with the notable exception of his fellow naval historian, Theodore Roosevelt, his American readers were generally strategic pupils. It was in England that he found his historical colleagues—and Mahan was above all a great historian.

Mahan, like Admiral Colomb, came to the writing and serious study of naval history relatively late in life. Indeed, he had three

[9] Mahan, *From Sail to Steam*, p. 280; J. L. Laughton, 'The Study of Naval History' *R.U.S.I. Journal* (1896), pp. 796–7. Mahan corresponded with Admiral Colomb and Laughton, see *Mahan Papers*, Library of Congress, Washington. D.C.
[10] Capt. A. T. Mahan, *The Influence of Sea Power upon History* (London, 1890); *The Influence of Sea Power upon the French Revolution and Empire*, 2 vols. (London, 1892); *Sea Power in its Relations to the War of 1812*, 2 vols. (London, 1905).
[11] Capt. A. T. Mahan, *The Life of Nelson*, 2 vols. (London, 1897).
[12] Capt. A. T. Mahan, *The Life of Admiral Farragut* (New York, 1892).
[13] Capt. A. T. Mahan, *The Gulf and Inland Waters* (New York, 1883).
[14] Mahan, *From Sail to Steam*, p. 310.

Admiral Alfred Mahan

discernable, if overlapping, careers. Until he was forty-five he was a relatively unremarkable officer in the United States Navy. Then, in the twilight of his naval career, a special appointment called forth his undoubted talents as a naval historian. Finally, after his retirement from the navy, the international reputation he gained as an historian made him *the* American naval expert. While the Government sought his advice and services on matters of high diplomacy and naval policy, the public of his country were instructed in the role of great naval power through a spate of articles and books that increasingly deserted history for the field of contemporary judgement and prophecy. Despite opinions to the contrary, it appears likely that Mahan's fame will rest on his historical ability rather than on his prophetic talents.[15]

Alfred Thayer Mahan was born on 22 September, 1840. His father, Dennis Hart Mahan, was Professor of Civil and Military Engineering at the United States Military Academy at West Point where Alfred was raised.[16] The father seems to have been something of a pedant, although a knowledgeable one, who had spent some time in Europe and was influenced by Napoleonic war concepts as embalmed by Jomini. He had a profound respect for scholarship. Although the younger Mahan toyed with the idea of a career in the Episcopal Church and spent some time at Columbia College, he finally entered the United States Naval Academy at Annapolis.[17] Despite the facts that his father pronounced him unsuited to a military career, that he possessed a rather overscrupulous and solitary temperament,[18] and that he lacked the hearty co-ordinated physique thought to be necessary to a military man,[19] Mahan's mental gifts were never in doubt and he graduated second in his class in 1859.

Almost at once the young graduate tasted warfare, serving in the Federal Navy during the War of Secession, as he invariably

---

[15] One writer has given him a debatable, but undoubtedly a contemporary, claim to greatness, i.e. 'Mahan's chief claim to fame is the fact that he guessed right about historical events, which I suppose is the ultimate test of a successful social scientist.' See Albert Lepawsky, 'A Tribute to Mahan, as a Social Scientist', *U.S.N.I. Proceedings* (1940), p. 1625.

[16] Major-General G. W. Cullum, 'Biographical Sketch of Professor Dennis Hart Mahan', *Register of West Point Graduates and Former Cadets* (U.S. Military Academy, 1953).

[17] Mahan discussed his reaction to the Naval Academy at length in *From Sail to Steam*. See especially Chapters III and IV.

[18] At Annapolis he displayed great reserve and indulged his solitary nature in long walks alone. These traits did not recede with the passage of time. See Puleston, *Mahan*, p. 37.

[19] He was clumsy. See Taylor, *Life*, p. 10.

referred to the Civil War. He served with credit but without special distinction in various vessels of the blockading fleet, and emerged from the conflict with the rank of Lieutenant-Commander. Between 1867 and 1869, in that rank, he enjoyed the broadening experience of a world cruise in USS *Iroquois*[20] visiting ports in Africa and Asia as well as those in China and Japan.[21] In 1870 he returned home by way of Suez and Europe, taking a few months to visit France, Italy and England. The year 1872 saw him both married and promoted to the rank of Commander. He served for a time off South America in command of USS *Wasp*[22] and then for a year at the Boston Navy Yard. Being temporarily retired for part of the year 1876, he lived in France during the summer, until his appointment as head of the Ordnance Department at Annapolis. After this spell of shore duty and more of the same at the New York Navy Yard, he went to sea in command of USS *Wachusett*[23] off the west coast of South America where he remained until he was called back in 1885, to teach naval history at the War College. He contracted to begin lecturing at the College in 1886.

It was at this point, in his forty-fifth year, that Mahan's career moved out of the customary waters of a serving officer and ventured into seas never before charted by a professional American sailor. Up to 1885 he was a well-read naval officer who occasionally had exercised his pen to good but not remarkable effect. After 1885, he rapidly became a writer to whom a return to sea duty appeared as an unwelcome interruption to his new and successful literary career. Although he had been unconsciously preparing for this work for some years, and indeed in some ways from birth, the change was nonetheless sudden. It is true that, in the eighteen-seventies, he read widely, that in 1878 he wrote a Third Prize

---

[20] USS *Iroquois*. Wood, screw-propelled, 3rd-rate steamer of 1,016 tons. Launched 1858 at N.Y. Navy Yard. See the delightfully detailed account of the early American steam navy in Frank M. Bennett, *The Steam Navy of the United States* (Pittsburg, 1896), Appendix B.

[21] He was particularly impressed with the extent of British influence in the world. Writing of the British soldier he remarked that 'It is not that there is so much of him, but that he is so manywhere...' *From Sail to Steam*, p. 222.

[22] USS *Wasp*. Wood, screw-propelled vessel. Formerly British register *Emma Henry*, captured at sea December 1863 by USS *Cherokee* and condemned by U.S. prize court for $294,869.01. Sold at Montivideo in 1876 for $2,548.47. Bennett, *The Steam Navy*, pp. 624, 627.

[23] USS *Wachusett*. Wood, screw-propelled, 3rd-rate steamer of 1,032 tons. Launched 1861 at Boston Navy Yard, *ibid*.

Naval essay for the United States Naval Institute[24] and that he was asked to write a history of the naval side of the Civil War that appeared in 1883.[25] Nevertheless his background did not give any clear indication of the power of his intellect.[26] In fact by 1885 his mind was mature, and only leisure time and some stimulation were needed to convert latent talent into profitable production. In 1885–6 these were provided by the strong personality of Commodore Stephen B. Luce[27] the founder of the Naval War College on whose conception of the value of history to serving officers rested both the inception of the college and the Mahan phenomenon.[28] Since both the dynamic Luce and the new college were in a hurry, Mahan was bullied (not unkindly) and thus forced to sacrifice definitiveness to the pressure of time. Hence the lectures which became *The Influence of Sea Power upon History* were compiled in less than a year. With the exception of an enforced spell of duty at Puget Sound in 1888[29] and a couple of years when the college did not function,[30] Mahan stayed at the Naval War College until 1892. His *Influence of Sea Power upon History* lectures were published in 1889. He also lectured on naval strategy, and when he left the college these strategy lectures were solemnly re-read to the collegians every year. The lectures finally emerged in book form in 1911.[31] The two leisure years between

---

[24] A. T. Mahan, 'Naval Education for Officers and Men', *U.S.N.I. Proceedings*, (1879) pp. 345–76.

[25] *The Gulf and Inland Waters*, see note 14.

[26] During his stay in France, in 1876, he wrote some historical material on French cathedrals, for which he could not secure a publisher. See Puleston, *Mahan* p. 71.

[27] Rear-Admiral Stephen Bleecker Luce, U.S.N. (1827–1917). Wrote textbook *Seamanship*, 1863; Founder of Naval War College (establishment secured 1884) and first President of that College; retired, 1889. The College was established at Newport, R.I.

[28] Though he was doubtful at first that it could be done there was no doubt of his intention to use history to throw light on problems confused by contemporary naval changes. See Puleston, *Mahan*, p. 89; Taylor, *Life*, p. 26.

[29] Mahan, *From Sail to Steam*, pp. 299–300.

[30] The Naval War College was not popular at first, either with the authorities in Washington or the naval service in general. A good proportion of Mahan's time was spent fighting for the continued existence of the College. See A. T. Mahan, 'Presidential Address at the opening of the 4th Annual Session of the Naval War College'. *U.S.N.I. Proceedings* (1888), pp. 622, 624–5.

[31] It is necessary to emphasize that, though revised somewhat for publication, this book embodied his thought and work of the late eighties when it was largely composed. Also note that Mahan kept the designation 'Captain' for writing purposes despite the fact that he had been promoted 'Admiral'. Captain A. T. Mahan, *Naval Strategy* (London, 1911).

1890 and 1892, saw the publication of *The Influence of Sea Power upon the French Revolution and Empire* and *The Life of Admiral Farragut*. While *Farragut* only reached a limited audience, the two 'Influence' books had a wider impact. Admiral Colomb at once admitted the superiority of Mahan's work over his own;[32] and Laughton wrote handsome reviews of the American's work in the *Edinburgh Review*. He had become famous in England.[33] At this point, and much against his will,[34] Mahan was sent to sea in command of USS *Chicago*[35] on a European detail. He was sent partly because he was due for more sea time, partly perhaps as official punishment for being a supporter of the unpopular Naval War College of which he was for a time President, and partly because a bureaucrat in Washington decided that 'it is not the business of a naval officer to write books'.[36]

The cruise of the *Chicago* in European waters produced some unpleasantness between the famous Captain-author and his shipmate, Flotilla Commander Rear-Admiral Henry Erben, who was a salty type.[37] Yet the cruise did bring home to Mahan the extent of his success as an historian, for when he visited England the red carpet was rolled out for him as sailors, writers, politicians including the Prime Minister, and Oxford and Cambridge vied with one another to do him honour. Furthermore, he was encouraged, and provided with much documentary assistance, towards writing a *Life of Nelson*.[38] As a result, he began work on *Nelson* while at sea in his cabin on the *Chicago*. Shortly after the European cruise was over Mahan solicited and obtained retirement from the navy; thus

---

[32] 'I think all our naval men regarded it as *the* naval book of the age' and 'my book comes a long way behind yours in literary merit.' Admiral Colomb to Mahan, 26 April, 1891, *The Mahan Papers*, Library of Congress.

[33] J. K. Laughton, 'Captain Mahan on Maritime Power', *Edinburgh Review* (1890), pp. 420–53; J. K. Laughton, 'Captain Mahan on Maritime Power', *ibid.* (1893) pp. 484–518.

[34] He did not attempt to conceal his displeasure then or later. See Mahan, *From Sail to Steam*, p. 313.

[35] USS *Chicago*. Steam warship. Dead weight 4,500 tons. Launched 1887, J. Roach and Sons, Chester. Cost $809,923.44. See Bennett, *The Steam Navy*, p. 778.

[36] Mahan, *From Sail to Steam*, p. 311.

[37] Mahan was a *competent* officer. However, Erben notwithstanding, he seems to have taken no joy in the details of command work during this cruise. See J. M. Ellicott, 'Three Naval Cranks and what they Turned', *U.S.N.I. Proceedings* (1924), p. 1623.

[38] He had a high regard for Nelson. He once said that it was impossible to do good biography without respect for its hero. See Mahan, *From Sail to Steam*, p. 306.

Admiral Alfred Mahan

he never reached flag rank during his active naval career[39] but he was at last entirely free to devote himself completely to the historical muse.

In point of fact, there was only one more serious book on naval history in Mahan's plans and by 1905 he had written *Sea Power in its Relations to the War of 1812* to complete his 'Influence' trilogy. He also published in 1902 *Types of Naval Officers*,[40] a collected series of biographies of British officers in the eighteenth century. This work was less intense than the 'Influence' books but still scholarly and historical. With these books his sustained *historical* book production ended, and, although his output for periodicals continued high and some of this was compiled in book form, he became increasingly preoccupied with the self-imposed occupation of national naval schoolmaster until his death in the autumn of 1914.

The schoolmaster, government-adviser role was partly due to the reputation his work earned for him, but it was undoubtedly also partly due to his friendship with Theodore Roosevelt. The latter had served as an instructor in Naval History at the Naval War College under Mahan.[41] He had been Assistant Secretary of the Navy just before the Spanish-American war and Mahan was called to Washington as a member of the Naval War Board in 1898. Also Roosevelt encouraged and consulted Mahan during his long pro-navy Presidency of the United States. The Roosevelt association undoubtedly increased the influence of Mahan on the development of American sea power.[42] Mahan remained a special lecturer at the Naval War College until 1912. In 1908 he was a member of the Commission to report on the reorganization of the Navy Department. He also served as chairman of a joint Commission on Naval Affairs and as a member of a Sub-Committee on Department methods. All this time he wrote both publicly and privately, and with missionary fervour and proliferation, to interest his countryman at large in the nature and application

---

[39] He was promoted Rear-Admiral in 1906 in a general promotion of retired ex-Civil War officers. See Puleston, *Mahan*, p. 263. The extra pay, £200 *per annum* pleased him. See Taylor, *Life*, p. 272.

[40] Captain A. T. Mahan, *Types of Naval Officers Drawn from the History of the British Navy* (London, 1902).

[41] Roosevelt lectured at the War College, particularly on the War of 1812, a subject about which he wrote a book and contributed a chapter to W. L. Clowes' *History of the Royal Navy*. For his history at the War College, see Mahan, 'Presidential Address, etc.', *U.S.N.I. Proceedings* (1888), p. 638.

[42] One can hardly use the word 'disciple' in referring to Theodore Roosevelt. He took what he wanted.

of sea power. In this connexion Captain Mahan has not gone unremembered.[43]

It was the historian, however, that made the publicist possible; and it is as historian that Mahan is chiefly to be considered here. In this connexion it is important to consider in more detail the genesis of the historical mind which suddenly flowered between 1885 and 1890. Aside from *The Gulf* and his prize essay of 1878 his literary production before 1885, as has been shown, was slight. He did, however, give some historical lectures to his ship's company off South America in 1874. One can only say that these were painstakingly done, that is according to his wife.[44] More revealing, perhaps, is the fact that he excelled more at academic than practical pursuits while at Annapolis. He had always exhibited a scholarly turn of mind. Still more important was the influence of Mahan's father. The elder Mahan had a considerable reputation as a teacher by historical example at West Point and this influence was acknowledged by Alfred to Captain J. M. Ellicott, on the quarter deck of the *Chicago* in response to a pointed question.[45] This quality of Mahan's mind appears to have impressed his influential supporter, Stephen B. Luce, as early as 1861 during a brief association of the two men at Annapolis.[46] Mahan's naturally reflective and active mind had also been quickened by foreign travel, and he is known to have subscribed to the *Manchester Guardian* in the eighteen-seventies.[47] Probably not many serving officers took a foreign periodical, and Mahan was undoubtedly a well-informed man on matters of general past and current history before 1883. But, as he himself has acknowledged, it was the sense of purpose that the War College appointment gave him that disciplined him as an academic writer.[48]

In addition Mahan seems to have had a natural aversion to that continual puddling in the technical elements of his profession that engrossed naval officers on both sides of the Atlantic Ocean in the eighteen-eighties. He undoubtedly looked upon the Naval War College appointment as an opportunity to demonstrate to his colleagues that technical or 'practical' (a word he hated) know-

[43] Comprehensive bibliographical reference to Mahan's works may be found in Puleston's *Mahan* and more completely in Livezey's *Mahan on Sea Power*. The contemporary commentator's flavour is immediately recognizable.

[44] Puleston, *Mahan*, p. 68.

[45] J. M. Ellicott, 'Sidelights on Mahan', *U.S.N.I. Proceedings* (1948), p. 1248.

[46] J. M. Ellicott, 'Three Naval Cranks, etc.', *U.S.N.I. Proceedings* (1924), p. 1625.

[47] Puleston, *Mahan*, p. 73.

[48] Mahan, *From Sail to Steam*, pp. 273, 274, 276.

ledge existed for the purpose of a higher application. By 1885 he had begun to think that the way out of the maze lay in understanding history, but he was not at all sure, at that point, just how universally liberating his escape valve would turn out to be. In a speech in 1892 he wrote revealingly of his neophyte trepidation: 'When I was first ordered to the College, before even I had begun to develop the subjects entrusted to me, an officer, considerably my senior in rank, asked what I was going to undertake. On my naming naval history, he rejoined, "Well, you won't have much to say about that".' Mahan went on, 'It struck, I am free to confess, a chord in my own breast.'[49] Well before that time, however, he had tasted of that happy conjunction of historical cause and effect so dear to the military historian. In his autobiography he has recorded:[50]

'During my last tour of shore duty I had read carefully Napier's *Peninsular War*, and had found myself in a new world of thought, keenly interested and appreciative, less of the brilliant narrative—though that few can fail to enjoy—than of the military sequences of cause and effect. The influence of Sir John Moore's famous march to Sahagun—less famous than it deserves to be—upon Napoleon's campaign in Spain, revealed to me by Napier like the sun breaking through a cloud, aroused an emotion as joyful as the luminary himself to a navigator doubtful of his position.' Such lyrical prose creates the impression that Mahan had recognized at first sight the kind of effect that he himself would strive to achieve.

Hence the man, the goal, the example and the call all came together in 1885. Mahan was additionally fortunate in that he took Jomini for his model, and in that he kept his published sources (he very seldom worked from direct documentary evidence) not preponderantly but none the less significantly French, for it was another legacy of his father's house at West Point that the naval historian was able to read French with ease. Jomini was helpful to Mahan as an example of how to introduce system into historical study in order to produce generalized rules or conclusions.[51] The idea that history has immutable, if difficult to define, 'principles' to offer her systematic inquirers was, as we shall see, both one of the secrets of Mahan's success as a naval writer and one of his more severe problems as a serious historian.

---

[49] Captain A. T. Mahan, 'The Practical Character of the Naval War College', *U.S.N.I. Proceedings* (1893), p. 156.
[50] Mahan, *From Sail to Steam*, p. 273.
[51] Puleston, *Mahan*, p. 90.

Jomini gave him guidance in facing that problem. This was of considerable importance, for it gave Mahan's work that cohesion and sense of universal applicability so lacking in previous naval histories and made it all seem 'practical' to the inquiring reader's mind.[52]

The use of French sources, especially for the purpose of filling in general European history, whether inadvertent or not, was a stroke of sheer genius. Any historian of the Royal Navy is immediately faced with the fact that he is dealing with what is, by and large, a fantastic success story, and as his subject reveals progressive improvement it becomes increasingly difficult not to become over-lyrical in bestowing the praise that the material virtually demands. This is easily exemplified by reference to the many American navalists who, in dealing with their two traumatic experiences of warfare with the United Kingdom, dwell in preoccupied fashion with single-ship actions in order triumphantly to demonstrate the fallibility of British naval power. Mahan, who saw in naval engagement something more than proof of individual ship and personal prowess[53] and who saw the significance of the power of naval pressure in the whole rather than the part, avoided the charge of being a worshipper of the Royal Navy as a consequence of the nature of his sources. He used French history and French historians to convict the French of their naval errors, and thus gave the impression that his pro-Royal Navy conclusions had been wrung from unwilling material by the sheer force of logic. It was this technique that gave rise to the words 'impartial authority'[54] that came so easily to the lips of his commentators both in England and America.

Since it was the tactical requirements of a new age of steam that were mainly responsible for Mahan's call to the War College, it is understandable and logical that his attitude to the study of history should be conditioned by that fact. Actually his practical approach was both the strength and weakness of his work as an historian. He never completely discarded this early attitude to the study of history. Therefore, although the wide range of his intellectual development often tends to mute and obscure the impression, Mahan's approach to the muse was fully as utilitarian

---

[52] Jomini was also important in showing Mahan how thin was the wall, if any, that divided military from diplomatic history; see *ibid*.

[53] Especially in his book on the war of 1812 he pointed up clearly the difference in significance of single-ship duels, and the later effects of a strong British blockade. See Mahan, *War of 1812*, vol. II, p. 208.

[54] From London *The Times*, 23 October, 1893. Reprinted in *U.S.N.I. Proceedings* (1893), p. 458.

as that of Admiral Colomb. Take his first, and in many ways his most important 'Influence' book as an example. It had two purposes: to show the impact of naval affairs on the shifts of European power politics for a hundred-year period;[55] and to expound the principles that emerged from a study of the main naval operations and battles during the same period.[56] It will be observed at once that the tactical incentive that originally sent him to the College had become subordinate to the demonstration of the strategic illustration. The reason for this inversion was a severely practical one. Mahan early concluded that the lessons to be drawn from strategic study tended to be more universally applicable than those derived from a concentration on a study of tactics. Because his expansive mind found the breadth of the diplomatic field more congenial, he was automatically attracted to it rather than to the narrow tactical one. At the same time Mahan was, as are we all, an instinctive child of his age; and although he objected to concepts of naval purpose being blurred by a too-ready reference to modern technical development, he was none the less influenced by current beliefs and found more release from these binding chains in dealing with strategy than with tactics.

Whatever its mental genesis, however, *The Influence of Sea Power upon History* was recognized by Mahan himself as being something more than an officer, and Navy Department, do-it-yourself kit. The new historian was very conscious of the fact that he was writing history. Like most literate non-academics he seems to have been inclined to believe, at least in the beginning, that scholars are accustomed to write with almost super-human detachment and omniscience, and he was unaware that such an attainment is a very rare scholarly gift. This *naïveté* disclosed itself in his intense desire to become academically respectable in the fulsome introduction to his first important book, as prolonged wrestling with the definition and acceptability of one word, 'principle', shows. Discussed in his first 'Influence' book, 'principle' was also the chief preoccupation in his Presidential lecture to the American Historical Association in 1902.[57] In *Naval Strategy*, published in 1911, he resurrected the vexed problem for discussion once more and in detail.

[55] Mahan, *Influence of Sea Power upon History*, preface.
[56] *Ibid.*, p. 2 ff.
[57] Captain A. T. Mahan, 'Subordination in Historical Treatment', Presidential Address to the American Historical Association, 26 December, 1902. Printed in *Naval Administration and Warfare* (London, 1908).

The use of 'principles' in the first 'Influence' book was obvious. Mahan stated bluntly that students of both tactics and strategy could absorb firm principles from a study of the lessons of the past. He used Hannibal's campaign against Rome and the Battle of the Nile (1798) to illustrate his contention that historical and strategic lessons could be applied to warfare in any age.[58] Although he conceded his inability to pronounce 'immutable' principles and felt strategy to be a more fruitful field for their illustration than tactics, he gave the impression of the novice attempting to convince his reader of the importance of his view through the blunt method of repetition. The argument was overstrained in detail and insufficient in depth for this purpose, but it was and is none the less convincing to the casual reader. Later on, in *Naval Strategy*, the discussion became more involved. He took a resolute plunge stating that naval strategy was based upon fundamental truths which 'when correctly formulated, are rightly called principles, these truths, when ascertained, are in themselves unchangeable.'[59] This was definite enough, but then Mahan proceeded to qualify the definition by stating that new technical development might affect the mode of application. 'This will constitute development,' he said, 'alike in the practice of Naval Strategy, and in that statement of its laws and principles which we call theory.'[60] He then conjured up that great panjandrum of the twentieth century, science, and stated that, as in science, strategic laws were immutable but that the application of those laws might change. He went so far as directly to compare experience of warfare to scientific experiment.[61] But evidently he was not so convinced of the immutability of principles as the foregoing would lead one to suspect. He also asserted that principles were of no use to a practitioner who had not reflected on their application.[62] Three pages later he made another stab at definition with the words 'study is simply the intelligent observation of incidents, of events, and drawing from them conclusions which we call principles.'[63] Again, not quite so definite. Then he justified the historian's use of 'principles' by stating that they were also used by Corbett, an inadvertant yet graceful compliment.[64] This was

[58] Mahan, *Influence of Sea Power upon History*, Introduction. Especially pp. 21–24.
[59] Mahan, *Naval Strategy*, p. 2.
[60] *Ibid.*
[61] *Ibid.*
[62] *Ibid.*, p. 9.
[63] *Ibid.*, p. 12.
[64] *Ibid.*, p. 16.

undoubtedly, however, the defence of one intent upon buttressing a breachable fortification in his thought by any means ready to hand. Finally, Mahan wound up in something of a rout from his original position when he went on to compare the value of the study of history and of principles.

Whether there are immutable principles in historical conclusion may be doubted. On the other hand the question of the utilitarian value of history is still, and is likely to remain, a matter on which thoughtful men and most historians will continue to disagree. It is for this reason that Mahan's rather unsatisfactory attempts to justify his approach are interesting. They reveal the serious student's concern with the credentials of his craft. Why did he take such pains?

Mahan, like his English fellow labourers, was faced with the task of proving that the study of history had uses for the naval officer. Thus, although he voiced contempt for the 'practical' approach that caused so much imbalance in the naval service of his day, he was at some pains not to run his new ship aground on that particular rock. In short, he directly took up the challenge and struggled to prove that his subject was of practical value and he made the attempt on ground that was familiar to his serving officer readers. This is observable in his flirtation with the word 'immutable' and in his daring, and unfortunately still not dead comparison of historical investigation to scientific experiment. Since both *The Influence of Sea Power Upon History* and *Naval Strategy* were books that emerged as edited lectures to naval officers one can see whom he was primarily attempting to convince. But he went further than that. In *Naval Strategy* he also discussed, perhaps unwisely from the naval service point of view, whether it would be more profitable to study history alone or principles alone. His conclusion was that it would be most profitable to combine the two, but that if the choice had to be made the study of history alone was to be preferred.[65] This admission qualifies Mahan for a benign smile from the historical muse.

It was, however, in the process of delivering his Presidential Address to the American Historical Association in 1902 that Mahan was forced to grapple directly with his status amongst historians. In this context one must realize that, while a military man might cause some fastidious academic eyebrows to be raised simply because he ventured into the academic field, he was not speaking to historians at a time when the pragmatic approach was generally unpopular with them. That great liberal,

[65] Mahan, *Naval Strategy*, p. 17.

Lord Acton, for instance, was shocked that Mandell Creighton should dare attempt a history of the papacy and give the impression of moral detachment.[66] Seeley always wrote with a purpose—'Narrative without generalization had no interest for him'.[67] In America Frederick Jackson Turner was not entirely without pre-set purpose in his researches. One could go on. Mahan, however, was concerned to justify himself. His books were renowned as sources of superb generalization and they were, as he admitted, dependent largely on printed secondary sources; therefore it is not surprising that he entitled his address 'Subordination in History'.

Although his development of the theme was scholarly and detached, Mahan based his central defence, almost defiantly, on practical results. With superb lack of modesty he contrasted himself, not unfavourably, with the renowned Lord Acton.[68] From the point of view adopted by Mahan, Acton was vulnerable. If the value of academic scholarship had anything to do with the business of communication then, when it came to the printed work, that great British scholar, lately deceased, had not been prolific outside the essay and periodical field. Undoubtedly, argued Mahan, Acton's mind was drenched with the wisdom of the ages. The shedding of some of this vast store of knowledge would have been of inestimable value to both scholars and mankind at large. Owing to a misguided passion for accuracy and completeness, however, only a few drops of this knowledge ever reached the general public. In contrast to this, Mahan had communicated; his books were written and distributed. This was his real defence and he went on to show how prolific historical production had been possible for a naval officer coming to the study of history late in life. Worthwhile production occurred, he said, through the proper use of certain questions which he addressed to history. By this means he was able to select and subordinate the material to produce valuable generalizations. Subordination of detail was thus important to achieving the desired pedagogical result. His purpose was pre-set. The method sometimes produced artistry as well. He used for an example the fact that one critic had accused him of giving the impression, in his *Life of Nelson*,

---

[66] Lord Acton said, 'It is the office of historical science to maintain morality as the sole impartial criterion of men and things, and the only one on which honest minds can be made to agree.' See G. P. Gooch, *History and Historians in the Nineteenth Century* (London, 1913), p. 376.

[67] *Ibid.*, p. 373.

[68] Mahan, 'Subordination, etc.', *Naval Administration and Warfare*, p. 248.

that the Lady Hamilton affair had cast a pall of gloom on Lord Nelson's last years. Mahan noted 'I confess that in reading this I thought I had unwittingly achieved an artistic effect',[69] For him then, the historian was the purposeful scholar allied to the artist. He went further and stated that the military historian found himself in a position of special advantage in that he 'naturally' applies his purpose (principles of war) to the writing of history.[70] Most of this, if not universally acceptable, is reasonable enough and not unworthy of men who have been classed above mere military scribblers. He extended his neck to the headsman somewhat when he attempted to argue that his conclusions were unlikely to be totally overthrown because of future original research in primary documents.[71] One can only state that twentieth-century historians have shown a great preference for original research and that not all their re-assessments have been negligible.

It should be noted here that Mahan's historical approach has been intelligently considered elsewhere as an integral part of his philosophical view of the universe. The sailor-historian was a very religious man and his spiritual convictions coloured all his thinking. As Francis Duncan points out, he looked on the universe as a place where God's plan was involved through the conflict between human beings, both singly and in groups.[72] He carried this conviction to such lengths that he could declare that arbitration, as a method of settling disputes, was immoral. Yet this view, limited as it may be because of its military-religious rigidity, in no way conflicted with his utilitarian approach to history—where generalizations could serve to show the sameness of man yesterday, today and for ever. In those days it was still possible for Mahan and millions like him to believe that it was safe to trust God and keep the powder dry. Today both assumptions enjoy less than universal acceptance.

If Mahan's writing had weaknesses in method, conclusion and logic, it had definite historical merit. Whatever the means he used, he pointed up the intimate connexion between naval events and national policy in a responsible manner. This contribution is only regrettably accepted by many historians today who tend to

[69] Mahan, 'Subordination, etc.', *Naval Administration and Warfare*, p. 257.
[70] *Ibid.*, p. 264.
[71] *Ibid.*, p. 269. It should be noted that Mahan appreciated the value of original research, yet in his emphasis he tended to downgrade its relative value to the total art of the historian. He was both defending himself and reacting against what he thought was over-emphasis in the other direction.
[72] Francis Duncan, 'Mahan—Historian with a Purpose'. *U.S.N.I. Proceedings* (1957), pp. 500–1.

look upon military historians and writers as supporters of death and destruction.[73] By tracing this interaction, however, Mahan was rendering a useful service to historians and other responsible thinkers; and if he had caused less revulsion and more study, the First, and perhaps the Second, World Wars might have witnessed more responsible civilian control. The men who detest the Pentagon and the War Office invariably also relegate to outer limbo the intrepid chroniclers of their follies.

Also, while the principles and their results were not neglected, Alfred Mahan took a genuine delight in the ascertainment of exact factual information and in the process of unfolding historical narrative. There is some indication of this in his reaction to Nelson. G. P. Gooch has commented upon the fact that Mahan's *Life of Nelson* was remarkable not so much for its portrayal of the genius in the flesh of action, as for its illumination of the prebattle training and reflection that went into the fashioning of the Nelsonic action into a work of military art.[74]

Mahan's biographic gift was great. Part of its strength lay in his frank recognition of inability to be objective about historical characters whom he disliked. Mahan was convinced that only the admirer should write biography. In his own case, at least, he was undoubtedly right. He thought like Nelson and the resulting *rapport* still makes felicitous reading. In addition, Mahan could, in some necessary circumstances, discipline his personal views in the service of his art. Contrast his attitude to the Neapolitan Revolution with his reaction to the extra-marital activities of his hero. In the Neapolitan affair Mahan's innate conservative mind, unfettered by any serious restraints, reacted to the tender but turbulent movement towards southern Italian liberty with conservative bluntness.[75] In the case of Lord Nelson's amorous pursuits, sympathy for the appreciated hero muted and softened, in seemly fashion, the necessary disapproval of his rigid conservative-religious mind.[76] It should be noted that he wrote when the revelations concerning the results of Nelson's persistent indiscretions first became known; and shocked incredulity was fashionable. The difference between the treatment in these two cases indicates that Mahan's mind was limited by his late arrival

---

[73] Opinions of Louis M. Hacker and Charles Beard mentioned in *ibid.*, p. 501.

[74] Gooch, *History and Historians in the Nineteenth Century*, p. 423.

[75] Mahan, *Life of Nelson*, Vol. I, pp. 439–43; Mahan, 'The Neapolitan Republicans and Nelson's Accusers', *English Historical Review* (1899), pp. 471–501.

[76] Mahan, *Life of Nelson*. The treatment is always disapproving but restrained. See especially Vol. II, p. 159.

Admiral Alfred Mahan

in the world of letters. Exposure to information produced balanced judgements from his pen. The reflection is unavoidable that study might easily have modified his arch conservatism. He was no special friend to liberal democracy, however, and his view of the state was in many ways childishly blinkered.

Mahan was, therefore, a successful writer who had claims to being considered as an historian of some status. What was his value as a formulator of strategic principles? It should come as no special surprise that his most glaring weakness as an historian, his over-rigidity, affected his value as a strategist. It was a great step forward to have linked naval activity and diplomatic purpose. Unfortunately, however, while his general assessment was accurate, the application of his discovery was static. It has been seen that Admiral Colomb sealed his campaigns off in watertight area compartments, in a manner that vitiated many of the conclusions he drew from supposedly static situations that were actually in a state of flux. In a broader sense Mahan was guilty of the same sin. He correctly grasped that the aim of national sea power drew relevance from its alignment to the national aim or objective, but he left the aim constant. Aims in warfare do not remain constant; if they did, Britain, no doubt, would have been at war with Russia after 1945 over the independence of Poland. The warlike aim of a state must be responsive to the capacity and successes of the nations involved. A lack of appreciation of the fluctuating, almost day-to-day, demands of war has caused more misery in this world than any other single strategic misconception. Mahan would take a struggle like the Anglo-Dutch Wars of the seventeenth century,[77] he would set the diplomatic stage carefully, and then set off cheerfully to chronicle the military encounters that either advanced or retarded the achievement of the aim he selected for the combatants to struggle over. This point of view led him, and he is not alone, to concentrate in a too facile manner on the 'principal object'—the annihilation of the enemy's armed forces—once he had paid lip service to the idea of a higher purpose. This, in turn, led him logically to advocate the idea of the 'big battle' as the principal object in war. Although there were other objects, this one took precedence.[78] A practical

[77] Mahan, *Influence of Sea Power upon History*, pp. 90–138.

[78] Mahan, *Naval Strategy*, p. 176; yet he did say that in the exceptional case of the conjunction of a great national upsurge with an 'incomparable' general, like Napoleon, the latter 'is not to be brought to terms by ordinary military successes, which simply destroy the organized force opposed'. That is to say, Napoleon presented a special case. See Mahan, *Influence of Sea Power upon the French Revolution and Empire*, Vol. II, p. 409.

result of this kind of approach caused his less intelligent devotees to believe that in the First World War the naval object was a big sea battle (Jutland) and in the Second World War that the strategic object was unconditional surrender. In short, this student of eighteenth-century limited war did not grasp the fact that it was limited, not only because of technology and manpower, but also because of shifting limited objectives as well.

Mahan was convinced that Jomini was as valuable a guide to the study of war as was Clausewitz—and that the two men were similar in outlook. This conclusion could not have come from a close and reflective reading of Clausewitz whose whole conception of war, tiresome and over-involved as it may be in detail, was constructed in the full appreciation that war, in both its petty and grand strategic senses, is dynamic and not rigid. The realization of this idea and its application to naval history was to render Julian Corbett both a more obscure, and yet a more profound, student of war than Mahan. Clausewitzian thought aside, Mahan's approach was the natural result of his disdain for detailed research. More research might have made for more solid scholarship. Cleo does not allow those who disregard her in detail to escape unscathed. Of course it must be admitted that if such detailed study was uncongenial to Mahan, it was also largely impossible[79] owing to a paucity of available sources, a situation that Laughton's work, Colomb's work and the effect of Mahan's success did much to remedy.

While the exaggerated reliance on principles led Mahan to pronouncements that were something less than universally valid, it would be a rash writer who went further and embarked on large-scale debunking. Much that he said was of extreme value to both the serving officer and the statesman. His repeated emphasis on the value of good military lines of communication,[80] the advantage of central position[81] and the reiterated statements of the value of concentration of force[82] are all conclusions that the strategist and tactician neglect at their peril. With the vexed question of the value of ships versus forts, he came down on the side of forts and incidentally Admiral Colomb[83] although his interest in the problem was not by any means sustained.

[79] In the eighteen-nineties at any rate.
[80] Mahan, *Naval Strategy*, p. 166. Referring to Mahan's general strategic and tactical precepts has been confined, where possible, to this book, which conveniently summarizes ideas developed in more detail in his historical studies.
[81] *Ibid.*, pp. 28–31.
[82] *Ibid.*, p. 47.
[83] *Ibid.*, p. 144.

On the question of the value of economic warfare applied by sea pressure he found himself in considerable difficulty. First there was his conviction that 'big battle' ensures success. Secondly, he went out of his way to prove the debilitating effects on a navy of overconcentration on economic offices.[84] However, once command of the sea was assured by battle he could understand the implications of blockade. When he wrote the history of *The Influence of Sea Power upon the French Revolution and Empire*, he began, he tells us, by considering the whole question of economic struggle first.[85] Because Napoleon, for reasons that Mahan generally regarded as discreditable, very often held the initiative, Britain was forced back upon a policy of security that led to the heavy application of blockade. Despite the fact that the struggle almost exhausted England, Mahan concluded that, inasmuch as it contributed to Napoleon's last acts of desperation on fields of battle on land, that policy was right and successful.[86] For this he handed golden laurels to the younger Pitt who had the courage to commit his country to a struggle in which the endurance required would be primarily economic, naval and diplomatic, and in which the final outcome would remain long in doubt. Despite the obvious reverence Mahan felt for the English Prime Minister,[87] his assessment will not appear extravagant to many readers even today. If the 'far distant ships on which the Grand Army never looked' get too much credit for Napoleon's overthrow from Mahan, once the 'big battle' was won, Mahan *did* look upon them as economic as well as purely naval instruments.

Mahan's actual influence on naval warfare, especially on British naval development after 1890, seems to have been more profound in its general stimulus than for its conclusions on particulars. It is true that he held decided views on the value of the size and speed of ships to be constructed.[88] He was not a big-ship advocate, but it is by no means evident that this conclusion of Mahan's was any more profound than that arrived at by the committed enemies of the Fisher revolution in England. When it came to establishing construction and strategic priorities he was as fallible as the

---

[84] Mahan, *Influence of Sea Power upon the French Revolution and Empire*, Vol. I, p. 179.
[85] He wrote the last, 'economic', chapter first. *From Sail to Steam*, pp. 303, 309.
[86] Mahan, *Influence of Sea Power upon the French Revolution and Empire*, pp. 407-11; Mahan, *From Sail to Steam*, pp. 303-10.
[87] Pitt helped Mahan by dying before war between the United States of America and Great Britain broke out.
[88] Taylor, *Life*, p. 212.

technological people whom he had condemned so early in his career. On the other hand, his reiterated view that sea-power effectiveness was in large measure dependent upon a naval nation taking pains to increase convenience of overseas bases[89] undoubtedly contributed in no small measure to that flood of expansionist chauvinism that characterized Great Britain at the turn of the twentieth century, and to which less obviously imperial nations were not immune. Nevertheless, this base-grabbing outlook was expressed as a general principle rather than as a recipe for specific action, and it is not possible to say that any particular idea of his was directly responsible for the acquisition of any particular plot of land. His real effect was to reawaken the British that upon the nurture and proper use of their naval power great military and political results had depended in the past, and to suggest convincingly that these past lessons might be instructive to confused military and political people in the (then) present. In short he linked by historical illustration and patient inference the idea of British imperial power with that of her naval prominence. It has recently been suggested by a military writer of some authority that the idea of naval predominance and the *Pax Britannica* might not stand up under critical examination.[90] This may be true. Few, however, would deny that this interconnexion caught the imagination of a large segment of pre-1914 influential British people, and that its most persistent and successful popularizer was Mahan.[91] For it must be said firmly that it was due more to their general acceptability than to their particular validity that the theories of this American writer influenced naval affairs and especially British naval affairs during his lifetime.

As a writer of prose Mahan was not strikingly gifted. People differ in opinion on his abilities in this respect.[92] Certainly it is true to say that while he exerted every effort to avoid the careless use of repetition and sometimes managed to create the classic descriptive passages, he never entirely evaded the wearying effect of long, involved sentencing and paragraphing. He himself claimed that this convoluted effect was a result of the passion for accuracy that motivated his writing. This may be true but the fact remains that his prose was stilted. Fortunately for him, he wrote

[89] A point continually stressed in his work. Specifically see Mahan, *Naval Strategy*, Chapter VII.
[90] Michael Howard, 'Bombing and the Bomb', *Encounter* (1962) p. 24.
[91] Taylor, *Life*, pp. 142–3.
[92] Very few writers agree on this and most have opinions. His latest competent critic, Livezey, thought him difficult. The matter is discussed in Taylor, *Life*, pp. 250–6. Mahan himself thought on the matter in *From Sail to Steam*, pp. 288–91.

at a time when readers were inclined to find virtue in obeisance to mammoth and difficult books.

Alfred Mahan was dynamic. It is true that his mind was set in a conservative mould, that his success depended a good deal on the overworking of a new approach to a receptive audience, that his prose was dull and that his addiction to over-simplification led him into errors of exaggeration and interpretation. Yet with all these limitations, and with a full appreciation that publication sales and contemporary impact are no guarantors of scholarly competence, it is clear that he has deserved the praise, both as historian and writer, that has been accorded him.[93] He improved with time. He came to the study of history late in life, and the three 'Influence' books, the writing of which was spread over some fifteen years, show a steady improvement in style, historical technique and respect for detailed and even primary sources of information. Sir John Laughton felt that *The Influence of Sea Power upon the French Revolution and Empire* was his best work.[94] The *War of 1812* work, however, is not only slightly easier to read but it is also the least general of the three. The reader of the '1812' book might even think the general discussion of Mahan as a researcher in this chapter a little harsh. There would be some justification for such a view since Mahan by that time had taken pains to obtain as much British, Canadian and American primary source material as he conveniently could—considering his mental habits and lack of academic training.[95] The resulting book was, therefore, more scholarly and more convincing than its predecessors. This point should not be overstrained, but it should be carefully noticed, since this capacity for scholarly self-improvement is remarkable in one whose mental outlook must have been influenced by his professional occupation. It is all the more remarkable if one realizes that when serving as a naval officer he deliberately set himself to increase his value as a ship commander by training himself to subdue his inclinations towards seeing all sides of a question. He held the view that too much study or 'closet work' inhibited a commander's necessary power of quick decision.[96] He was finally unsuccessful in this attempt at self-discipline and became instead a great naval historian.

---

[93] For a balanced critical summary see Francis Duncan 'Mahan—Historian with a Purpose', *U.S.N.I. Proceedings* (1957) p. 503.
[94] Taylor, *Life*, pp. 49–50.
[95] He consulted a wide range of sources including Canadian and American State Papers.
[96] Puleston, *Mahan*, p. 72.

Mahan's impact on the growth of naval history was greater than any of the other of these pens behind the fleet. He found it a record of battles, and left it as a subject that was intimately connected with foreign policy and the general history of the nation state.

5

THE EDITOR

Sir John Laughton

JOHN KNOX LAUGHTON was born in Liverpool, the son of a seafaring father, in 1830. His father had left the sea before John was born and, in Sir Geoffrey Callendar's picturesque but unrevealing phrase, 'took to Calvinism'.[1] Whether this new passion of the elder Laughton's was responsible for the interest in learning that took John Knox from the Liverpool Royal Institution School to Gonville and Caius College, Cambridge, is not apparent. What is certain is that young Laughton sat the mathematical Tripos successfully. On the outbreak of the Crimean War he entered the Royal Navy as a civilian instructor and he served first in the Baltic, in war-time, and later in the East Indies in HMS *Calcutta*.[2] Civilian though he was, he saw action and displayed gallantry in the Chinese conflict, as he had in the Baltic, and was awarded the campaign medals. In 1859 he served in the *Algiers*[3] in the Mediterranean and by 1866 he was ashore instructing at the Royal Naval College, Portsmouth. Here, in the course of his teaching duties, he developed enough interest and proficiency in geography and meteorology to remain a respected expert in those subjects to the end of his life.

When the Royal Naval College opened at Greenwich in 1873, Laughton moved from Portsmouth, and became Head of the Department of Meteorology and Marine Surveying. In 1876 he

---

[1] Biographical details of Laughton's life, before 1874, are, unless otherwise acknowledged, drawn from Sir Geoffrey Callendar's article in the *Dictionary of National Biography* and his *The Times* 'obituary'—14 September, 1915.

[2] HMS *Calcutta*, 84. Flagship of the East Indian Station. Laughton joined her on 4 March, 1856, when she flew the flag of Rear-Admiral Sir Michael Seymour.

[3] HMS *Algiers*, 90. Screw-propelled, 2nd-rate warship.

gave the first lecture at Greenwich on naval history, and thereafter history dominated his life. He retired from the naval service in 1885 and thereupon became Professor of Modern History at King's College, University of London, a position he held until 1914. In 1893–4 he became Secretary of the Navy Records Society. Laughton was knighted in 1907, and in 1910 this pioneer in the revival of naval history was honoured with a testimonial and address presented by important people, including many Admirals on the flag-list and the Prince of Wales.

In Laughton's case, however, a description of the positions he held only scratches the surface of his life. He was an historical beehive. Callendar states that he produced some *nine hundred* 'lives' for the *Dictionary of National Biography*. He wrote between eighty and a hundred articles, a large proportion of which were historical review articles for the *Edinburgh Review*. He spoke to the Royal Historical Society, the Royal Institution and the Royal United Service Institution.[4] He edited or wrote upwards of twelve books, all but one of which were on naval subjects and most of which were done for the Navy Records Society of which he was Secretary between 1894 and 1912. During a visit to the Near East in the eighteen-sixties, he made himself an expert on the geography of the Holy Land. A good proportion of his review articles were concerned with French books and he read German. Since he was obviously well acquainted with the Spanish records concerning the Armada Campaign, it is probable that he read Spanish as well. His interests and accomplishments were catholic.

Formidable though his work may have been, it was not, as one might suspect, forbidding. Although his prose occasionally and understandably took on that quality one associates with a pen everlastingly on the march, it never became completely pedestrian. The bulk was divided and shafted by the arrows of his critical mind. What was missing was the quality of playing imagination, the lyrical quality of the prose artist and the completeness of approach which comes from the mind that is naturally philosophical. His mastery of language, however, was equal to the important task of discovering and editing historical documents. He was, in short, a man with a purpose, and his readers, while they may regret the absence of carefree wit in his prose, are compensated by his stimulating and faithfully critical approach. It is some measure of his critical watchfulness that, in his review of the

[4] Laughton himself collected his articles and published lectures, and bound them together in three volumes. These volumes are now in the library of the Royal Military College of Canada.

Sir John Laughton

Lord Acton lectures, he should choose to criticize one who stood out as a principal exponent of the scientific method in history, on the grounds that Acton was guilty of drawing broad conclusions from insufficient knowledge. This daring judgement was seconded by Acton's successor as Regius Professor of Modern History at Cambridge, George Macaulay Trevelyan.[5]

Although his industry was not confined to naval history, and about half of Laughton's work for the *Edinburgh Review* was on non-naval subjects, it is as a naval historian that he is best remembered, and as such he finds a prominent place in this survey. In this field he was very much a pioneer.[6]

Laughton began the study of naval history in the eighteen-sixties, and an article on the French Admiral Suffren appeared in the *United Services Magazine* in 1867 (the same year as John Colomb's first).[7] In 1874 he read a paper to the R.U.S.I. on the 'Scientific Study of Naval History'. There he tried to show a military audience not only that the study of naval history was practical and that the past contained lessons for the future, but also that naval history consisted of a good deal more than simply hero- and battle-worship. He thought that it was quite wrong and positively dangerous to write as if British sea control was in the natural order of things. It was, said the Greenwich lecturer, the

[5] In Volume III of his collected articles Laughton inserted what purports to be an extract from a letter of George Macaulay Trevelyan to Arthur Elliot, the editor of the *Edinburgh Review*. The extract reads: 'In the exceedingly able and interesting article on Lord Acton's lectures [Ed. Rev. Ap. 1907] I notice on p. 275 the reviewer doubts whether Lord Acton's [word missing?] about *The Man in the Iron Mask* was as categorical as is represented in the published edition of his lectures. In this point, however, the Editors are not to blame. I was present at the lecture—I remember as well as if it was yesterday the thrill of excitement with which I heard a categorical statement about the solution of the famous mystery. I remember thinking to myself—"Well, if he says so, it must be true: but why doesn't he tell us how he knows it?"

'I do not remember absolutely about the Casket Letters, but I can assure the reviewer that such categorical statements on any doubtful points were quite common with Lord Acton. He was much more of an artist and less of a scientific historian than the world thinks, when he was talking or lecturing at large. He used to say, in private conversation, the strangest things sometimes, for example, that the Jesuits murdered Rossi. It is now *known* that the Republicans did it.

'No doubt on subjects he had really mastered—as the Reformation—he was safe and knew everything: but the reviewer is right in supposing that he did *not* know everything about everything: and he liked to come out with a telling story and make your flesh creep. It was one of many reasons why we all loved him.'

[6] He began writing for the *Edinburgh Review* in the 1880's.

[7] 'Le Bailli de Suffren' appeared in print in May and June, 1867. The article was reprinted as Chapter IV of Laughton's book *Studies in Naval History* (London, 1887), pp. 94–148.

result of carefully nurtured development, and its successes rested at least as much upon national intelligence as on national pluck. Using the sacred figure of Nelson as a touchstone, he remarked the fact that it was superior tactical skill, and not single-handed individual feats of bravery that made Nelsonic fleets great. In this way history in Laughton's hands was valuable in pointing up the *real* rather than merely the *heroic* reasons for past British naval success. Once this fact was grasped he felt that people would begin to see how the modern equivalent of wooden-wall seamanship was intelligent fleet direction and improved scientific know-how on the part of fleet personnel.

The lecturer then gave his diagnosis of why such apparently obvious conclusions took such a long time to gain acceptance in service thinking. It was a direct result, he felt, of the sluggish mental habits of naval officers. Undoubtedly this was an oversimplification, since accurate historical appreciations did not exist and therefore were not available for study. Nevertheless he was surely not unfair in suggesting that extreme conservative attitudes within the service tended to stifle any sense of inquiry that did develop. A tendency to reverence tradition, characteristic of the conservative mind, had real uses in a service that had three centuries of generally successful experience behind it, and Laughton certainly recognized the fact.[8] What he was concerned about, however, was the tendency of unchallenged traditions to harden into dogma. Dogma is dangerous in any aspect of life, but it is doubly dangerous when rigidly applied to the flexible requirements of war, and its dangers are even more intensified when it rests on a remembrance of past events that is inaccurate or misunderstood. That is to say traditionalism tended to produce naval officers who attributed past successes to past history that they believed, rather than knew, to be fact. Laughton's view was that the conversion of a misunderstood appreciation of the past into dogma for the solution of difficulties in the present might easily cause terrible disaster in a future war. When one remembers that Laughton was speaking in the presence of naval men for whom opposition to innovation was almost a way of life, as he well knew from personal experience, then his courage in advancing such views stands out. Therefore it was natural that Laughton should try to impress his military audience with the practical value of history by suggesting that principles of war could be culled from its study. As an example, he dwelt on the way in which historical

[8] J. K. Laughton, 'The Scientific Study of Naval History', *R.U.S.I. Journal* (1874), pp. 1–18.

examples showed the value of 'concentration of force' in naval warfare.[9] He remained much addicted to this particular maxim all his working life. However, although Mahan, as we have seen, 'was to make much of the idea of principles deduced from history', Laughton himself, strangely enough, never became a persistent formulator of such rules.

This lecture was an important landmark in the development of naval history. For the first time services audiences were specifically told, in public, that history could be of use to them and that it might help solve some of their practical problems. It was certainly an event when technically minded 'practical' service officers were informed that if historical investigation were properly performed it could yield precise or 'scientific' results. Naturally neither all nor even a large proportion of the listeners were impressed with the arguments but a start had been made, and Laughton followed up this beginning with another lecture from the same platform in 1875.[10] Furthermore, the lecturer did arouse the interest of a few influential listeners. The support of Admiral Sir A. Cooper-Key in particular[11] proved to be very important for both naval history and Laughton. At that time Key was President of the Royal Naval College and his initiative made it possible for Laughton to begin lecturing on naval history at Greenwich in 1876. Judged from this practical approach, the R.U.S.I. lectures were a great success, for Laughton probably had aimed his remarks more at the ears of the Naval College President than any others. His actual aim was to have a special naval historical Professorial Chair set up at Greenwich but he was forced to be content with the more limited objective reached. The lectures were also important because Mahan had his interest aroused by them.

When Laughton began to teach his new subject it became clear to him, almost at once, that really valuable history lectures would require a more solid factual base than one could draw from available source material. Where was that material to be found? The

[9] J. K. Laughton, 'The Scientific Study of Naval History', *R.U.S.I. Journal* (1874), p. 523. This idea had been developed as well in the article on Suffren. See *Studies in Naval History*, pp. 117-8 (the reference here is *tactical* concentration).

[10] These lectures and their reception were discussed years later by Laughton at the R.U.S.I. See J. K. Laughton, 'The Study of Naval History', *R.U.S.I. Journal* (1896), p. 796.

[11] Sir Astley Cooper-Key (1821-88), Admiral. Early in career Key elected to seek promotion in service on the new ships of the modern steam navy: Director of Department of Naval Ordnance, 1866-9: President, Royal Naval College at Greenwich, 1873-6: First Naval Lord at Admiralty, 1879-85. His biography in *D.N.B.* was written by Laughton.

obvious neglected source was the official Admiralty records which were preserved in the Public Records Office.[12] When he attempted to consult these records he was informed that they were not automatically available to him. The proper procedure required an application for permission to investigate a particular man, upon which each application was considered on its merits. Furthermore he found that while permission to consult pre-Napoleonic material was generally granted material after 1792 was infrequently released. Not only did it appear to him, as to others since, that documents were often restricted long after the need for such restriction was immediately apparent, but he was also faced with the problem of not knowing the extent of the existing material. Under such circumstances, research was bound to be circumscribed by more than the usual uncertainty. Consequently Laughton twice applied for a general permit to enable him to gauge the extent and nature of the material. Both requests were refused. In 1879, however, the sympathetic Cooper-Key became Senior Naval Lord at the Admiralty and he suggested that the Professor try again. The result was that Admiralty records until the year 1815 were laid open for Laughton's investigations, and for five years he was the only person to have access to them. Laughton, however, was no dog in the manger, and he realized the need to make these historical materials more generally available. It was largely due to his efforts that the Admiralty records were generally open to scholars by the year 1887.

The swift response of Key to Laughton's need was partly due to the impact of the professor's earlier lecture on naval history on the professional sailor. Was the Admiral convinced by Laughton's personality and the logic of his arguments? Doubtless both were contributory factors, but it appears likely that Laughton was regarded as a no-nonsense, reliable man because of his mathematical proficiency. At a time when mathematical knowledge was considered vital in the new steam navy, he was a man who understood it all and taught it. Key, early in his career, had staked his future on the proposition that technological change lay at the base of Britain's naval future. Therefore he would have been naturally inclined to give heed to an expert in mathematics who talked the language of science. Indeed both the solid methods of Laughton's research and the support he received from certain people in the Royal Navy undoubtedly owed much to the mathematical proficiency that placed him in *rapport* with technological

[12] For a description of these events see Laughton, 'The Study of Naval History', pp. 800–8.

minds in a scientific environment. Between 1880 and 1885 Laughton continued to burrow away at the mass of material in the Admiralty records. During those years he built up the detailed specialized knowledge of naval history that made him such a productive and knowledgeable writer in the future.

Before and during this period of intense activity in the Public Records Office Laughton wrote a few articles, but his first book was not published until 1886.[13] From that year his output increased phenomenally. Undoubtedly his scholarly abilities had ripened considerably by that time. He was stimulated as well by a change of academic environment. It was in 1885 that he retired from the naval service, and only six months later he took up his new post as Professor of Modern History at King's College, London. Then in 1886 he married for the second time. His new wife was Spanish and came from Cadiz. He had one son and three daughters by his first wife, and three sons and two daughters by his second. This second marriage had an influence on his work, not only in the sense that his Spanish researches were intensified, but his growing family made progressively increasing demands upon his financial resources and Laughton did not have a private income. Hence his historical writing, which was largely an interesting additional occupation while he was at Greenwich, became a vital source of income when he was at King's. Thus, abruptly, Laughton became not only an historical scholar but a full-time professional writer as well. The financial pressure under which he worked helps to explain the fact that he was never able to write books that showed the results of time-consuming reflection on general principles, historical patterns or the widespread connexions of grand strategy. While he always had a passion for accuracy, the bulk of his work bore the recognizable imprint of deadlines that had to be met. For instance in a review article on the American Civil War[14] written as early as 1883, he demonstrated that although he was aware that political and military events influenced one another, he had not thought out clearly the precise nature of the connexion between them.[15] In general it seems clear that he was kept so busy writing an enormous number

[13] J. K. Laughton, *Nelson's Letters and Despatches* (London, 1886).
[14] Review 'Article VIII' the *Edinburgh Review* (1883), pp. 510–47. This article reviewed M. le Comte de Paris, *Histoire de la Guerre Civile en Amérique* (Paris, 1883), *Campaigns of the Civil War*, 12 vols. (New York, 1882). Abner Doubleday, 'Chancellorsville and Gettysburg', Vol. VI, and Francis V. Greene: 'The Mississippi', Vol. VIII: *The Navy in the Great War*, 3 vols. Commander A. T. Mahan, 'The Gulf and Inland Waters', Vol. III.
[15] *Ibid.*, pp. 546–47.

G

of short pieces that he was unable to develop a real strategic line of his own.

During the eighties he wrote for the *Edinburgh Review*,[16] he contributed to discussion at the R.U.S.I.[17] and produced three books.[18] In all of them he increasingly urged on the British nation the necessity of a real, as opposed to an heroic, understanding of naval history. As we have seen, his first published work comprised selections from Nicholas's massive collection of Nelson's correspondence. He stepped boldly up to the contemporary picture of the infallible Nelson and strove to present him as an intelligent manufacturer of victory and not as its lucky show-piece. His second volume was a collection of previously printed articles that devoted sympathetic attention to some prominent French naval personalities. His third book dealt with Lord Torrington, the Admiral who had first advanced the 'fleet-in-being' concept as a means of preventing the invasion of England by an army supported by a superior naval force. What these volumes had in common was their timely nature. Widespread and unintelligent concentration on a largely mythical past, the contemporary tendency to underrate continental enemies and wrong thinking about invasion were precisely the ghosts that needed to be exorcised if both the navy and naval history were to be properly used and appreciated in the new naval age.

In the nineties, the climate of opinion towards the navy and also towards its history veered from apathy to intense interest.[19] Furthermore, by 1890 Laughton was in a position decisively to influence the course that the development of naval history was to take. He had reached a position of some eminence in the civilian academic world and had formed important associations with non-military historians. In the navy he was something of a legend. He was a familiar figure to two generations of sailor-students who had been through the Greenwich system and this gave him some support among naval officers generally. More important, he had friends in high places, since the officers he had instructed during

---

[16] He began to do reviews for the *Edinburgh Review* in the 1870s. The first of these dealt with Arctic exploration. His first dealing with a marine subject appeared in October, 1878 when he reviewed two books on the Indian Navy.

[17] He was a supporter of Philip Colomb's ideas regarding the defence necessary against invasion. See P. H. Colomb, 'The Relations between Local Fortifications and a Moving Navy', *R.U.S.I. Journal* (1889), Discussion, p. 197.

[18] *Nelson's Letters and Despatches* (London, 1886), *Studies in Naval History* (London, 1887): *Memoirs Relating to Lord Torrington* (London, 1889).

[19] A. J. Marder, *The Anatomy of British Sea Power* (New York, 1940), pp. 44–8.

Sir John Laughton

his educational services afloat in the eighteen-fifties and sixties were now coming into positions of power. Between 1890 and 1910, seventeen of the pupils he had instructed on board *Calcutta*, years before, became active Captains and of this number eight reached flag rank.[20] On top of this his investigations of Admiralty records, undertaken during the eighties, made him the most knowledgeable man then alive on the details of naval history.

These special advantages made Laughton the ideal man to instigate the formation of a society to promote the study of naval history. His frustrations, both as a researcher and teacher, had made him acutely aware of the need to make historical materials concerned with the development of the Royal Navy available to a wider public. As he began to advocate this need, support came from W. L. Clowes, the naval correspondent of *The Times*[21] and from David Hannay, a student of naval history.[22] Aside from this support from naval publicists, he aroused the interest of a number of senior naval officers, including Admirals Bridge,[23] Hornby,[24] Fanshawe,[25] Hamilton,[26] Hoskins[27] and Captain Prince Louis of Battenburg.[28] General and academic support came from J. R.

---

[20] Quoted by G. A. R. Callendar in the *Dictionary of National Biography*.

[21] W. L. Clowes (1856–1905), was naval correspondent of *The Times*, and a very influential writer on naval affairs. Clowes was educated at King's College, London. He became a Fellow of that College in 1895—and thus a colleague of Laughton's.

[22] David Hannay (1853–1934), journalist and writer in naval subjects. He wrote especially for the *Pall Mall Gazette* and the *Saturday Review*.

[23] Sir Cyprian Arthur George Bridge (1839–1924) from Newfoundland. Admiral and student of war. Studied growth of German naval strength, and the fleet dispositions required for Imperial Defence. Retired 1904, after having commanded at important stations. Bridge was an opponent of the *Material* school of naval planners. It is interesting to note that Bridge served in the *Algiers* in 1859, a ship in which Laughton had served only a few years before.

[24] Sir Geoffrey Thomas Phipps-Hornby (1825–95), Admiral of the Fleet. Expert on strategy, tactics and fleet manœuvres, due, in Laughton's words, to the fact that 'almost the whole of his service was in flagships', despite his never having 'seen a shot fired in actual war'.

[25] Sir Edward G. Fanshawe (1814–1906), Admiral. His highest naval appointment was Commander-in-Chief, Portsmouth, 1878–9: G.C.B. 1887.

[26] Sir Richard Vesey Hamilton (1829–1912), Admiral. An officer with a wide and distinguished service record: First Sea Lord, 1889–91 and President of the Royal Naval College, Greenwich, 1891–4: retired, 1895.

[27] Sir Anthony Hilroy Hoskins (1828–1901), Admiral. Wide service; Senior Naval Lord at Admiralty, 1891.

[28] Louis Alexander Mountbatten, first Marquis of Milford Haven (1854–1921), Admiral of the Fleet. Became First Sea Lord, but this able influential aristocrat was forced to resign in 1914 owing to publicity given to his Austrian birth. During the period 1890–95 he was Naval Adviser to the Inspector General of Fortifications

Seeley[29] and S. R. Gardiner,[30] the historians. The patronage of such socially and politically important people as the Duke of Norfolk,[31] Earl Spencer[32] and the Marquess of Lothian[33] gave the idea immediate prestige and good reason to hope for some success. The variety of the sponsors, indeed, was indicative of the fact that naval history had come to be regarded as of national, rather than merely of specialist, importance.

Laughton and his fellow planners were by no means without precedent to guide them in determining the form that the new Society was to take. Both the Hakluyt and the Camden Societies were examples of how other groups of scholars had organized themselves for the purpose of publishing documentary material. Laughton, for instance, had himself edited a volume for the Camden Society, and Seeley and Gardiner were both undoubtedly knowledgeable concerning the operation of such an essentially academic activity. Actually, the formation of organizations devoted to similar projects was very much a feature of the age. The tendency was most obviously represented in the remarkable career of F. J. Furnivall[34] who between 1864 and 1881 founded the Early English Texts Society (which had published 146 vols. by

---

and later Secretary of the 1895 Defence Committee. From the first he was a supporter of the Navy Records Society and later became the first President of the Society for Nautical Research.

[29] Sir John Robert Seeley (1834–95): Historian. Regius Professor of Modern History at Cambridge. The close interest taken by this historian in 'The Expansion of England' and its naval support was founded on Seeley's knowledge of Napoleonic Europe, and served his constant purpose of showing the pedagogical value of history. Seeley used history to illuminate generalizations.

[30] Samuel Rawson Gardiner (1829–1902): Historian. Professor of Modern History at King's College, London. Colleague of Laughton's. Historian of Jacobean and Interregnum times. Gardiner was (in 1893) editor of the *English Historical Review* and Director of the Camden Society, both of which posts made him an invaluable supporter of the new Navy Records Society.

[31] Henry Fitzalan-Howard, 15th Duke of Norfolk (1847–1917), Earl Marshal of England. Public servant, and 'the first Catholic layman, since the death of More, who had played a great and honourable part in English public life'.

[32] John Poyntz Spencer, 5th Earl (1835–1910), Politician. Spencer was 'insistent on the requirements of national security', and between 1892 and 1895 was First Lord of the Admiralty.

[33] Henry Schomberg Kerr, 9th Marquis of Lothian (1833–1900): Diplomat and long-time Secretary of State for Scotland. Patron of learned pursuits. A member of the Historical Manuscripts Commission and, for a time, President of the Royal Society of Antiquaries. He was a member of the governing body of the Imperial Institute.

[34] Furnivall, Frederick James (1825–1910), Editor, oarsman, social reformer, and English scholar.

1910), the New Shakespeare Society, the Chaucer Society and the Browning Society. All of these helped to do for English literature what Laughton wanted to do for naval history. The then Director of Naval Intelligence, Rear-Admiral Sir Cyprian Bridge, suggested that money should be raised through individual subscription.

It was Bridge who took the Chair for the preliminary or exploratory meeting,[35] Since fifty-six promises of support had been received, it was decided to proceed with the founding of a Society 'for the purpose of printing rare or unpublished works of naval interest [and] which aims at rendering accessible the sources of our naval history and at elucidating questions of naval archaeology, construction, administration, organization and social life'. The formal constitution of the Navy Records Society was adopted on 14 July, 1893. At that time some ninety-five members had enrolled. Earl Spencer was elected President, and the patronage of H.R.H. Duke of Saxe-Cobourg and Gotha[36] and H.R.H. the Duke of York[37] was secured. Laughton was elected Secretary and H. F. R. Yorke[38] of the Admiralty became Treasurer. Other distinguished supporters were Vice-Admiral Colomb and J. R. Thursfield, together with such noted authors as C. H. Firth,[39] Sidney Lee[40] and Sir Alfred Lyall.[41] It was agreed that Laughton himself would launch the enterprise by editing *State Papers relating to the Defeat of the Spanish Armada*, Volume I of which he completed in

[35] Information on the formation of the Society is to be found in the endpapers attached to the first volume published by the Navy Records Society, and in Laughton, 'The Study of Naval History', pp. 795–820.

[36] Alfred Ernest Albert, Duke of Edinburgh and Duke of Saxe-Cobourg and Gotha (1844–1900), 2nd son of Queen Victoria. Admiral of the Fleet. Fleet manipulator of considerable ability.

[37] Later King George V, George Frederick Ernest Albert (1865–1936). Had been a naval officer and reached the rank of Commander in 1891 when he left the navy to take up duties as heir-apparent on the death of his elder brother, the Duke of Clarence.

[38] Sir Henry Francis Redhead Yorke (1842–1914), Civil employee at the Admiralty. Sometime Director of victualling.

[39] Sir Charles Harding Firth (1857–1936): Historian. Specialist in Cromwellian era. Became Regius Professor of Modern History at Oxford, 1904. Interested in problems of preservation and publication of manuscripts. Founder and first President of Historical Association, 1906–10.

[40] Sir Sidney Lee. Editor of *Dictionary of National Biography*, and Shakespearean scholar. Biographer of Queen Victoria and King Edward VII.

[41] Sir Alfred Comyn Lyall (1835–1911): Indian Civil servant and writer. In 1893 he published *Rise of British Dominion in India*. Later biographer of the Earl of Dufferin and Ava.

1894.[42] Thereafter things moved swiftly, the numbers increased to four hundred members late in 1895 and five hundred in 1896. David Hannay, Sir Clements Markham[43] and T. A. Brassey,[44] the wealthy naval-minded politician, undertook to edit papers. The historical materials published by the Society did not by any means all come from public repositories. Private collections were also used. In this connexion it is important to note the importance of the patronage of men of high social position, like Lord Spencer. Not only did Spencer's personal interest lead to his turning over large chunks of his family papers for the Society's use,[45] but the example set by this nobleman had its influence on other possessors of important manuscripts. In a country where social position is considered important, any patronage on the part of influential families is not to be lightly dismissed.

In retrospect, it is apparent that the Society has lived up to the hopes that animated the breasts of the founder members and its actual achievement does not fall short of the prediction made by Laughton in 1896 when he said, 'Those of you who are here fifty years hence may say to your grandson or great-grandson that what they know of the art of naval war, and of the glories of our country, they owe to the Navy Records Society'. To this growing position of influence Laughton himself contributed a great deal. Aside from being the chief founder, he held the Secretary's position between 1893 and 1912. During that interval the Society released forty-two edited volumes of historical materials. Of the forty-two, Laughton himself edited seven, he had an acknowledged hand in the preparation of two more, and there were undoubtedly others in which he displayed more than a secretarial interest. Clearly, Laughton supplied the major part of the initiative, enterprise and continuity to which the Navy Records Society owed its success.

The significance of this Society, however, was not merely that it

---

[42] J. K. L. Laughton, *State Papers relating to the defeat of the Spanish Armada, Anno. 1588*. Vol. I (London, 1894). Endpaper to this volume gives description of the founding and purpose of the Navy Records Society.

[43] Sir Clements Markham (1830–1916): Geographer and historical writer. Served in Royal Navy 1844–51. Active in the Royal Geographical and Hakluyt Societies. Vital interest in Polar exploration. He was 'in all things an enthusiast rather than a scholar'.

[44] Thomas Brassey, 1st Earl Brassey (1836–1918). Heir to railway contractor's fortune. Philanthropist, politician, and indefatigable writer on naval subjects.

[45] The Spencer papers were later edited for the Society by Julian Corbett and Herbert Richmond.

catered for naval historians. It brought the serious study of naval history to the attention of non-military historians.[46] During most of the nineteenth century historians tended to confine their accounts and explanations to the concentrations and transfers of political power. When economic or military factors impinged heavily on these political activities, historians, if they took these factors into consideration at all, tended to handle them in amateurish fashion, or more precisely without documentary reference. The work of the Navy Records Society represented a long step forward in removing one of the reasons for this lack of balance, at least as far as naval events were concerned. This is an important point, since the growth of social, anthropological and economic factors in the twentieth century when properly used and handled with perspective have immeasurably enriched the historian's understanding of past events. The Navy Records Society was one of the pioneer bodies in this kind of development that has transformed the study and teaching of history. It provided the raw materials that enabled historians accurately to assess the effects of naval war on politics in England's past. Those who today still disdain to take advantage of this accumulated documentary evidence, on the ground that it is mere military specialism, might well ponder these developments. There is still today a tendency for academics to abandon the specialist field of defence study either to the lunatics who think that military and political arrangements can be divorced or to their equally dangerous opposite numbers who are paid to think in certain ways by their governmental employers. That the field of knowledgeable critics is not more vacant than it is owes much to the enterprise of men like Laughton and societies that have provided the materials to conquer such dangerous ignorance. It should also be carefully noted that Laughton's work, added to that of Admiral Colomb, had a good deal to do with making history respectable amongst practical sailors. As the Navy Records Society produced its volumes, it was also providing historical examples to strengthen the navy case in the growing competition for larger shares of the public purse that distinguished army–navy relationships between 1885 and the First World War. The growing interest in historical example and evidence of the kind provided by the Navy Records Society were invaluable allies of the Admiralty in the coming Fisher era, when that body was

[46] In the same way that 'science' was used to make naval history respectable to the Admirals, so the documents were used in an attempt to make it respectable to the professors.

defending itself against Lord Roberts and the National Service League.[47]

Also the Society provided a place where men of differing background and interests could work together for scholarly purposes. To find Admirals like Bridge and Hamilton editing books along with historians like Charles Firth, J. R. Tanner[48] and S. R. Gardiner emphasized the inter-mixture of professional and academic that from the first characterized the volumes issued by the Society. Much of the reason for this junction can be found in the peculiar hybrid position Laughton had established for himself.

The main ideas that were developed by Laughton's naval history contemporaries, John Colomb excepted, were developed at some length and emerged in book form. Each of them submitted themselves with varying degrees of success to the discipline of weaving the results of detailed historical investigation into lengthy and sustained narrative. Thus the main lines of their thought are relatively easy to discern. From a study of Mahan's and Corbett's books, for instance, one can follow their individual progressive mental development. In Laughton's case, his salient ideas are much less fully revealed, even to the close student.

The reason for this obscurity is the form in which Laughton chose to express himself. Although he produced upwards of a dozen books, the vast majority of them were either edited by him, or else they were composed of collections of previously published articles. Only three of them contain book-length sustained narrative written by himself. One of these was an extremely descriptive and unrevealing biography of Henry Reeve, the long-time editor of the *Edinburgh Review*.[49] This cautious work revealed Laughton's abilities as an editor; it was not good biography. The other two were biographies of Lord Nelson; one a slight volume for the 'English men of action' series[50] and another entitled *The Nelson Memorial*.[51] The preface in the latter volume explicitly stated that

---

[47] During the first decade of the twentieth century the National Service League, calling for conscription, challenged naval claims that invasion could be prevented by sea forces alone. Field-Marshal Lord Roberts lent his immense prestige to the army argument.

[48] Joseph Robson Tanner (1860–1951). Fellow of St. John's College, Cambridge and lecturer in the University. Interest in constitutional and naval history.

[49] J. K. L. Laughton, *Memoirs of the Life and Correspondence of Henry Reeve*, 2 vols. (London, 1898). Laughton explained his approach to biography in the Preface.

[50] Published in London, 1895.

[51] Published in London, 1896.

it had no pretensions to be an important work of historical interpretation and claimed justification on the basis of the number of attractive illustrations that it contained. Furthermore both the Nelson biographies were obviously by-products of the selection of Nelson documentary material that Laughton had earlier culled from Sir Harris Nicholas's large work, and published under a separate cover. Much more typical of Laughton's book production was *From Howard to Nelson* which he edited for Heinemann's in 1900. This book detailing the lives of British Tudor sailors contained one chapter written by the editor, and the other eleven by various admirals.[52] The extent of his personal contribution, however, was not to be found in the proportion of the book actually penned by him, but rather in the indirect influence he exerted. In the preface, he admitted that the book did not make a great contribution in the form of original research, but he pointed out that most of the historical facts were taken from the *Dictionary of National Biography*, 'for which, indeed, the Editor, in another capacity, is mainly responsible'.

It can be seen then that temperament, the pressure of other commitments or the need to write swiftly for money, or all three together, kept Laughton from developing a sustained philosophy of history. His strategic ideas and general attitudes towards naval history must be deduced from a reading of the formidable number of short pieces that he wrote. Consequently it can be seen that the very bulk of his production, its extremely fragmentary nature, and its diversity, all militate against an easy and coherent assessment on the part of the military analyst.

Also, the constant pressures on him to produce material quickly kept him from writing works comparable to those written by Corbett, Richmond, Mahan and even Admiral Colomb. Nevertheless he did influence historical writing in his era in a most decisive fashion; for within his limits he displayed qualities of judgement and professional craftsmanship.

It may well be that a tendency towards romantic fancy, and there are considerable overtones of romanticism in all of Laughton's work, first led him to investigate naval history while at Greenwich. Nevertheless he retained a service viewpoint all his

[52] Although another chapter was written by the Chichele Professor of Modern History in the University of Oxford, Montague Burrows, a former naval officer. This book had a strange subsequent career. It was reissued long after Laughton's death, in 1923, by Bickers and Son, Ltd. In this edition the names of the naval contributors were omitted. This made Laughton's introduction a meaningless ramble. Also Laughton's first initial 'J' was replaced by the letter 'T' and so stamped on the hard cover: a most curious publication.

life, and when he advocated the study of naval history to young naval officers at Greenwich, his supporting arguments were based on the practical utilitarian value that such a study held for the profession.[53] It was his view that from the study of such things as the way in which naval organization developed, of how manning problems were met and how tactical general principles were applied in the past came the real knowledge upon which improvements in the present and future could be based. Laughton's main purpose, in short, was to maintain and improve the Royal Navy as an efficient national instrument of war. He would have been the last to regard a utilitarian approach to history as an academic sin. This approach had its uses. For instance, it is clear in retrospect that the tactical confusion that existed as a result of contemporary naval changes invited practical solutions. It was a part of Laughton's special strength that while generally resisting the temptation to prostitute history in favour of predetermined conclusions about the tactical patterns of the future, he was still able to convince people that history had something useful to say about the problem. It is likely that, had Laughton not taken the time to carefully explain its importance, naval history would have enjoyed a good deal less support amongst naval officers than it ultimately commanded.

In addition it was this practical mentality that had led Laughton to the recognition of the importance of manuscript and archives material. As he made use of it he was the craftsman rather than the artist. Unlike so many craftsmen, however, he had the capacity to see true artistry in the work of others. As powerful thinkers like Mahan and Corbett revealed their rare abilities on the scaffolding he was instrumental in erecting, Laughton never let a petty jealousy blind him to their accomplishments. The same expert craftsman who was easily able to recognize genius, however, was also capable of spotting the incompetents who ventured on the field that he had pioneered. As the market for naval history expanded with the increasing naval pressures of the age, more writers tried their hand at it and those who did not do their homework were unmercifully attacked by Laughton. It is true that in his later years Laughton tended to view any new naval writer with an automatic suspicion that bore hard on some young authors, and the number of those whom he held to have written a 'mendacious chap-book'[54] increased. Nevertheless in earlier and more charit-

[53] Laughton, 'The Scientific Study of Naval History', pp. 512–22.
[54] A phrase used by Laughton to characterize out-of-balance naval history. Personal information.

able days, his majestic castigations were reserved mainly for those who entered the field labouring under the assumption that specialist investigations were unnecessary. It was well for naval history that this ever vigilant and formidable guardian of standards was constantly on the watch. Laughton felt a downright contempt for the publicists who masqueraded as historians. This was the view he took of David Hannay's work.[55] Hannay is best remembered for his two-volume short popular history of the Royal Navy. In this he mentioned his sources generally but did not bother to reinforce specific statements by particular references. Hannay's biography of Admiral Rodney was reviewed by Laughton. He acknowledged that there was merit in the book, but on the other hand he pointed out that 'the rule not to quote authorities' deprived otherwise able works of much of their value.[56] Hannay was not alone in incurring displeasure on the grounds of method. He quarrelled with Sir George Clarke's[57] book *Fortifications*.[58] Although he was in sympathy with Clarke's conclusions, and despite the fact that he recognized Clarke's literary and technical competence, he objected to the book's apparent twisting of historical evidence to fit previously determined conclusions.[59] In short, it was important to him that historical fact should be properly and honestly handled.

He defended the methods of history strongly against the sallies of the pure naval propagandists. Of the Navy League he wrote firmly and acidly that it 'does not strengthen its arguments by the suggestion of impossible contingencies'.[60] The League was obviously the lunatic fringe of navalists, yet even in dealing with the great Mahan he defended the craft. While he was quick to point out that Mahan's general conclusions appeared to be sound, he nevertheless found that some arguments based on slight or select evidence were overplayed. For instance, one of Mahan's most sweeping arguments had to do with the far-reaching naval planning of

[55] J. K. L. Laughton, 'Rodney and the Navy of the Eighteenth Century', *Edinburgh Review* (1892), pp. 166-200.
[56] *Ibid.*, p. 167.
[57] George Sydenham Clarke, Baron Sydenham of Combe (1848-1933): soldier administrator and military thinker. Later Secretary of the Committee of Imperial Defence.
[58] Published London, 1890.
[59] J.K.L. Laughton, 'Forts and Fleets', *Quarterly Review* (April, 1891), p. 352.
[60] J. K. L. Laughton, 'The National Study of Naval History', *Transactions of the Royal Historical Society* (1900), p. 92.

Colbert. Mahan strove to show how Colbert and his ideas were slowly submerged in the grand army designs generally associated with the name Louvois during the reign of Louis XIV in France, and the American had claimed that this change of emphasis reduced the effectiveness of France's responses at sea for the next hundred years. Furthermore, Mahan had argued, the change in emphasis was the direct result of a personal decision taken by Louis XIV himself. Laughton agreed that French military emphasis changed as Mahan had asserted, but felt that the transition was much more gradually achieved than Mahan had indicated. With specific references to the sixteen-nineties, he showed that vast sums were still being poured into the naval force as late as 1692, and this indicated a sustained Royal interest in nautical affairs. Then Laughton went on to claim that inefficient administration, rather than the lack of Royal interest, was at the base of French naval impotence.[61] Laughton used specific references to qualify conclusions that Mahan had arrived at in his more general reading. Laughton also criticized Mahan for his tendency to rely heavily on Nelson's personal letters when arguing cases in which Nelson's reputation was involved. He made the pertinent observation that Nelson's letters often revealed his emotional reactions rather than his mature professional judgements.[62]

Corbett, as well, came in for his share of criticism. In *Drake and the Tudor Navy*, Drake's opponents in England were often given short measure, and it could be argued that Corbett drew exceptionally sweeping conclusions about the tactical methods employed in the Armada campaign. Laughton's criticism was based on the manner in which Corbett had used the available historical evidence.[63] True to form as a man who was a craftsman and a bibliophile, rather than an analyst, he sought for error in the use, manipulation or referencing of historical fact with a passionate dedication. Since it cannot be said that either Mahan or Corbett were entirely without their preference for fiction over fact, Laughton's criticism was valuable. This is especially apparent to the professional historian who, when he turns to works that have merited much public acclaim, is often appalled to find a paucity

[61] J. K. L. Laughton, 'The Battle of La Hogue, and Maritime War', *Quarterly Review* (1893), pp. 473–7.
[62] J. K. L. Laughton, 'Captain Mahan's Life of Nelson', *Edinburgh Review* (1897), pp. 87–90.
[63] J. K. L. Laughton, 'Mr. Corbett's Drake and his Successors', *Edinburgh Review* (1901), pp. 8–9, 18–9.

of fact behind the dazzling theoretical exposition. When in doubt one wants the facts. So did Laughton.[64]

As might be expected from a man who set much store by the accurate determination and correct assessment of historical fact, Laughton was prepared to sacrifice patriotic exhortation on the altar of historical evidence. To this extent, he displayed a certain originality. It has been mentioned that he was not above attacking Corbett for undue partiality to Drake, whom J. A. Froude had previously invested with that aura of sanctity which nineteenth-century Protestants customarily reserved for their anti-Catholic heroes. Drake was not a solitary example of this candid approach. Admiral John Jervis's victory over Spanish forces at the Battle of Cape St. Vincent, and Lord Howe's triumph over the French Revolutionary Navy on the 'glorious First of June, 1794',[65] were both a part of the revered military folk-lore of the United Kingdom in the nineteenth century. Nevertheless Laughton, on close investigation, was unimpressed and came to the conclusion that both Jervis and Howe had bungled their battles.

Despite these various declarations of independence Laughton cannot be regarded as a revolutionary thinker. His long exposure to the thought patterns in a service that had its natural conservative tendencies reinforced by a century of fossilization did not leave him unmarked. Also like many self-made men he approved and reflected the class prejudices and *mores* of aristocratic Victorian England. The influential supporters of his indefatigable editorial efforts were men of high social position. Their support could never have been won by a revolutionary mind from outside the upper classes.

His essential conservatism, therefore, permeated all his writings and took many forms. When dealing with personal relationships he demanded high standards. Nowhere was this tendency more evident than in his approach to the great love affair between Lord Nelson and his 'beloved Emma'. If he made reluctant allowances for Lord Nelson, he made none for Lady Hamilton. For that tragi-comic flamingo figure he had nothing to offer but the public judgement of his self-satisfied masculine age. He wrote, ungallantly, that 'her falsehoods clung to her even in the grave'.[66] Even Mahan, who was seldom unconventional in issuing

[64] J. K. L. Laughton, 'Notes on the Last Great Naval War', *R.U.S.I. Journal* (1885), pp. 909–19, especially p. 912.
[65] *Ibid.*, p. 913.
[66] J. K. L. Laughton, 'Emma, Lady Hamilton', *Edinburgh Review* (1896), p. 407.

moral judgements, was more charitable than that. It is today difficult to appreciate the shock with which the late-Victorian public received the long-delayed public revelation of the true parentage of Nelson's 'ward'. In justice to Laughton it must be said that few commentators were equal to the occasion.

Laughton's essential conservatism also showed itself in the way in which he looked upon the international situation of his time. The possibility of vast changes in the world's power system did not appear likely to him, and he did not appreciate the significance of the growth of American and Japanese naval power in the Pacific for Great Britain. His essential pragmatism inhibited his imagination. Again in this tendency to regard the world order, and Great Britain's paramount place in it as more or less fixed, he was no different from thousands of other Englishmen. Also typically, he gave no serious thought to the social and humanitarian implications of warfare in an increasingly technical age.

This fixed outlook on the world naturally made him no friend to movements at home or elsewhere that aimed at sweeping political or social changes. For the aspiration of national groups who desired political freedom in the flowering age of the British Empire, he showed scant sympathy. Suffice it to say that his judgements on these matters were invariably conservative. The most extreme of these views was applied to the Maltese. Since they were not really, historically, an indigenous people, they had in Laughton's judgement 'not the slightest claim to political rights of any kind'.[67]

Laughton was also conservative when he came to consider the main effects of increasing democratic tendencies within the British nation on its own naval service. His natural reaction, as one might expect, was to distrust the effects of this influence. He contrasted the British situation where naval changes were taking place in response to national panics, with the French system where military and naval affairs were left in the hands of professional and technical experts. The French system, he thought, was better than the British.[68]

Yet there was a real problem. It has become fashionable amongst both historians and practising politicians of the present day to suggest that politico-military difficulties in the pre-1914 era could have been largely obviated by a mere rearrangement of

[67] J. K. L. Laughton, 'Hardman's History of Malta', *Edinburgh Review* (1910), p. 214.
[68] J. K. L. Laughton, 'Sir Thomas Brassey on the British Navy', *Edinburgh Review* (1882), p. 504.

bureaucratic processes. To Laughton and his contemporaries, the virtues of the organization men were not so apparent. To guarantee that the vast imperial and naval functions of the fleet would be met in the eighteen-nineties required an extensive outlay of public funds. Public support was required for more naval expenditure. On the other hand increased public support meant more public interest in the details of naval development and function. This increased public interest, however, was not related in an obvious way to the competence of the public to judge the value of such detailed changes. The tremendous increase of naval building that commenced after 1885 spawned untold numbers of naval 'experts', few of whom were reticent. This did not make for ease of planning at the Admiralty and it is by no means apparent that, if the Committee of Imperial Defence or a Naval War Staff had been instituted in 1890, this conflict would have been resolved. The effective working of special governmental machinery requires the sympathetic attention of political men. It would have been difficult to find men in positions of power who had a disposition to operate such organizations in the eighteen-nineties.

Laughton's ideas in response to this situation were more straightforward than workable. His viewpoint was that capricious public opinion pushed the navy forward on undesirable courses every time a naval 'scare' occurred. These 'scares' forced naval planners at the Admiralty, urged on by nervous politicians, to plan naval changes on the basis of the latest scare evidence rather than on the basis of carefully considered naval need and potential over a long period. The resultant development was distinguished by its piecemeal rather than its perspicacious nature. To counter this pernicious development he felt that it was necessary to educate the civilian and the naval officer at different levels. History should be used for this teaching purpose. The civilian should be informed of the part that the navy had played in the development of England as a premier power;[69] the naval officer, on the other hand, should be instructed in the naval details of how the fleet should be used to maintain and exploit that position in the present and the future.[70]

This kind of thinking showed little understanding of the historical relationship between the civil and military powers in Great Britain and the jealous control maintained by the civilians. Actually, it was clear that when he had to choose Laughton trusted the naval officers more than either the general public or

[69] J. K. L. Laughton, 'The National Study of Naval History', *op. cit.*, p. 82.
[70] *Ibid.*, p. 81.

the politicians. This is observable in his reaction to the Naval Defence Act of 1889. He supported the measure because it provided for a large enough naval budget to allow the professional planners to operate for at least three years unhampered by the deleterious chopping and changing usually engendered by public debate.[71] Laughton in his support of the professionals went even further than this. He stated that public response to excited revelations about foreign navies nearly always tended to be on a quantitative level. This generally produced a graded response from politicians who, already inhibited by too much Treasury control, would nearly always make quantitative adjustments in times of crisis. A more useful approach, in his view, would be to introduce a naval budget of such staggering size that it would discourage foreign rivalry by its very expansiveness[72] and at the same time allow naval planners to proceed without continual public interference. In short, his solution was to offer the naval professionals a national blank cheque. Whatever one might think of Laughton's assessment of the problems that called forth this idea, it is distinguished neither by its democratic tendencies nor by its practicality. Behind the attempted response to a real problem there lurked the basic disdain of the military for the political man. Service environments did not train up flexible political scientists in those days, not even in the case of an exceptional personality such as Laughton.

Laughton's distrust of democracy also led him to accept the prevailing view of naval function; that the fundamental purpose for which the navy existed was the battle, resulting in the big victory from which countless happy benefits would emerge. He shared this view with both Mahan and Admiral Colomb. Behind the big-battle theory there lay the view that once the aim of a particular war or even part of a war had been decided upon, then the military should be allowed to pursue that aim without interference from the politicians. There was some merit in this view, but unfortunately Laughton's concentration on detail, like Colomb's, did not at once allow him to consider with comparable intensity that behind, for instance, an Admiral Russell in the Mediterranean, an Admiral Rooke at Gibraltar and an Admiral Saunders in North America lay the flexible political minds of William III, Marlborough and the elder Pitt who with consummate skill adjusted political aims to fit changing military and political situations. Not only were these political aims giving rise to military cause and effect, operating

[71] J. K. L. Laughton, 'Naval Armaments', *Edinburgh Review* (1894), p. 466.
[72] *Ibid.*, p. 474.

Sir John Laughton

crudely for long or short periods of time, but in reality they rested upon a system of delicate inter-relationships between the state and its agents that was constantly changing and that required constant re-appraisal and adjustment. It was this sort of inter-relationship that Clausewitz had made clear to those who took the trouble to read him. Clausewitz was not in vogue in England at that time, and British naval interpretation suffered from the resultant insular separation from Continental thought. The British naval writers up to this point believed that war was a struggle fought according to reasonably fixed rules and not an art that involved all the facets of the state, together with high powers of imagination in the minds of its directing personnel. To this day the lecturer in military or naval history is caught in the dilemma of whether to attempt to picture the wholeness of the demands of war on the state, despite the fact that a truthful attempt often leads to a weak conclusion, or to inspire his hearers with clear-cut cases of cause and effect ripped from history to elucidate 'principles of war'. The temptation is not easy to resist.

Laughton did not develop a body of tactical thought. As we have seen, the one fixed tactical rule that he 'discovered' in 1874,[73] and that he returned to with frequency, was the idea of the concentration of force on the enemy's weakest or most vulnerable point. He saw examples of this in the careers of Suffren, Rodney and of course Nelson. His pre-occupation with one point, no matter what the reason, was understandable in an age when officers were mesmerized by the Nelsonic maxim 'Engage the Enemy more closely'. Laughton at least asked the additional question: How?

In the same way, his strategic thought was neither highly developed nor profound. What there was of it is best illustrated by his references to the Battle of Trafalgar. Piers Mackesy has recently properly pointed out that the strategic results of Trafalgar were not clear-cut.[74] Laughton was obsessed with the idea that powerful results flowed from England's greatest victory, but his conclusions, when he came to pin-point them, were nerveless. Writing in 1905[75] he concluded that Trafalgar had conclusively frustrated Napoleon's attempts to come to grips with Britain by the use of French regular maritime forces, and he held that this frustration caused him to attempt the Continental system which

[73] Laughton, 'The Scientific Study of Naval History', see p. 523.
[74] Piers, Mackesy *The War in the Mediterranean, 1803–1810* (London, 1957), pp. 77–99.
[75] J. K. L. Laughton, 'The Centenary of Trafalgar', *Edinburgh Review* (1905), p. 630.

required the domination of all Europe. This over-expansion led to his inevitable defeat. The long years and the thousands of dead stretching from 1805 to 1814 seem not to have stirred Laughton's imagination. What Trafalgar did was to convince Napoleon of the futility of attempting to defeat the British by effecting a masterly concentration of force at sea to support an invasion of the island kingdom. In the sequel, taking the long view, British sea power gave the small British Army the mobility to do effective work despite its size; its activity gave encouragement to the formation of European coalitions and it did useful blockade work. The most certain conclusion about post-Trafalgar sea power was the length of time it took to produce results. It was not a preferred method for beating Napoleon; it was merely all the British had to offer. However, Laughton returned to this theme in 1907. The French historian, Edouard Desbrière, in his *La Campagne Maritime, 1805*, annoyed the English naval historian with the conclusion that Bonaparte broke up his north-coast invasion of England force, and took the road to Austerlitz, two months before Trafalgar was fought. This struck hard at the theory of Trafalgar's decisive importance. Laughton, reviewing Desbrière, elaborately revealed the depths of Napoleon's design by following the complicated nature of his movements of fleets in preparation for invasion of England.[76] This was useful analysis even if it did not show that Napoleon's designs were practical. At the very end of the review, however, he applauded Desbrière for calling Nelson's battle decisive.[77] Since Desbrière obviously did not think the battle decisive for the reason that it prevented invasion, one must assume that Laughton was determined on the word 'decision' regardless of the proofs. This kind of logic was not characteristic of Laughton but the lack of completeness in his views certainly was.

Actually Laughton's views on the broad issues of strategy and tactics were very much caught up in the practical quarrels of navalists of his day. He ranged himself on Admiral Colomb's side in the ships-versus-forts controversy. He was concerned to improve and broaden naval education. He strongly supported the building of many small, as opposed to a few larger, warships. He was concerned to combat the soldiers who claimed that the navy was unable to protect Great Britain from invasion. On these matters, the topical winds of the time shifted him, and he never

[76] J. K. L. Laughton, 'La Campagne Maritime de 1805', *Edinburgh Review* (1907), p. 344.
[77] *Ibid.*, p. 370.

Sir John Laughton

wrote with the calm detachment that characterized the more philosophic approaches of Mahan and Corbett.

It is clear that Laughton's contribution to the development of naval history, like his approach to the subject, was mainly practical. Nevertheless his contribution to the revival of the subject was immense and his personal accomplishment was astounding. To appreciate the force of these judgements, his career as a writer must be seen in perspective against his life and background. During his lifetime he was certainly regarded as a formidable eccentric. Considering the shifts that his life took this is not surprising.

Laughton came originally from a seafaring family, and one that had no established position in society. His parents were not wealthy so that it was on the basis of his abilities rather than his family background that he went to Cambridge. His exposure to mid-nineteenth-century academic life and his success with his studies undoubtedly accounted for the continuing scholarly bent of his mind, but Cambridge did not alter that as a social outsider a brilliant career was by no means assured him. He wrote at a time when men particularly required a secure position within society from which to operate and, for whatever reasons he turned to it, Laughton found social security in the navy. It must be remembered, however, that to join the navy as a civilian naval instructor was a far different thing than to enter the service as a midshipman and therefore he could never look forward to holding rank, let alone high command. Thus the career he chose was not one that held out hopes for personal advancement, while at the same time, despite his educational function in the fleet, he had cut himself off from the main stream of scholarly activity in England. This conflict must have frustrated him somewhat.

If it is evident in retrospect that the scholarly instincts implanted by Cambridge never left him, it must also be remembered that Laughton's mind was inevitably moulded by over thirty years' continual contact with that set-apart breed of men, Britain's nineteenth-century naval officers. This fact assumes greater significance when one realizes that he served initially in wartime on fully rigged ships of the line that held within them men whose knowledge of the age of Nelson was not derived from books. In other words Laughton's first and great impressions of the naval service afloat were derived from an association with an essentially eighteenth-century Royal Navy. For a novice the reconciliation of strong naval tradition, crude life and Cambridge memories must have been difficult. This is not to imply that Laughton was a delicate flower who suffered severe shock on exposure to the facts of shipboard life, but rather to emphasize that in such circumstances one adapts or goes under. Laughton adapted and as a result his outlook on life seems to have remained that of a naval officer. He spent thirteen years afloat in all and after that eighteen more years in close association with naval officers during his various naval shore appointments. Also his service time included the years of the steam revolution. All in all he was the repository for a unique combination of conflicting impressions.

When he came to serve ashore, his old academic instincts now directed in an historical direction were revived and expanded, yet the fact remains that when King's appointed him to a Professorship, they were appointing a naval person as well as a Cambridge M.A. It is also worth noting that his interest in history came about while he was a naval Professor, so that even his new academic knowledge was encrusted with the salt of the sea and was further conditioned by the practical purpose that had launched him on his new line of investigations. Finally the new King's Professor remained financially insecure.

It is against this background that Laughton's scholarly accomplishment must be assessed. The remarkable thing is not that he often looked at academic problems from the point of view of a naval officer but rather that he often so successfully escaped from that essentially non-intellectual viewpoint. When he began to write on naval history he was 45 years old. When he took on his new civilian career he was 55. Yet it was at this stage in life, generally not regarded as a time of beginnings in most men, that he invaded the world of civilian academics. Within a ten-year period (1880–90) he had convinced editors of learned publications, prominent writers of history, a proportion of the members of his own profession and some men of social importance, of the value of naval history. He was able to write it with a respect for historical evidence and an appreciation of the historical method. As a result of his own experience he was able to see the need for making historical evidence more readily available and to attack writers who ignored the existence of that evidence. On top of that he was able to keep up an interest in a wide range of non-naval subjects and to adapt the techniques he saw at work there to the advancement and enhancement of his own speciality.

Laughton writing on naval history never approached the rounded completeness that characterized the work of Mahan, Corbett or Richmond, but his contribution to naval history cannot be rated as being less important. His obituary in *The Times* stated that he had had much to do with naval history being taken out of the hands of 'mere specialists or analysts'. This owed much to the application of critical methods to primary source material. Laughton encouraged criticism by his example and through his industry vast stores of historical records were opened up.

6

HISTORIAN IN UNIFORM

Admiral Sir Herbert Richmond

On 15 December, 1946, the Master of Downing College, Cambridge, died. His death brought regret not only to the Cambridge academic community, but also to the ward-rooms of many ships of the Royal Navy. Herbert William Richmond had come to Cambridge from the sea. He was an Admiral. He was also a naval historian and it was this activity as a naval historian that had been the cause of his move from the bridge to the Master's Lodge.

Admiral Sir Herbert Richmond passed the bulk of his life in the Royal Navy and, even when he left the service, his attempts to improve the navy, especially by influencing attitudes towards strategic policy, continued. From this purpose he never wavered. Unfortunately, as with many clever men in a hurry, especially those that are forced by circumstances to deal with a bureaucracy, his efforts did not always elicit unqualified approval from his sometimes less perceptive and certainly less experimental naval superiors. His professional life could not be described as a smooth voyage.

Richmond was born to a family that boasted three generations of artists.[1] His father, Sir William Blake Richmond, R.A., was an artist of some ability. Equally important, Sir William had combined his artistic ability with a successful career both in the social

[1] Richmond's life is described by H. G. Thursfield in the *Dictionary of National Biography, 1941–50* (Oxford, 1959), pp. 723–5: by George Macaulay Trevelyan. *Proceedings of the Royal Academy, 1946*, pp. 325–37: and more particularly by Arthur J. Marder, *Portrait of an Admiral* (London 1952), see especially Chapter I, 'A Biographical Essay'. The writer is much indebted to both Marder's informed judgements and to the results of his published research, to which this chapter aims at being a complement rather than, in any sense, a displacement.

Admiral Sir Herbert Richmond

and the financial sense. As M. H. Bell put it, he 'was conspicuously in favour with the peerage and the bench of bishops', as well as figures of 'more important interest' such as W. E. Gladstone, Prince Bismarck, Charles Darwin and Robert Browning.[2] Indeed, his circle of acquaintances was wide as well as being socially respectable, for Richmond was aware of England's developing social problems through exposure to the ideas of Ruskin. He succeeded Ruskin as Slade Professor of Fine Arts at Oxford, and thus he had close connexions with the academic community as well. The artist's son, Herbert, who was brought up in such a secure social position and who was exposed from an early age to the personalities of the great men of the day, naturally developed an assurance that matched his apparent intellectual capacities. In the course of time it developed that one of Richmond's remarkable qualities was his loyalty to the profession he chose. The fact that he was free to choose that career liberated him from regarding it with uncritical adulation. His enlistment was in a sense a concession rather than a solicitation.

He possessed a definite talent for drawing. Yet he does not seem to have been strongly inclined towards the galleries of the Royal Academy. What artistic gifts he possessed revealed themselves, in later years, in his talent for caricaturing his messmates. On his second try at the entrance examination, he went to the training ship *Britannia* in 1885. His first posting as a midshipman was to the Australian station where he served on HMS *Nelson*,[3] a battleship that was designated for commerce protection despite the fact that it was neither powerful enough to be able to engage a modern battleship with hope of success nor fast enough to catch a frigate. He next joined the Hydrographic Branch, but despite the fact that he found service on a hydrographic ship interesting, it did not promise advancement. The ambitious Lieutenant then transferred to the Torpedo Branch. Admiral John Fisher, who was interested in torpedo work, was at Portsmouth at the time, and encouraged torpedo men. When he graduated from Torpedo School[4] he went to the Mediterranean in 1897 for service on HMS *Empress of India*.[5] This ship was new, having been completed in 1893, and she was fitted with the new 18-inch torpedo

[2] M. H. Bell, *D.N.B.* article on Sir William Blake Richmond (1842–1921).
[3] HMS *Nelson*, Battleship, 7,473 tons. Completed 1881. The general information concerning *battleships* on which Richmond served is taken from O. Parkes, *British Battleships* (London, 1957).
[4] HMS *Vernon*, Torpedo School Sloop, 5,481 tons, at Portsmouth.
[5] HMS *Empress of India*, Battleship, 14,150 tons. Completed 1893.

tubes. After two years in the *Empress of India*, Richmond joined the Mediterranean flagship, *Ramillies*,[6] of the same class and carrying the same torpedo equipment as his previous ship. In 1899 he transferred to the *Canopus*.[7] She had just been completed that year and was the most modern battleship afloat. The *Majestic*,[8] which he joined in 1900 was not quite as modern as the *Canopus*, having been completed in 1895, but she was the flagship of the Channel squadron and thus Richmond was at the very centre of naval sea-going affairs. Hence when the newly appointed Commander came to the Admiralty, as Assistant Director of Naval Ordnance, he came with considerable technical experience and he had formed contacts with important sea-going officers. While at the Admiralty he took part in the reforming work that Admiral John Fisher was promoting. In 1904 he took up a new sea appointment as executive officer on HMS *Crescent*, the flagship of the Cape of Good Hope station. She was a 7,700-ton protected cruiser that had been completed in 1893. The appointment could hardly have been considered a plum. In 1907 he returned to the Admiralty as Assistant to the First and subsequently to the Second Sea Lord. This period, which saw an Admiralty association begun with high hopes on both sides dwindle into a relationship of scarcely veiled hostility between the young officer and established institutional methods, also saw him begin both his marriage[9] and his first book.[10] The latter, begun in 1907, was not in complete form until late 1914 and its publication was interrupted by the war. He next left the Admiralty for the challenge of naval command as captain of the revolutionary battleship HMS *Dreadnought*.[11] This vessel, the first of its kind, was one of the most important commands at the Admiralty's disposal for a Captain. It must have appeared to Richmond that his swift advancement was secured. It was not to be. For two years after 1911 he served in command of 2nd-class cruisers.[12] This was the result of his having offered too much advice to his superiors. He consoled himself

[6] HMS *Ramillies*, Battleship, 14,150 tons. Completed 1893.
[7] HMS *Canopus*, Battleship, 12,950 tons. Completed 1899.
[8] HMS *Majestic*, Battleship, 14,900 tons. Completed 1895.
[9] To Elsa Bell, daughter of the industrialist Sir Hugh Bell. Richmond's wife's sister married George Macaulay Trevelyan, the historian.
[10] *The Navy in the War of 1739–48*, 3 vols. (Cambridge 1920).
[11] HMS *Dreadnought*. Revolutionary all-big-gun battleship of 21-knot speed. Launched Portsmouth, 2 February, 1906. Fully completed in a year and a day. The centre of a controversy not yet dead with which Lord Fisher's name was and is connected.
[12] HMS *Furious*, Twin-screw, protected, 2nd-class Cruiser, 5,750 tons. HMS *Vindictive*, Twin-screw, protected, 2nd-class Cruiser, 5,750 tons.

Admiral Sir Herbert Richmond

with naval history, by editing a volume for the Navy Records Society,[13] occasionally lecturing at the Portsmouth War College on tactics and strategy. He returned to the Admiralty as Assistant Director of Naval Operations. For two years beginning in 1913 Captain Richmond watched appalled while, as war clouds gathered and broke, corporate naval planning at the Admiralty was discouraged. Many of his gloomy prognostications, especially those concerning the force of Admiral Cradock,[14] proved only too accurate. At his own request he went, in May, 1915, to the Italian Navy as a liaison officer where he found his initial enthusiasm for the appointment evaporate in the face of persistent Italian inaction.[15] Back home in October he went to the Grand Fleet in command of HMS *Commonwealth*.[16] The *Commonwealth* was one of the *King Edward VII* class battleships of pre-Dreadnought vintage. These eight ships comprised the Third Battle Squadron under Rear-Admiral Sir Edward Bradford. Known as the 'Wobbly Eight' they were detached from the Grand Fleet and based on Sheerness to guard against a repetition of the recent German raid on Lowestoft. They arrived in the Thames on 2 May, 1916, and this disposition caused them to miss the Battle of Jutland at the end of the month.[17] Richmond remained in this inactive situation until April, 1917, when he was given command of HMS *Conqueror*[18] in the Second Battle Squadron of the Grand Fleet. Meanwhile Admiral Jellicoe, in November, 1916, had left the Grand Fleet to take up the post of First Sea Lord. His place as Commander-in-Chief of the Grand Fleet was given to Admiral Beatty. Richmond had formed strong opinions on the way the Battle of Jutland had been fought and he blamed Jellicoe for the lack of a decisive victory.[19] He had no confidence in Jellicoe's leadership and he did not hide his poor estimate of the First Sea Lord and the Admiralty from Beatty. His views were not all based on conclusions he drew up by himself. He kept up a fairly regular correspondence with other officers, such as Commander K. G. B.

---

[13] *Papers Relating to the Loss of Minorca*, ed. Captain H. W. Richmond, R.N. Navy Records Society, Vol. XLII, 1913.
[14] Marder, *Portrait*, p. 123. Rear-Admiral Sir Christopher Cradock, whose force on the South American Station was annihilated by Admiral von Spee's squadron at Coronel, 1 November, 1914.
[15] *Ibid.*, p. 154.
[16] HMS *Commonwealth*, Battleship (*King Edward VII* class), 16,350 tons. Completed 1905.
[17] Julian S. Corbett, *Naval Operations*, Vol. III (London, 1923), pp. 317, 324.
[18] H.M.S. *Conqueror*, Battleship (*Orion* class), 22,500 tons. Completed 1912.
[19] Richmond, *Diary*, 27 May, 1917. See Marder, *Portrait*, p. 253.

Dewar[20] and especially with Julian Corbett at the Historical Section of the Committee of Imperial Defence. Corbett was important in this matter since he had access to his chief, Maurice Hankey, who early in 1917, in addition to his duties as Secretary of the Committee of Imperial Defence, became Secretary of the Imperial War Cabinet. Richmond was thus somewhat knowledgeable about both Grand Fleet and Cabinet opinion. In any event, Richmond came to the attention of both Lloyd George, when he became Prime Minister, and the First Lord, Sir Edward Carson. He had interviews with both these politicians in 1917,[21] and it may be confidently surmised that the battleship Captain said nothing likely to either enhance Jellicoe's reputation or to diminish that of Beatty.[22]

Doubtless Richmond's activities were mostly motivated by a desire to improve the war-making machinery at the Admiralty, but it is undeniable that he was frustrated at not being able to take part himself in the London planning processes. When, finally, Jellicoe was supplanted it was by one of whom Richmond approved, Admiral Wemyss.[23] Shortly afterwards Richmond returned to the Admiralty as Head of the Naval Training Division. Unfortunately, new wielders of power, once successful, tend to be suspicious of their more active supporters. Furthermore, Richmond was saddled with a reputation as a troublemaker. Hence the impatient Captain found the new First Sea Lord friendly but guarded.[24] In January, 1919, Wemyss told him that he was too outspoken and sent him back to sea. This might have been the end of his career and he was aware that the First Sea Lord had saved him from retirement. His new command was HMS *Erin*,[25] one of the battleships completed in 1914 and, at the last minute, held back from delivery to Turkey. She was a good ship, and such a posting was probably a necessary one as a preliminary to advance-

[20] Then Commander K. G. B. Dewar who in 1917 was in the Operations Division of the Naval Staff, and was charged with making 'weekly appreciations of the situation and any criticisms or suggestions for the War Cabinet', Marder, *Portrait*, N.23 p. 388.

[21] Richmond, *Papers*. National Maritime Museum, RIC/9/1 (Henceforth N.M.M.).

[22] 'By the end of 1917 there was a distinctly revolutionary atmosphere at Scapa and Rosyth.' Marder, *Portrait*, p. 25. In December, 1917, Jellicoe was dismissed from the Office of First Sea Lord.

[23] Rosslyn Erskine, Baron Wester Wemyss (1864–1933). At the time the then Sir Rosslyn was a Vice-Admiral.

[24] Richmond, *Diary*, 7 December, and 20 December, 1918, in Marder, *Portrait*, pp. 327–9.

[25] HMS *Erin*, Battleship, 23,000 tons. Completed 1914.

Admiral Sir Herbert Richmond 115

ment to flag rank. Nevertheless Richmond was not optimistic about his future in the navy. Beatty's elevation to First Sea Lord[26] changed all this. Early in 1920 Richmond was made Rear-Admiral and placed in charge of the Naval War Course at Greenwich.[27] This congenial occupation was cut short by the economies commonly referred to as 'Geddes Axe'.[28] Between 1923 and 1925 he was Commander-in-Chief, East Indies Station, and on his return was given a K.C.B. Then two years spent as First Commandant of the new Imperial Defence College gave him scope for his lecturing talents. However, during these years it became increasingly clear that his critical views of Admiralty policy were estranging him from the current leaders of his service. He was particularly vehement in his support of smaller vessels in the then current big-versus-small ship controversy. Hence, though he was promoted full Admiral in 1929, neither Richmond nor the Admiralty can have been very surprised when his public airing of independent views eventually precipitated his retirement.[29] He retired of his own volition, but only after events had made it clear to him that the top commands were not within his reach. As Marder says, the materialists in the ascendant at the Admiralty 'looked with scorn on officers with a "theoretical approach", and particularly one who had spent much of his professional life telling them what materialist blockheads they were'.[30] Naval history saved him from being a mere *The Times* letter writer. In 1934 he was appointed to the Vere Harmsworth Chair of Imperial and Naval History at Cambridge.

The Vere Harmsworth Chair had originally been a chair of naval history, but the statute was changed and the scope of the Professorship broadened when J. Holland Rose, who was not primarily a naval historian, retired.[31] Thus Richmond inherited the task of pioneering the movement of this subject into the main

---

[26] Then Admiral of the Fleet. He was appointed First Sea Lord in November 1919, and held that post until 1927.

[27] 'I am more delighted than I can say to be getting away, and to a job in which I feel I shall be doing the kind of work that my way of life has let me into doing.' Richmond to Corbett 19 May, 1920. *Corbett Papers* in the possession of W. C. B. Tunstall, Box 13 Section (a). Henceforth rendered CP 13 (a).

[28] Notorious, if necessary, economies recommended by a Treasury Committee headed by Sir Eric Geddes and carried out in 1922.

[29] Two articles entitled 'Smaller Navies' *The Times*, 21 and 22 November, 1929.

[30] Marder, *Portrait*, p. 31.

[31] E. A. Walker, *The Study of British Imperial History* (Cambridge, 1937), pp. 6–9.

stream of Tripos activity. For a man who had very little university experience, despite his natural academic turn of mind, this was not an easy assignment. Two years is not sufficient time to measure his success at the task. However, he did impress university people as an all-round public figure who might with dignity and effect manage the affairs of a Cambridge college. He was elected to the Mastership of Downing College in 1936. Here, despite his lack of real university administrative training, he was more at home. Both his early experiences and his family traditions fitted him to occupy a public position in the university, whose colleges had on their walls portraits of many famous Victorians painted by his father and grandfather. In this position he was a smashing success. He attempted to make the Master's Lodge at Downing a more important social centre than were most Masters' Lodges at that time. He played his part as Master by inviting undergraduates to these gatherings, using all his social skill to draw them easily into conversation with older and interesting people. In no time he personally identified himself with the successes and failures of his new home. This sailor had found his true anchorage. He must have found Cambridge all the more congenial as it threw him into regular association with his brother-in-law, the historian George Macaulay Trevelyan, who was first Regius Professor of Modern History and later Master of Trinity.

Richmond's mature views of the navy and his naval history interests were intertwined, and were thus partly the result of his early naval environment. Examination of his early naval career is, therefore, rewarding. He had begun as a critic of the cadet system.

First-hand experience of naval entry examinations and naval education showed him as he experienced it that there was a good deal wrong with a system that decided a boy's fate, regardless of motivation, on the basis of a mere 'cram' examination in mathematics.[32] The system was wasteful, unfair and inefficient. As his midshipman's training continued he became more and more alienated by activity that was narrowly mathematical in content, that pre-supposed everyone to be a potential technician and yet neglected such things as chemistry and physics, that put a premium on learning by rote, that failed to explain the seamanship relevance of a subject so taught (often because it had no relevance to anything but an outdated qualifying standard), and by neglecting

[32] Richmond, *Diary*, 30 October, 1894, N.M.M. RIC/1/4. Note that Marder did not print the whole of Richmond's *Diary*. Where Marder's book is not mentioned the reference is to the original.

history that totally failed to teach a boy why he was valuable to the navy and the nation.[33] Richmond's complaints will not strike either service or academic instructors as novel. They are the standard complaints of a mind that cannot, will not, or perhaps should not, come to grips with technical and mathematical detail for its own sake. It is not surprising, at a time when pettifogging and technical concerns over-occupied the small minds of the impressive men on the great ships, that a clever boy from a family of high intellectual ability should feel the need of some changes.

This is not to say that Richmond's early reactions to the Royal Navy were rounded and complete or even academic. Indeed, he shared many of the typical, or what many people feel are typical, prejudices of the naval officer. He was intensely nationalistic; foreigners he did not regard as quite 'gentlemen'.[34] He set great store by 'general ability' and 'all-roundedness'.[35] He approved of birching and caning as punishments, and he had nothing but contempt for those who would judge promotion qualification on book-learning—especially mathematical book-learning. These views were to change somewhat when his mind became informed and disciplined by serious research, but he remained interested in the naval training of young officers all his life, and he never wavered from his original impression that it should be 'practical'.

Richmond first commented on the general inadequacy of naval education in 1894. It was his fate to influence the service in improving it. This was made possible through Richmond's contact with Julian Corbett, since his family and the Corbett family were friends of long standing. In March and April, 1902, Corbett wrote two articles[36] for the *Monthly Review* castigating the prevailing system of midshipman and young officer education and suggesting improvements. Much of the material that the articles were based on came into Corbett's hands from the young naval officer;[37] indeed, in their emphasis on practical training, their deprecation of cramming mathematics, their unhappiness with instructional methods, and in fact in their whole general approach, they bear the marks of Richmond's reflections.[38] Corbett wrote a third article in September,[39] and the combination of Richmond's reflections, Corbett's ability as a publicist and the Second Sea Lord,

[33] Richmond, *Diary*, 30 October, 1894. See also *ibid*, 11 March, 1901.
[34] *Ibid*, 2 October, 1891, N.M.M. RIC/1/1.
[35] Richmond to Corbett 20 November, 1904, CP 13 (a).
[36] Entitled, 'Education in the Navy'.
[37] Richmond was promoted Commander on 1 January, 1903.
[38] Richmond, *Diary*, 13 April, 1902, N.M.M. RIC/1/6.
[39] For the *Monthly Review*, also entitled 'Education in the Navy'.

Admiral Sir John Fisher's quick grasp of the calibre of the ideas generated, produced the famous Selborne Education Scheme which was promulgated in December, 1902.[40] At a time when a a man with ideas was generally labelled as either a 'faddist' or a 'dangerous lunatic',[41] such quick acceptance must have been pleasing. It may also have been deceptive. Although, perhaps, this success came to Richmond too soon and too easily there seems little reason to deny him substantial credit for it, despite that, when Richmond commented on the Selborne Scheme, he pontificated that he was not 'in absolute concurrence' with all the details 'but I think the corners will be rubbed off with further consideration and the whole scheme a success'.[42]

It is impossible to understand the general background to Richmond's Admiralty career at this time without some comment on the fact that his stay there partly coincided with Admiral John Fisher's term as Second Sea Lord. Even in this secondary post Fisher dominated his environment. Although Fisher was clever, and although the sum total of his attributes placed him almost in the genius class, it would be wrong to think of him as an original thinker of outstanding ability. He had of course tremendous energy. Equally important was his ability to detect new ideas. Furthermore, he was able to assign priorities to these ideas, and to play the game of administrative and political power astutely enough to ensure that these ideas were carried out in their proper sequence. This is what distinguished Fisher from his contemporaries: that he was able to see the naval service and its problems whole and, within a short space of time, to translate theoretical ideas into practical policy. That he was often both ruthless and wrong is obvious. That he dominated the British naval scene between 1900 and 1914 is equally clear. It probably explains much of Richmond's future service frustration to say that he was one of the many people who served Fisher's turn, for a time.

When Richmond came to the Admiralty early in 1903 he brought with him a plan for improving the system for educating navigation officers. This plan had been worked out on board the *Majestic*, in conjunction with his friend, Henry Oliver,[43] the

[40] For a discussion of the scheme see Arthur J. Marder *Fear God and Dread Nought*, Vol. I, (London, 1952), pp. 243–7: Marder, *From the Dreadnought to Scapa Flow* (Oxford, 1961), pp. 28–32. Michael Lewis, *The Navy of Britain* (London, 1948), pp. 197–9.
[41] Richmond's own words. *Diary*, 11 March, 1901, N.M.M. RIC/1/6.
[42] Richmond, *Diary*, 26 March, 1903, N.M.M. RIC/1/6.
[43] Then Commander, later Admiral of the Fleet Sir Henry Oliver, Navigation Specialist.

navigation officer. He first considered giving the plan to Corbett, but perhaps because he was slightly put out that Corbett published a third naval education article without soliciting his advice and help, Richmond decided to try the authorities at the Admiralty. 'So I asked Oliver if I might take them and give them to J. Fisher as they stood. He agreed: and this bundle of papers I gave Jacky.'[44] Fisher knew Oliver and seems to have had a high opinion of his professional ability.[45] As a result he appointed a Navigation Education Committee, of which Richmond and Oliver were both made members, and used the Richmond–Oliver plan as the committee's point of departure. The young commander wrote exultantly, 'Oliver is delighted, naturally. It really is wonderful to have a man at the Head of Affairs who can take up a matter as Fisher has, who is so absolutely approachable and ready to listen to suggestions and act on them.'[46] Years later Oliver recalled these committee days, and gave Richmond credit for promoting the committee and the subsequent founding of the Navigation School. Oliver also had a wistful word for Fisher, writing that 'in the everlasting war against Downing Street ... old Jack, could handle Civil Servants and Cabinet Ministers and get things done whatever his faults may have been'.[47]

Richmond, who made himself useful by proselytizing for Fisher's big Selborne Scheme amongst the influential doubtful,[48] was able to influence Fisher concerning two other appointments to the Navigation Committee.[49] Not only did Richmond, along

[44] Richmond, *Diary*, 26 March, 1903, N.M.M. RIC/1/6. The collaboration is mentioned in Admiral Sir William James, *A Great Seaman* (London, 1956), pp. 99–100.
[45] James, *A Great Seaman*, pp. 96–7.
[46] Richmond, *Diary*, 26 March, 1903, N.M.M. RIC/1/6.
[47] Enclosure in Richmond *Diary*. Oliver to Richmond 9 April, 1935, N.N.M. RIC/1/6.
[48] He doesn't say who, but mentions that Fisher thanked him 'very cordially' for his 'missionary work'. Richmond, *Diary*, 26 March, 1903, N.M.M. RIC/1/6.
[49] Then Captain Henry D. Barry (formerly in command HMS *Duke of Wellington* as of 21 January, 1903), whom Oliver recommended to Richmond: then Commander Arthur Hayes-Sadler (navigator HMS *Empress of India* as of 16 September, 1902). Richmond, *Diary*, 3 May, 1903, N.M.M. RIC/1/6.
The composition of the Committee follows:
(1) Captain H. D. Barry, R.N., Director of Naval Ordnance and Torpedoes.
(2) Commander Francis S. Miller promoted Captain 30 June, 1903 (formerly Navigation HMS *Revenge* from 1 September, 1900).
(3) Commander H. F. Oliver. In command of HMS *Mercury* 'Instructional School Ship for Navigating Officers' as of 18 June, 1903, promoted Captain 30 June, 1908 (formerly Navigator HMS *Majestic*) as of 31 December, 1899. [*continued overleaf*

with Oliver, do most of the work of the committee,[50] but also sat on the executive committee for the Selborne Scheme.[51] Fisher chaired those meetings and however much one may feel that in building up the Selborne Scheme he picked from the brains of others, it is clear that the idea of making Engineers 'entirely interchangeable with other Lieutenants and rise to the command of ships and fleets' was Fisher's alone and was sprung on the committee as a surprise.[52] Richmond had his doubts but was induced to support Fisher in his 'broad big idea'.[53]

Fisher had read the Navigation Committee's Report by 3 May, as had the First Lord, Selborne.[54] Considering the composition of this rather typical Fisher Committee, it is not surprising that it reported in overwhelming support of Oliver's ideas. Fisher at once announced his intention of promoting Oliver and giving

(4) Commander Arthur Hayes-Sadler, navigator.
(5) Commander H. W. Richmond.
(6) P. Dale Russell (Private Secretary to Rear-Admiral John Durnford). Secretary to the Committee.

[50] Since the others had wives 'in port'. *Diary*, 3 May, 1903.
[51] The 'New Scheme' Committee comprised:
(1) Commander H. W. Richmond.
(2) Hugh O. Arnold-Forster, Esq., M.P., Parliamentary and Financial Secretary to the Admiralty.
(3) Sir Evan MacGregor, K.C.B., I.S.O., Permanent Secretary to the Admiralty.
(4) Eng. Rear-Admiral Sir A. John Durston, Engineer-in-Chief of the Fleet.
(5) James A. Ewing, Esq., M.A., LL.D., F.R.S., M.I.C.F., Director of Naval Education—appointed in 1903 under the New Scheme.
(6) Cyril Ashford, Esq., Headmaster at Osborne under the New Scheme.
(7) Captain Rosslyn E. Wemyss M.V.O., appointed Captain of HMS *Racer* and Commandant of Royal Naval College, Osborne, under the New Scheme, 25 November, 1902.
(8) Captain the Hon. Horace L. A. Hood, Executive Officer on HMS *Ramillies* from 3 January, 1900. Appointed Captain HMS *Hyacinth*, 21 July, 1903.
(9) Commander William C. E. Ruck-Keene, appointed Executive Officer HMS *Racer*, i.e. Royal Naval College, Osborne, from 12 March, 1903, under the New Scheme.
(10) Chairman, Admiral Sir John A. Fisher, G.C.B. Second Sea Lord. *Ibid.*, and *Navy Lists*.

[52] *Ibid*. It was one of the most important features of the Selborne Scheme that naval officers were to be so trained that specialization would not replace interchangeability as an ideal goal for Royal Naval Officers. They were not trained to interchange in ordinary circumstances, but rather trained so that interchangeability was a *possibility in emergency circumstances*. See Marder, *From the Dreadnought to Scapa Flow*, p. 47.
[53] *Ibid.*
[54] Richmond, *Diary*, 27 May, 1903, N.M.M. RIC/1/6.

him command of the new Navigation School 'as Jack said, we want this school to be a success and Oliver is the man to start it well'.[55]

Some time has been spent on this period of Richmond's career because it is partly based on hitherto unpublished material, and also because it appears to have been a crucial time in Richmond's professional development. Although he had succeeded in making himself valuable to Fisher he was incapable of remaining a mere disciple. There can be little doubt that Fisher wished his chosen satellites to pursue their careers in the ways he suggested. Richmond was offered an opportunity to go to Antarctica for which he had once expressed interest.[56] He avoided that. He refused the command of the 2nd Class Cruiser *Iris*. Finally he gave up a chance to go to the United States Naval Academy at Annapolis to study American officer training methods.[57] Then in July his sponsor, Fisher, left the Admiralty to become Commander-in-Chief, Portsmouth, and Richmond's chance to influence his own immediate posting vanished with the Admiral. He attempted to secure first a posting to the battleship *Prince George* and then one as captain of the *Albermarle*, in the Mediterranean. In both attempts he was blocked by his superiors in the Naval Ordnance Department. Fisher wrote sympathetically that 'it is not the way to encourage officers to come to the Admiralty' but, for the moment, he could do nothing.[58]

As we have seen he finally was sent as Executive Officer on HMS *Crescent* at the Cape of Good Hope.[59] Two-thirds of the basis for Richmond's difficulties with his own service are discernible in the background to this posting. First, he exhibited a rather over-selective attitude when offered work by a Chief who manifestly possessed the ability to look after his supporters swiftly. Secondly, the quick and repeated frustration of the young Commander's hopes when Fisher left the Admiralty indicates that for

---

[55] Richmond, *Diary*, 27 May, 1903, N.M.M. RIC/1/6.
[56] *Ibid.* 16 June, 1903. N.M.M. RIC/1/6. He had earlier (1895) expressed a desire to go there—at least in his *Diary*. HMS *Iris* was a twin-screw second class cruiser of 3,730 tons whose complement was borne on HMS *Duke of Wellington*. Richmond declined this less than alluring appointment.
[57] Richmond, *Diary*, 27 May, 1903. N.M.M. RIC/1/6.
[58] Enclosure in Richmond *Diary*. Fisher to Richmond 6 July, 1903, N.M.M. RIC/1/6.
[59] HMS *Prince George*, was a *Majestic* class battleship. When consoling Richmond for failing to get the *Prince George* posting Fisher wrote 'I will take care you don't suffer eventually and in some ways it will do you good'. See Fisher to Richmond, 6 July, 1903. N.M.M. RIC/1/6.

I

reasons of personality or jealousy, or both, he had not endeared himself to his brother naval officers in positions of power. This made his future look somewhat bleak so long as his personal files were being handled by people outside the 'fishpond' as the environment of Fisher's supporters was aptly named. Also it is clear in retrospect that when Fisher came again to the Admiralty Richmond would need to make himself more acceptable to his brother officers if he was to be of any use to Fisher in the great man's reforming work.

As early as his service in the Mediterranean, Richmond seems to have taken an interest in naval history which his contact with Corbett strengthened.[60] For a couple of years before 1907 he had begun to make a serious study of the War of the Austrian Succession.[61] His leisure time while in the Cape Station was given over to historical-strategical reflection. Fisher had become First Sea Lord in 1905 and in 1906 he sent for Richmond who became, for a time, his aide; later he served the Second Sea Lord.[62] His temperament, his past experience and his growing preoccupation with strategic problems all made him disinclined to play a modest role in his new position. In particular, he held strong views about the need for a Naval War Staff at the Admiralty.

The conception of a Naval War Staff, and this includes Richmond's view of it, was not directly analogous to any army General Staff. The Board of Admiralty ran the navy; the Army Council did not have such wide powers over the whole army. Rather the envisaged Naval War Staff would assist the Admiralty Board by providing it with war plans based on its own investigations and those of the newly established Committee of Imperial Defence. The office of the Director of Naval Intelligence was often thought of as a substitute for a Naval War Staff. Actually that office was not a war planning body, but rather an information collection centre whereby information about foreign navies could be fed to the Board to assist them in formulating scrapping and building policies for the Royal Navy. As Richmond emphasized, active war plans might result from the D.N.I.'s information, but it was not his function to formulate such plans. Consequently, such planning was invariably postponed. Although Richmond felt that 'with Fisher at the Admiralty questions will not be allowed to be top shelved as they were', nevertheless 'a service like ours should

---

[60] Letters from Richmond to Corbett from Cape Station CP 13 (a).
[61] Richmond, *The Navy and the War of 1739–48*, Vol. I, Preface.
[62] Vice-Admiral Sir W. H. May (1849–1930).

not be dependent on the energy of one man'.[63] Fisher did not share this latter view.

It is, at first sight, rather surprising that Fisher's reforming plans did not include the formation of a Naval War Staff. Two reasons may be surmised for this. Fisher did not like the idea of a continuous body invested with definite authority and specified function that might limit his own personal power. He no doubt felt this for both personal and service reasons, caught as he was in the midstream of his reforming movement. Secondly, he was probably enough of a traditionalist to resent the setting up of a body to take away, or limit, the time-honoured war-making power of the venerable Board of Admiralty.

Consequently, when Richmond, his mind reinforced by historical study, began to agitate this great question, he was to find that not only was the usual weight of service opinion against a young man's advice on remaking the whole war directional apparatus of the navy, but this time his principal stumbling block was the First Sea Lord himself. Arthur Marder has written that Richmond stated in conversation that the falling out with Fisher was due to disagreement over Fisher's educational scheme and Richmond's refusal to use his literary talents to support the First Sea Lord's policies in the Press.[64] The latter explanation may very well be true. Regarding education, however, it has been seen that Richmond and Fisher seem to have been in agreement over education as late as 1904.[65] Richmond's memory was, after all, fallible.

It is, therefore, possible that Richmond's views on the need for a general Naval Staff contributed to his break with Fisher. These views undoubtedly stemmed from his historical reading, and by holding on to them tenaciously he kept himself opposed to the majority of his brother officers all his life. There his views are worth noting more extensively. His comments on this subject were set down in his diary in April, 1907.[66] He said that he had no important work to do at the Admiralty, being compelled to spend

[63] Richmond to Corbett 20 November, 1904. CP. 13 (a). See also *ibid.*, 13 July, 1905, when Richmond stated that he was preaching the General Staff idea. He also stated that he deplored the 'Jackyite' and 'anti-Jackyite' controversy then raging in the service.
[64] Marder, *Portrait*, p. 18—also, note I, Chapter I, p. 367.
[65] That is to say, Richmond's views were in process of change between 1904 and 1907. It should be noted that his disagreements with Naval Education after 1906 turned on the lack of *strategical* teaching, a subject on which he was only slightly fanatical in 1903.
[66] Richmond, *Diary*, General Entry, April, 1907, N.M.M. RIC/1/7.

his time in arranging visits of Dominion and colonial dignitaries, a task he disliked and the value of which he did not rate highly. He characterized the Navy–Admiralty organization for war as being 'beneath contempt'. Because of the Admiralty system war plans were impossible to concoct. 'The War Course College is an instructional establishment and the officers working there are officers under instruction learning the very elements of the strategic side of their profession. . . . The Intelligence Department has no executive functions. The Commander sitting in the Foreign branch, for instance, spend their [sic] time cutting extracts out of foreign papers,' blue-pencilling newspapers or adding estimates. He noted that the 'M' or military branch, that dealt with preparation for war, did not have a single naval officer on it. 'Meanwhile *nothing* is being done. Fisher makes no move . . . we have no one trained to think of the problems of war, the organization required and the multitudinous details. I know only too well how ignorant we are, not only of modern wars but even of wars in History . . . Fisher, clever as he is, has not made a study of it, and in reality has no knowledge. He is a genius, and a genius may do things not within the compass of an ordinary man: but his predecessors have not been, nor may his successors be geniuses.' Britain would, he felt, drift into war without considering 'what we like to call abstract considerations'. Captain Sir Charles Ottley,[67] the Director of Naval Intelligence, was keen on a General Staff but felt his hands tied while in office. Captain Edmond Slade,[68] at the War Course, thought the time was not ripe. Why not? Who was more forceful than Fisher—only convince him and the game was won; but 'he shows no inclination to accept the principle'. Part of the difficulty was that a General Staff meant the supercession of many civilian employees, and this would have met with strenuous opposition from the Civil Service as a whole. Richmond was very perturbed at the quantity of civilian influence at the Admiralty.

This diary fulmination is as shrewd an appreciation of the wrongs at the Admiralty as it is a charter for Richmond's future

[67] The Naval Intelligence Department was directed by the then Captain Sir Charles Ottley, between 1905–7. His subsequent appointment under Fisher's influence to the post of Secretary of the Committee of Imperial Defence (1907–12) blocked the aspiring Colonel Sir George Sydenham Clarke, R.E. (Colonial Governor, Engineer and Fortification expert, Imperial Defence pioneer—later Lord Sydenham of Combe), see F. A. Johnson, *Defence by Committee* (Oxford, 1960), pp. 70–1.

[68] Captain Edmond J. W. Slade, Commandant Royal Naval War College at Portsmouth.

frustration in trying to surmount the obstacles catalogued. Questions of civilian influence aside, it is clear that he had an understanding of the serious deficiencies in naval planning that were not remedied in time for the First World War—for despite the creation of a Naval Staff there was much justice in Slade's view[69] that the men to operate it did not exist in any selectable quantity. Richmond, however, in his rigid theoretical approach, neglected to allow for Fisher's being surrounded by enemies. The First Sea Lord, considering the opposition he was facing both within and without the service, would have been less than his usual canny self to have thrown naval strategy open to service debate at that time.[70] Nevertheless, the plea that perhaps Fisher was caught in an impossible situation does not alter the fact that it was a bad situation, and that the navy and Britain saw a tremendous technical creature rear itself up without it being generally realized that the monster's brain was not commensurate with its body. This unfortunate state of affairs may have had its genesis in the era of Victorian educational ignorance but it did exist. Richmond was right but he too was trapped by fate. The sadness of his story, and that of the Royal Navy in the twentieth century, is that in a way he remained so to the day of his death.

It will have been observed that it was the study of history that led him into his major conflict with the majority of his chosen profession. History taught him above all else that truly significant naval war plans are those that are formulated against the background of clearly defined objectives. He also perceived that objectives themselves might be in conflict, and that a sense of balance must be imposed in selecting theatres of war. To do this adequate planning machinery was required. These were basic ideas that informed all of Richmond's writing, both historical and propagandist.

It should be noted that a War Staff was established in 1912 at the direction of Winston Churchill. However, it did not become an efficiently used or trusted part of the service establishment for a very long time. This was mainly because naval officers holding important Admiralty posts resented any attempt to inhibit their power of direct action. Richmond was on the War Staff before and at the beginning of the First World War, and he was well aware that its powers of operation were circumscribed by officers

[69] Richmond, *Diary*, General Entry, April, 1907, N.M.M. RIC/1/7.
[70] However overbearing one may feel that Fisher's personal autocracy was, it is difficult to see how a continuing reform policy could have taken place without it. This is undoubtedly Marder's view and I support it.

jealous of their position.[71] The idea of personal responsibility so ingrained in the naval character does not easily give way to modern joint planning procedures. In fact when Richmond was on the War Staff he found that he had virtually no work to do,[72] and this added to his sense of frustration even though it allowed him time for historical research and correspondence with historians. The Naval War Staff, indeed, was used as a place where bright but unsettling officers could be sent to keep them quiet and prevent them from effecting anything.

While Richmond easily recognized the difference between a piece of historical research and a piece of naval propaganda or naval commentary on international affairs, he never doubted that history was an utilitarian craft. In 1921 Captain Alfred Dewar stated, at the Royal United Service Institution, that history was not a worth-while study for its own sake; its real use was as a help towards understanding a particular occupation. He advanced the view that only naval officers could really understand naval history and write it successfully.[73] Richmond would have agreed, at least in so far as he believed that history was chiefly useful as an instrument of self-improvement for the navy and the naval officer. As early as 1899 he had written that naval officers should be rounded practical men who could apply historical precedents, and that no one really knew what the precedents were.[74] He constantly acknowledged his debt to Corbett, but when ashore in 1903 he introduced Corbett to Charles Trevelyan[75] and Walter Runciman,[76] both Members of Parliament, and then commented: 'My time ashore will not be all wasted if I can get some naval knowledge into these shoregoing men and M.P.'s.'[77]

Since the gulf separating serving officers and interested civilians was greater then than it is now, this viewpoint was more representative of the practical naval officer rather than the young historian.

During the same period, and while busy on the educational scheme he penned a tirade against those who wanted knowledge for its own sake, stating that it was a naval officer's business to

[71] Richmond, *Diary*, in Marder, *Portrait*, p. 92.
[72] *Ibid.*, p. 126.
[73] Captain Alfred Dewar 'The Necessity for the Compilation of a Naval Staff History', *R.U.S.I. Journal* (1921), p. 374.
[74] Richmond, *Diary*, 30 October, 1899, N.M.M. RIC/1/4.
[75] Charles P. Trevelyan, b. 1870, 3rd Bt., 1928. Liberal and later Labour M.P.
[76] Walter Runciman, First Viscount Runciman of Doxford (1870–1949), Liberal politician and shipowner.
[77] Richmond, *Diary*, 26 March, 1903, N.M.M. RIC/1/6.

Admiral Sir Herbert Richmond

acquire knowledge for the navy's sake.[78] While Richmond was at the Cape he was offered a post on the staff of the Naval War Course College at Portsmouth.[79] He turned it down, perhaps because, if his later strictures on that institution are any guide, he did not believe that the lecture system in use then had real educational value. What one got there, he stated later on, was lectures by experts describing the fine points of high strategy to men who had not already been given basic strategic training. What was needed was intensive reading, followed by free discussion by informed minds.[80] Strategic lectures were lost on men whose appreciation of the historic basis of strategy was largely confined to tales of service 'courage'. One might as well, he wrote, say 'that a class of men learning logic are the best people to write a textbook on the subject'.[81]

Thus in all of these ways he sought to improve the preparation for war of naval officers and the organization of the naval service for dealing with war. Although his ideas gradually gained in acceptability, his immediate practical success was limited. Most significantly, however, his service viewpoint was shaped by his historical study.

The establishment of the *Naval Review* to which he gave the initial impetus was another matter. As we have seen, Richmond was convinced that the general training for officers was not only badly planned and delivered at too elementary a level, but also that it was administered in disconnected, if prescribed, doses. To impart education by a free interchange of views, especially in a way that would allow the junior officer to voice his opinion without fear of reprisal against his career, was ideal, and it was partly achieved through the *Naval Review*.

Richmond and 'a half-dozen young officers' met together, on 12 October, 1912, to launch 'a correspondence Society for the Propagation of Sea-Military Knowledge'.[82] This group included such able men as Commander K. G. B. Dewar, R.N., Commander the Hon. R. A. R. Plunkett, R.N. (later R. Plunkett-Ernle-Erle-Drax), Lieut.-Commander H. G. Thursfield, R.N., Commander Thomas Fisher, R.N., and Captain Edward D. Harding, R.M.A. The plan evolved was that each of the group would write articles,

[78] Richmond, *Diary*, 22 May, 1903, N.M.M. RIC/1/6.
[79] Enclosure in Richmond *Diary*, Slade to Richmond 30 April, 1906, N.M.M. RIC/1/7.
[80] Richmond, *Diary*, 18 November, 1919, in Marder, *Portrait*, p. 359.
[81] Richmond, *Diary*, General Entry April, 1907, N.M.M. RIC/1/7.
[82] The founding of the *Naval Review* is described in Richmond, *Diary*, 27 October, 1912, in Marder, *Portrait*, p. 89.

the whole would then be printed and circulated to prospective members—especially the 'younger men'. The founder wrote that 'what I hope to develop is the mental habit of reasoning things out, getting at the bottom of things, evolving principles and spreading interest in the higher side of our work'. Characteristically, he added, 'I wonder what the authorities will say when it reaches their ears.' They were not overjoyed, but the *Naval Review*, contrary to Richmond's fear, survived their displeasure and their war-time censoring.[83] It even recovered from a short suppression in the First World War and still goes regularly to print to the enlightenment and pleasure of at least a good section of the senior Service. Candour and freedom of discussion are preserved in the *Naval Review* through the double safeguard of restricted membership on the one hand, and guaranteed anonymity of authorship on the other. Although not fool-proof, the system, especially under strong editorial control,[84] has done its protective duty fairly well and the chief difficulty with the publication, for a layman at any rate, has been that articles of more scholarly merit than security danger have been embalmed there owing to an additional safeguard that forbids public quotation from it. It is not, therefore, an easy periodical to discuss intelligently, since much of the strength of its message has depended on the personality and abilities of its contributors. It has certainly allowed young naval officers to write radical and provocative essays upon occasion, rather than remain addicted to the fawning effusions that so often are submitted for, and win, naval prizes. Since its first publication, the *Naval Review* has been, next to shore leaves and ward-room privileges, the greatest release valve for officers in the Royal Navy. One has no hesitation in stating that it was Richmond's most lasting contribution to the service he loved.[85]

The *Naval Review* work was also, in a way, a safety valve for Captain Richmond, since he was incapable of subduing his critical faculties. This undoubtedly gave him the reputation in the service of a man who would always find fault and disturb the *status quo*. Since his superiors were often less intellectually able than he was, this did not make him popular with them. Thus while his cleverness ensured his promotion, as Marder's work has shown, it also

[83] Richmond, *Diary*, 1 September, 1915, in Marder, *Portrait*, p. 194.
[84] For an attempt to victimize an author see Richmond, *Diary*, 18 May, 1919, in Marder, *Portrait*, pp. 342–3.
[85] Richmond did not, of course, found the *Naval Review* unaided. Since the evidence used here is drawn from his own *Diary*, his part may appear to be exaggerated. Nevertheless, at the very least, he worked hard for the inception of the periodical.

made certain that positions of real influence, and eventually the highest positions of influence where Service policy was determined were denied to him. This remained true despite the fact that open disagreement with the Admiralty Board did not occur until 1926–8, when he was Commandant of the Imperial Defence College. Up to that time Richmond's influence on naval policy was indirect.

It has been seen that strong views concerning ship construction policy finally barred Richmond from the highest naval appointments. These opinions had been formed as a part of his general strategic thinking and of his appreciation of 'Imperial Defence'. Following the J. C. R. Colomb view of the importance of maritime communications tied to a network of strategic bases, he advanced a theory of war that was strategically sound for an Empire, but politically antiquated for a Commonwealth. Even a late Victorian like Sir John Colomb was realistic about Empire political developments; being wise enough to see that local loyalties were strong. Much had happened to the Empire since Colomb's day, and yet Richmond's method was to decide upon ideal military situations and exhort political support for those ideas.[86] Whatever the logic of his military appreciations may have been the result was that he wrote out strategical patterns to fit a situation that no longer, politically speaking, existed. It must be said that if Englishmen like Richmond tried to prepare for war on a misconception, much of the new Commonwealth never tried to prepare at all.

The unpreparedness of the various Commonwealth forces for war prior to 1939 made the old Imperial Defence formulae less than reliable. This lack of preparation also encouraged the tendency of British planners, including Richmond, to think in terms of a war policy centralized in and directed from London. For instance, if Canada's share, both in the air and on the sea, of the Battle of the Atlantic, was slight in 1939, by 1943 it had become vital to the defeat of the German U-Boat offensive. British over-control of planning and Canadian unpreparedness together contributed to the delay of effectiveness. Despite its keenness in matters of naval policy, a mind like Richmond's was ill equipped to deal with the changing nature of Commonwealth relationships that lay at the base of changing strategic conceptions.

[86] Richmond's general defence ideas are discussed in his *Imperial Defence and Capture at Sea in War* (London, 1932). For an example of an exhortation to prepare for the defence of Empire trade see pp. 113, 114. For a typical example of Richmond's treatment of colonial nationalism see p. 30.

More controversial, and more interesting, were Richmond's pre-Second World War uses of air power. Like many sailors and soldiers, he saw the prime value of air power as an auxiliary support arm and protection for the army and navy. Outside naval circles the one hostile witness that Arthur Marder quotes, regarding Richmond's value as a lecturer, was, not surprisingly, an air force officer who had found his style pedantic and his views all predetermined by his major pedagogic point—that the navy was the most important fighting arm possessed by Great Britain.[87] No doubt the dissenting airman resembled the top of an iceberg and the majority of his airmen colleagues lay dissentingly submerged beneath the ocean of the naval strategist's erudition and formidable personality. This point is worth noting since it is likely that Richmond had his share of anti-air force prejudice in a service that never has lacked it. However this may be, it is well to notice that Richmond's views on the importance of air power were taken in opposition to those who advocated the use of air power to subdue an enemy through the means of the massive terroristic strike at the general population of large urban centres.[88] Richmond was not above questioning the moral propriety of such a conception. His most serious objection, however, was based upon a conviction that the indiscriminate use of terror, due to its lack of specific military objective, would not produce any specific result and was, therefore, a wasteful and unrealistic way to make war. In historical assessments, both in the United States of America and in Great Britain, of the usefulness of such tactics in the Second World War, the weight of opinion seems to support those who advocated the specific attack on the military-industrial target rather than those who advocated the mass bombing of urban areas.[89] However that may be, if Richmond was right for the forties, the usefulness of his views for the sixties would not pass muster without argument, verified by computors, in the strategists' judgements today.

Thus the need for size limitations on warship construction, the

[87] Marder, *Portrait*, Note 8, Chapter I, p. 367.

[88] Richmond, *Imperial Defence*, etc., pp. 135–40. The subject is treated in other works, nearly always in connexion with the need for co-operation between the Services and the need to concentrate on the decisive object. The subject is discussed retrospectively in his *Statesmen and Sea Power* (Oxford, 1946), pp. 314–18.

[89] Sir Charles Webster and Noble, Frankland, *The Strategic Air Offensive Against Germany*, H.M.S.O. (London 1961). Although the conclusions of this work are tentative, the evidence presented gives support to the strategic bombing of specific industries.

Admiral Sir Herbert Richmond

value of imperial communication and co-operation (both interservice and inter-'empire'), and the danger of adopting an air force panacea idea of winning war by terror dominated Richmond's extra-service propaganda thinking during the twenties and thirties. During the war he helped to explain the intricacies and possibilities of naval strategy to his less instructed countrymen, mainly through the pages of the *Fortnightly* magazine.[90]

What shall be said, however, of Richmond the historian? Before going on to discuss his main historical work it must be re-emphasized that he was never concerned with the question of history's intrinsic merit as opposed to its utilitarian value as an instructor and a manufacturer of principles. Although his views may have changed in Cambridge days, it is clear that until 1935 he never seriously doubted the superior value of the man of action, who must bend academic knowledge to his own ends. At the conclusion of the First World War, when his name was discussed in connexion with an academic opening at Cambridge, he stayed out of the running and penned the revealing statement that 'I think I can do more than that with my life'.[91] He clearly thought of himself as a sailor who wrote history rather than an historian forced to go to sea. The contrast to Mahan is clear; for Richmond history was a vehicle rather than a destination.

Furthermore, Richmond's scholarly output was not high. Until his retirement from the Service he did not produce many articles. In this respect again he differed from Mahan. His two detailed historical studies were *The Navy in the War of 1739–48*, published in 1920 after nearly fifteen years of interrupted labour, and *The Navy in India*, a history of British–French naval conflict in the Hughes–Suffren period, the research for which was done on the spot during his East Indies Command (1923–5) and which was published in 1931. In the meantime he produced *National Policy and Naval Strength*[92] which brought together some occasional addresses to which he added one or two new chapters. Although some chapters in the book are scholarly, its main purpose was undoubtedly propagandist. The 'Introduction' was

[90] He wrote a few articles for this publication before the war. Between 1939 and 1943 he became the regular contributor on the developing naval war.
[91] Richmond, *Diary*, 18 May, 1919 in Marder, *Portrait*, p. 343. Yet Richmond seriously considered the post and, in a letter to Corbett, was much less flippant. His decision was based on a calculation as to whether the Admiralty would ever properly use his talents. He decided to chance it. Richmond to Corbett, 24 January, 1919. CP 13 (a).
[92] Sir Herbert Richmond, *National Policy and Naval Strength* (London, 1928).

written by Lord Fisher's arch-opponent, Lord Sydenham of Combe.[93] *Imperial Defence and Capture at Sea in War* was not primarily an historical study.

Richmond's first work on the war of 1739–48 was his most detailed and comprehensive. Corbett's judgement when writing to Richmond that it was 'your war' is not likely to be altered.

The war Richmond chose to discuss was an integral part of the general French–English struggle for maritime and imperial power that continued with interruptions for the whole of the eighteenth century. Some idea of how such a subject should be managed had been revealed by Corbett in his *England in the Seven Years War* which came out as Richmond began his researches. However, *Seven Years War* was, in the main, a success story to which the career of the elder Pitt gave a distinct sense of unity, that the earlier war lacked. That Richmond was able to surmount these difficulties is a measure of the achievement his book represented. Part of this triumph was due to the lack of pressure on him to write for any deadline and the consequent 'hobby' approach he followed. He had formulated ideas on how such a history ought to be done, and he wrote the book, as he afterwards told Sir Julian Corbett's wife, 'to please himself'.[94] However, pleasing himself involved a singularly meticulous search for documentary evidence both in England and on the Continent. Thus, when the 'amateur' book appeared, it revealed the kind of careful assessment and utilization of evidence that one would have associated with a trained historian. Such a production would have been highly regarded if it had come from the pen of an Oxford don; as a product of a naval Captain of the *Dreadnought* era it was, and is, a remarkable book. He was the first Englishman to approach that complicated war whole, and to discuss its strategic and tactical features with an eye to their historical perspective.

The references he used were impressive. For strategic discussions he used Parliamentary Records and availed himself of the papers of prominent men of the age such as the Duke of Newcastle. He went to Paris to complement his British materials with French documentary sources. He also followed strategic ideas through from the planning to the active stage. Admiralty materials were used, and in this connexion he made public important material from the *Diary* of that venerable fleet commander and

---

[93] Who had attacked Corbett in the House of Lords in 1916. Corbett to Richmond 30 September, 1916, N.M.M. RIC/9/1.
[94] Corbett family information.

Admiral Sir Herbert Richmond

Admiralty adviser, Admiral Sir John Norris.[95] He used the Hawke and Sandwich papers as well.[96] At the fleet and single ship levels he supported his accounts of naval actions by direct references to the journals of ships and, when available, those of ship captains and fleet commanders. All of this was given credibility by Richmond's patent ability to identify himself with the sailing ship era; showing a great 'feeling' for his selected period, especially in its professional aspects. A good example of his range of ability is shown by his account of the controversial Battle of Toulon.[97] Outside the work done on the Armada and Trafalgar this account represented the first attempt to deal with a big battle, its causes, nature and consequences from all points of view. He plunged resolutely into the task of assembling and evaluating the contemporary relevant documents concerning the subsequent court-martial of the British Commander in Chief, Mathews.[98] The resulting comprehensiveness of view kept him from approaching Mathews superficially, as a man who should be judged simply as a battle leader of greater or less acumen, or of more or less technical skill or bravery. Mathews was influenced, if not controlled, by the strategic framework within which he worked. Richmond's assessment took into account the purpose for which Mathews was sent to the Mediterranean in 1744, together with the instructions he had been given and the means he had at his disposal with which to accomplish the predetermined objective. Consequently the historian was able to show that Mathews had been unfairly treated, and that the investigation of his conduct was inadequate, both as a means of establishing the truth of what had happened and as a guiding body of information to help shape naval decisions in the future.[99]

Although Richmond doubtless prided himself on his ability to move easily in the realms of high strategy and political significance, the soundest portions of the book are undoubtedly those that show such meticulous care in their handling of the minutiae involved in the descriptions of ship dispositions, movements and actions.[100] A predilection of strategic evaluation never caused

[95] In the British Museum. AD. MSS. 28132–5.
[96] See Richmond, *The Navy in the War of 1739–48*, Preface.
[97] *Ibid.*, Vol. II, pp. 1–57.
[98] Admiral Thomas Mathews (1676–1751). Mathews was dismissed the Service as a result of the court-martial verdict.
[99] Richmond, *The Navy in the War of 1739–48*, Vol. II, pp. 55–7.
[100] A random and representative example is his notation of Admiral Nicholas Haddock's Force in the Mediterranean in April 1741.   [*continued overleaf*

Richmond to lose sight of the need for detailed supporting information, without which other scholars are incapable of forming independent judgements and incapable of using the material for independent studies in specialized areas. If Richmond learned the value of citing authorities and utilizing methods for treating them from Laughton and Corbett, he none the less combined the two in logical detailed narrative in a unique way.

Richmond was, of course, determined that his book should have relevance for the *Dreadnought* age.[101] In this case it missed the mark somewhat because, although completed in 1914, it was not published until the First World War was over. However, even if the book had been available it is unlikely that practising sailors would have derived much practical knowledge from it. This was so because Richmond's utilitarian bent was never allowed to dominate his highly developed sense of the need for strict attention to the facts. That is to say, what lessons Richmond drew from his studies emerged from the material on investigation rather than having been determined in advance and then supported with masses of historical evidence. His was not the handy compendium approach, and to understand his views one must read his books and not just his chapter headings. Although it is apparent that *The Navy in the War of 1739-48* reveals how the conditions and even actions of past wars have a relevance for the present day, the author was much too sophisticated a writer to allow this fact to dominate his recording purpose. In fact, to have linked detailed narrative and breadth of strategic approach, in an artistic balance to convey a strong total impression, was perhaps Richmond's greatest achievement as an historian.

Similarly, since he appreciated the complicated nature of the war he was easily able to show how the politician's attempt to use

---

Haddock's Force at this date consisted of:

Large ships: *Somerset*, 80; *Lancaster*, 80; *Warwick* 60; *Dragon*, 60; *Advice*, 40—with Haddock. *Ipswich*, 70; *Pembroke*, 60; *Sunderland*, 60; *Plymouth*, 60; *Oxford*, 50—with Martin.

Small: *Dursley* galley, 20; *Aldborough*, 20; *Salamander* 6. 8: *Ann*, 8. 6: *Mercury*, 8. 6—with Haddock. *Kennington*, 20; *Guarland*, 20; *Duke*, 8. 6—with Martin.

The *Guarland* rejoined Haddock in January. See *The Navy in the War of 1739-48*, Vol. I, note 2, p. 154.

[101] *Ibid.* See the concluding pages of Vol. III, which constitute a twentieth-century warning, as well as a commentary on the wayward eighteenth. See also Vol. I 'Introduction', especially p. xi, in the references to lack of study of war 'in its higher aspects'.

Admiral Sir Herbert Richmond 135

the same man, Admiral Sir John Norris[102] as both principal naval adviser in London and principal commander in the Channel area, was foolhardy.[103] It is true that in this case, as in that of Mathews, he tended to support the naval officer's point of view, and to deal harshly with politicians and civilians. However, this was understandable in a man of his temperament and background. What is remarkable is not his bias, but rather that his conclusions were drawn from such a wide body of evidence, that they were put forward in such a restrained thoughtful way.

In this book Richmond had a good deal to say about the defence of trade. His detailed researches emphasize that strategic dispositions were seldom made without having taken into consideration the need to protect British commerce and to inhibit that of the French and Spaniards. Indeed, the war had its origins in commercial ambitions and frustrations. Yet the way in which the significance of this trade should be discussed, in strategic terms, was by no means clear either to Richmond or to any other naval writers prior to 1914, with the special exception of Sir John Colomb. It was not until the later researches of such men as J. Holland Rose[104] and Richard Pares[105] devoted particular attention to this subject that its true significance was realized. The researches of Laughton and Mahan had inhibited useful study of this aspect of naval diagnosis, for a time. This was because they had not approached the topic from the point of view of determining what proportion of the naval forces should be devoted to the protection of commerce and consequently they had not attempted to determine how the general strategic patterns had been modified by trade requirements. What they had done was to ask 'can a trade war decisively and victoriously end a conflict?' With the benefit of hindsight one may assert first that this depends upon the nature of the enemy and the circumstances of the conflict. Secondly, it presupposes that trade war deals only with attempts to inhibit enemy trading activities and neglects trade

[102] Sir John Norris (1660–1749), Admiral of the Fleet. Commander-in-Chief, Channel Fleet, 1739–44.
[103] The whole Admiralty Board signed a letter of protest against the Secretary of State communicating direct with Norris and by-passing them. Their reasoning was sound on general principles, but the difficulty pointed up the fact that the politicians trusted Norris's judgement above that of the Board. See *The Navy and the War of 1739–48*, Vol. II, pp. 87–8.
[104] See such treatment as is given in J. Holland Rose, 'The Struggle with Napoleon'. *The Cambridge History of the British Empire*, Vol. II (London, 1940), p. 83.
[105] Richard Pares, *War and Trade in the West Indies* (Oxford, 1936).

war activity as it relates to the protection of national commerce, and the consequent impact of this activity on national ability to finance and wage the war. Thus when Mahan dealt with trade war, especially in relation to Napoleon, he was concerned to show that maritime commercial pressures were not sufficient in themselves to bring France to her knees.

This approach had led Mahan, supported by Laughton, to assign a low strategic priority to trade protection.[106] In a sense, Richmond was the inheritor of that viewpoint and he continued the tendency to give trade conflict on the sea a low priority category in strategic planning. At the same time his remarkable attention to detail ensured that specific instances of fleet movements for the purposes of trade protection were not omitted from his book. This produced the consequence that, in an age more susceptible to economic agreement, a present-day reader is surprised that the author did not make more attempt to draw inferences from the material presented. Paradoxically, Richmond's lack of conclusions on this topic are emphasized by the thorough nature of his research.

The book abounds in examples of this trade-protection problem. The merchants, of course, continually advocated increased naval attention to the movement of trading fleets. This reached the point at one stage where it was suggested that a fleet, separate from the Western Squadron, be set up to ensure more trade protection.[107] The Admiralty did not accede to this request and their decision was supported by the historian on the basis that a separate fleet would reduce over-all strategic flexibility and hence over-all efficiency. No doubt Richmond was correct in his conclusion since the number of disposable vessels was limited.[108] Nevertheless the importance of the fact that the suggestion was made seems to have escaped him, even though it was clear to him that trade protection was an important matter.[109] Similarly re-

---

[106] Just as the climate of thought in the 1914-8 period, partly derived from a study of Mahan, led the Admiralty to undervalue commerce protection until it was almost too late.

[107] *The Navy in the War of 1739–48*, Vol. I, p. 189.

[108] In 1743 there were persistent complaints from the merchants about lack of trade protection to which the Admiralty replied by pointing up merchants' shipping indiscipline with regard to convoy, and mentioning the severe shortage of sailors to man extra ships for the fleet.

[109] In the year 1741 Richmond listed strategic priorities for the Mediterranean Squadron as trade attack, watching the Spanish Cadiz Fleet, 'the protection of Minorca', protection of the West Indian Squadron from a surprise attack, and the support of Austrian-Italian armies on land. Trade protection is not men-

ferring to the Mediterranean, he mentioned that it was trade that often deflected the fleet from important Allied co-operation and naval offensive duties. He even went so far as to say that a fleet that left the Spanish Cadiz Squadron unblockaded in order to convey merchantmen through the Mediterranean was obliged to do so unless the Admiral was willing to incur 'the severest censure'.[110] Nevertheless, the impression remains that he regarded such an operation as a diversion from the main task.

All this is to say that when priority choices had to be made by fighting Admirals between 'military objects' and the protection of national merchant shipping, the merchant shipping usually won. In an age when many fleet commanders were also often members of the House of Commons, the mercantile attitudes and vindictive nature of Parliament would not be ignored. When the rich hulls were threatened, prudent Admirals deployed to protect them. Richmond, however, failed fully to appreciate this fact and its consequent determinant effect on strategy. This was partly due to a natural unfamiliarity with a form of historical interpretation not yet current when he wrote. It was also due to a somewhat overdeveloped romantic view of war. This is revealed most clearly in his other books where he deplored the tendency of the Dutch to prefer trade with the enemy to complete support of their allies when they had to make choices. It is true that the Dutch often sacrificed 'honour' when their trading requirements were threatened. Their existence as a nation was bound up in their choice.[111] To Britain as well, though in a lesser degree, trade was important in war. It was not vital for survival in the eighteenth century but it was essential to provide the profits on which both prosperity and war-making revenue depended. Indeed, the growth of the naval service had depended upon mercantile prosperity almost from its beginnings. Like his contemporaries, Richmond did not clearly see this connexion but unlike them he did not neglect the evidence of its existence.

If Richmond was incapable of up-grading the trade war, he was clear-sighted in realizing that priority choices were made both more necessary and more difficult by the over-extension of the

---

tioned at all! See *op. cit.* Vol I, p. 175. See also p. 186, where he states firmly that trade defence depended upon what offensive operations 'were in train, and would occur' as the exigencies of those operations permitted.

[100] *Ibid.*, Vol. I, p. 156.

[111] This was a favourite theme with Richmond. Specifically see Richmond, *Statesmen and Sea Power*, p. 119 (the reference is to the 1739–48 war).

Royal Navy during these years.[112] Manning and material problems left the Service unable to perform all that the war demanded of it. Although this was directly traceable to a lack of due responsibility on the part of the politicians, it must be admitted that it was extremely difficult in the circumstances for them to assign realistic naval priorities. Richmond was unrelenting in his placing of blame for this state of affairs on political shoulders and in this he was a little unfair. It is surely reasonable to expect that a war will throw up a few leaders of genius to redress political miscalculation. In that war, with the possible exceptions of Peter Warren[113] and Edward Vernon,[114] the politicians were not especially fortunate in their sea commanders.

When it came to dealing with that most difficult form of military activity, combined operations, the book revealed Richmond at his superb best. This best is particularly observable in his accounts of the unsuccessful attack on Cartagena 1740[115] and of the victorious operation against Louisburg in 1745.[116] His well-documented presentation of the requisite ingredients for a successful combined operation could hardly be bettered. Luck aside, he showed how combined operations on any large scale are not merely area operations but involve politicians and military men both at home and overseas in a truly national endeavour. Both careful planning and operational genuis are required for this sort of work. Other problems peculiar to combined operations were dealt with as well. The vital nature of *rapport* between sea and land commanders, the importance of swift movement once the operation is in the active stage (especially in the West Indies), the importance of respectful avoidance or flanking of fixed defence by the assaulting forces, the requirements of local and general sea command, the influence of naval containment in one area on the success of landing operations in another are all well defined, explained with understanding and illustrated with enough reliable material to make it all credible—and instructive.

The question of the efficiency of trade war and blockade used

[112] For example, his criticism of the Mediterranean Squadron being given too many tasks to perform in 1744. See *The Navy and the War of 1739–48*, Vol. II, pp. 138–40.

[113] Sir Peter Warren (1703–52), Vice-Admiral. Naval commander at the capture of Louisbourg 1745, and Commander-in-Chief of the Western Squadron in 1747–8.

[114] Edward Vernon (1684–1757), Admiral. Commander-in-Chief West Indies 1740–1 and in North Sea, 1745. Cashiered for insubordination, 1746.

[115] *The Navy in the War of 1739–48*, Vol. I, pp. 101–37.

[116] *Ibid.*, Vol. II, pp. 200–16.

against an enemy was discussed by Richmond. Again like Mahan and Laughton, he did not regard this as a particularly decisive form of war. However, the problem of the historian in deciding on the efficacy of this kind of war was more complicated for the chronicler of the 1740 period than for the Nelsonic era.

One reason for this was that national statistics were not generally available for the pre-1780 period, and hence an estimate of damage done to trade had to be arrived at by reference to the estimated tonnage of the enemy that was sunk or captured. This made conclusions highly tentative. A second reason lay in the fact that the British blockade was not applied close to French ports in a consistent manner, indeed the technique of close blockade was a development of a later era, and so anti-trade measures were less than air-tight in their efficiency. There was also the well-known fact that France was not as dependent on trade as was Great Britain. Finally, the long French coastline made successful bottling-up operations extremely difficult. The unimpeded escape and return of the Duc d'Anville's[117] ill-fated expedition in the face of forces determined to prevent its movements is a commentary on the relative ease with which individual trading vessels might move undetected.[118]

The problem of stifling enemy trade in this war was further complicated by a lack of guiding policy from London. Even when decisions were made on the spot, however, it was not certain that they were the best decisions. For instance, during the latter part of the war, Admiral Peter Warren determined to concentrate his Western Squadron and make blockade his principal object. Richmond remarked that, 'if the enemy is met, an adequate commander will obtain a crushing success; but if he is missed, it is possible that the fleet, the reliefs of which may have been disorganized, may be crippled and rendered incapable of further service for some—perhaps a long time'.[119] The best Richmond could say about this kind of war was that, imperfectly pursued as it was, it contributed to the general exhaustion that finally forced the French to sue for peace in 1748; but it was not a decisive form of war against France.[120]

All of this probably indicates a disposition on Richmond's

---

[117] Roye de La Rochefoucauld, Duc d'Anville, led abortive expedition to reconquer Louisburg in 1746. Most of his men died of smallpox in Bedford Basin, Nova Scotia.
[118] Richmond. *The Navy in the War of 1739–48*, Vol. III., pp. 20, 47.
[119] *Ibid.*, Vol. III, p. 230.
[120] *Ibid.*, Vol. III, pp. 246–47.

part to argue the value of military as opposed to purely economic pressure; the natural preference of the professional for the military encounter and a too-rigid tendency to seek for a definition of the 'decisive object'. This does not alter the fact that his conclusions were based on a realistic appreciation of the technical, administrative, geographical and maritime difficulties involved in pursuing a trade war against an enemy like France effectively. As happened so often with him, the thoroughness of his research made him see clearly the complications and difficulties involved in either formulating policy or historically assessing its usefulness.

Richmond's history was not nearly as convincing to the casual reader as an authoritative, ready, rule-of-thumb guide for Captains and Admirals—and even politicians—as was the work of Mahan. Although determined that history should instruct, his respect for historical evidence was such that, sometimes inadvertently, he allowed the real difficulties in the way of definitive judgement to qualify his conclusions. To some this may appear to indicate either failure in the face of what Mahan called the problem of subordination in history, or simply a lack of organizing ability. However, as a naval officer Richmond was in a position to understand the professional aspects of the problems he dealt with. Furthermore, his historical investigations corroborated his professional appreciation of the myriad forces that made strategic decisions difficult. To have realized the complexity was a considerable achievement since this aspect of naval history has been only gradually developed by other historians.[121] He was conscious, as were Nelson and other eighteenth-century sailors, of the restrictive effects of the almost perpetual lack of small vessels for use in probing enemy dispositions and maintaining fleet liaison. He was constantly aware of the manning problem that plagued Admiralty plans, and he showed the nature and effect of this chronic difficulty. He gave weight to the personal peculiarities of his *dramatis personae* and the resulting 'friction of war' between leaders. Although perhaps over-simplifying the problem of securing agreement on the 'decisive object', he was well aware of, indeed his researches laid bare for the first time, the conflicting area demands on the navy of America, the West Indies, India, the Mediterranean, the Western Approaches, the English Channel

[121] Especially and progressively by J. R. Tanner, *Samuel Pepys and the Royal Navy* (Cambridge, 1920); R. G. Albion, *Forests and Sea Power, the Timber Problem of the Royal Navy* (Cambridge, Mass., 1926); John Ehrman, *The Navy in the War of William III, 1689–1697* (Cambridge, 1953), in the author's opinion the best study of the organic nature of the basis of sea power ever written.

and the North Sea. He also considered how the strategic planners were faced with making priority decisions between trade plundering, island and base capturing, blockade, invasion protection and support of Allied land forces in the Mediterranean and in Northern Europe. All this was new thinking about the 1739–48 war and indeed about eighteenth-century war in general.

Taking a more organic view of war than Mahan, he was wise enough to see that objectives change, noting carefully that this war, begun as a 'purely commerical one', changed to a war for the 'balance of power' in Europe when the French entered the contest. It has since been stated that in reality trade war was also 'balance of power' war in 1739.[122] Agreement with this argument only slightly alters Richmond's judgement, since the extra enemy provided by France's entry certainly changed the degree of attention that had to be given to purely European questions. Richmond was not blind to the solid military advantages gained by France through adopting a belligerent posture stopping short of war before 1743. He understood the close connexion of diplomacy with war.[123] While he seems to have disliked the hampering influence of parliamentary moods and pressures on the Government in its execution of war policy, he carefully and imaginatively set out its existence and nature in detail.[124] Like Colomb, he had the gift for illuminating much in telling phrases. For instance, after trailing on through chapters chronicling the lack of responsiveness of the ships to home direction, he humorously remarked of the ministers that 'they seem to have accepted the strange belief, so often prevalent in public affairs, that once an order is given the thing is accomplished'.[125] Also in discussing the possibility of invasion, he refused to dogmatize as did Admiral Colomb on the impossibility of such an event taking place, conceding a possibility of success in certain circumstances. He was not a Blue Water dogmatist. At the same time in discussing the sighting of the French invasion flotilla by two of Vernon's cruising 'hired privateers' he pointed out that this was not the result of luck, but of careful planning.[126] Naval historians will join in labelling this judgement as sound, for one of the banes of their existence is the casual observer of sea affairs who thinks that successful conjunction and intelligence at

[122] G. S. Graham, *Empire of the North Atlantic* (Toronto, 1950), pp. 113–14.
[123] *The Navy and the War of 1739–48*, Vol. I, p. 172.
[124] For example see *ibid.*, pp. 183–92.
[125] *Ibid.*, p. 165.
[126] *Ibid.*, Vol. II, p. 180.

sea is, when convenient to his thesis, the result of chance alone.
That luck operates in sea warfare is beyond doubt, but that its
operation does not consistently decide great issues was Richmond's view.

By far his most intelligent strategic conviction in the study was
his dissent from the idea that the big battle was the decisive
object of naval or any kind of war. He did not deny its efficacy in
certain circumstances but at the same time he understood that it
could not easily be forced on an unwilling enemy. He emphasized
the value of concentration at the Channel approaches, not only
for protection of trade and against invasion but also the vital
area in which to deploy should the enemy decide to offer a battle.
It was a question of emphasis, and too much emphasis on battle
led to the deplorable situation whereby commanders were
commonly valued by the service as big-battle men. A naval man
who held excessively to the latter concept was often, in Richmonds' view, 'a mere fighting blockhead'.[127] The duty of naval
commanders was to execute strategic plans, and in his judgements on Admiral Mathew's behaviour at Toulon Richmond was
prepared to excuse a seeming lack of ardour in the face of the
enemy by reference to multifarious prescribed duties.[128] He thus
defended Mathews's need to take all factors into consideration,
even in sight of enemy sails, before he offered battle. In so doing
Richmond was striking a blow for making rational decisions about
priorities in war. What his contemporaries preferred was the ceaseless repetition of Nelsonic comments imperfectly understood.
Many still do. Richmond's historical work, taken as a whole, had
much to impart to the riders of Jacky Fisher's mechanical monsters before 1914. What a pity they missed it!

In the eleven years that elapsed between the publication of the
1739–48 history and that of *The Navy in India*[129] Richmond's
own powers had matured considerably. He was also, at the latter
date, clearer in his own mind about the message that he wished his
history to deliver. The First World War had provided him with
plenty of additional evidence for the tendency for men to be subordinate to their machines, and for strategic thought to be subordinated to routine and then ignored by mighty wearers of gold
braid. His experience at Greenwich and in the East Indies did nothing to modify these impressions. Hence in his plan for this book on
the Hughes–Suffren naval duel during the American Revolu-

[127] *The Navy and the War of 1739-48*, Vol. I. 'Introduction', p. xii.
[128] *Ibid.*, Vol. II., p. 145.
[129] *The Navy in India* (London, 1931).

tionary War, he deliberately avoided tactical detail and resolutely applied himself to extract an assessment of the contemporary sea strategy both locally and in relation to the war as a whole. He worked from primary sources, English and French, both in the Indies and in Europe.[130] The book was planned in a careful and orderly fashion. First he showed how, from 1778 to 1783, the Royal Navy was over-stretched and how this highlighted India's role as an area of distraction—one envisaged by the French as a potential drain on British war shipping. Intelligent application of this power of distraction would help to make their ultimate object, the invasion of Britain, a possibility.[131] English strategists were aware of this danger. Thus the abortive British plan to take the Cape Colony[132] appeared not as a mere colonial grab but a sound strategic plan to capture a base commanding the French line of communication to Mauritius, and hence ultimately to relieve British over-extension in the Indian Ocean.[133] He once again pointed up the necessity to attack towards the attainment of the principal object of the war, and he noted that his object had shifted in 1778, from that of reducing the American Rebellion to 'the distressing of France and securing His Majesty's own possessions against any hostile attempts'.[134] This was a broad enough object, certainly, but it reflected accurately the dire straits of Great Britain in the near invasion year, 1780.[135] In the Eastern war theatre Hughes's immediate objective was the main French fleet. The French naval commander, Bailli de Suffren, was eager to fight Hughes. This being so, the results turned primarily on the relative merits of the two fleets and the chances of combat. For the British it also depended upon the degree to which their fleet was involved in an army support role, or tied to its bases. Timing was a great factor, and Richmond showed how Hughes was often denied the power to command the favourable moment by the failure of his East India Company associates and superiors to comprehend the need for periodic refits,[136] by their

[130] To mention a selection: *Journal* of Admiral Hughes, P.R.O.; Suffren Correspondence, Colombo Archives; India Office Records: Archives de la Marine, Paris; Archives of the Cape of Good Hope.
[131] Richmond, *The Navy in India*, pp. 27-9.
[132] In 1780-1. See *ibid.*, pp. 126-7.
[133] *Ibid.*, pp. 121-6.
[134] *Ibid.*, pp. 120-1.
[135] For a detailed discussion of this year in home waters, see A. Temple Patterson, *The Other Armada* (Manchester, 1960). Patterson does not mention *The Navy in India*.
[136] Richmond, *The Navy In India*, pp. 30, 301, 302.

disinclination to spare troops in time to take necessary bases for the fleet by combined assault, and by their further reluctance to garrison and arm such bases properly once they were obtained.[137] Richmond had thereby demonstrated that, militarily, bases are only as significant as floating naval power makes them, and that base support effectiveness depends upon their being sufficiently armed to free the fleet from guarding its own supplies, in or near harbour. John Colomb's ideas were thus given historical support.

Although he gave Suffren his due, which was only proper, Richmond's interest in the campaign lay largely in exploring Hughes's difficulties; his lack of ships, his bickering over objectives with the East India Company officials (not with the military commander Sir Eyre Coote, who was an exemplary colleague), with his difficulties over naval bases and with Hughes's tendency to value material more than time. He showed how these difficulties were increased by the lack of army–navy co-operation over which the various British commanders had little personal control.[138] In short, his real object was to show why Hughes's success was limited, allowing for the fact that Suffren was a great commander and Hughes an adequate one. Having discussed Hughes's problems thoroughly he was able to conclude that the war had largely turned on the 'human factor' which was 'the most influential of all the elements in war, transcending that material factor which tends to dominate the minds of superficial men.'[139]

The Navy in India was the last of Richmond's campaign histories. The last two he wrote dealt with questions of sea power on a more grand scale, and both were written while he was Master of Downing College, one *Statesmen and Sea Power*, published in 1946, the other *The Navy as an Instrument of Policy*, edited by E. A. Hughes, and was published after Richmond's death, in 1953.

These two books do not reveal any significant alteration of Richmond's general views on strategy. Neither do they reveal changed attitudes in historical approach to his subject. What is different in them is a move away from the close campaign study to the broad general survey. To Richmond's mind many of the errors of the First World War and certainly the painful adjustments that had to be made at the beginning of the Second World War were

[137] Richmond, *The Navy in India*, p. 182.
[138] The British land commander was Sir Eyre Coote whose strategic appreciations were never seriously at variance with those of Hughes. For instance, in desiring the capture of Negapatom by combined operation Coote supported Hughes against the Madras Council, not a strategically brilliant body. See *ibid.*, pp. 154–72, especially p. 173.
[139] *Ibid.*, p. 298.

the direct result of lack of proper preparedness and war planning. He was convinced that the complacency producing such difficulties had its roots in a general lack of appreciation for his view that national policy war planning and Service preparedness were continuing and interacting requisites in the life of a healthy state. The purpose of *Statesmen and Sea Power* was to show how statesmen nurtured and used the elements of sea power. The editor of *The Navy as an Instrument of Policy* stated in his preface that Richmond wrote that book to help prevent what he greatly feared—'that what has happened before will repeat itself, and the nation, even if it survives—and the Empire, will again relapse into complacency'.

To illustrate these themes he tackled the whole sweep of English history from 1559 onwards. It was a Mahan-like concept. Although the first of these books was based on the Ford lectures given at Oxford in 1943 and was more general than its successor, it is safe to assert that both, while not exhibiting concentrated research into new documentary materials, reveal a wide-working knowledge of available documents. The results of this approach are particularly well revealed in the book Hughes edited, where the influence of the Baltic nations on British policy is discussed with a thoroughness seldom reserved for wars that are not noteworthy for the size of the fleet actions to which they give rise.

Thus Richmond's last books connected, in a vivid way, the foreign policy of Great Britain with the growth and utilization of sea power. By excursions into areas outside the main or dominating patterns of European diplomacy and naval action, he demonstrated the multifarious nature of British naval commitments. This emphasized his view that all-round preparedness must take precedence over the natural desires for peace-time economies arrived at by the setting up of short-term priorities. Furthermore, although his viewpoint continued to be more professional than civilian oriented, these works taken together constitute one of the most formidable attacks of the century on the idea that war is for professional military men alone.

The sum total of his achievement was considerable. He was not, in the same way as Corbett and Mahan, an original thinker. Yet he surpassed both of these men in his capacity to do detailed, thorough, revealing research. His prose exposition, while sometimes given to over-simplification, was direct and striking in its impact. Above all he combined in his person a rare union of the man of action and the responsible scholar to a degree that excites the admiration of both naval officers and professional historians.

Previously the Royal Navy had produced men capable of understanding, and sometimes of gloriously fulfilling, the role that the state cast for them, but never before had it produced a man with the capacity to explain both the navy to the nation and the nation to the navy: to the mutual advantage of each.

7

CIVILIAN HISTORIAN

Sir Julian Corbett

ALL of the men hitherto discussed in this book had, at some stage in their careers, practical military experience. Julian Corbett was a civilian. Furthermore, until he took up writing in a serious way, he was not engaged in any settled civilian profession. Indeed, it was almost by accident that he became a naval historian.

Julian Stafford Corbett was born at Imber Court, Thames Ditton, in 1854, his father, Charles Joseph Corbett, being a successful and worthy architect.[1] There were five other children in the family including one girl. Charles, who was the eldest, ran the family business and was for a time M.P. for Lewes. The family was generally Liberal in politics and in varying degrees they were all disarmers, suffragists and reformers. Although his brothers had intellectual abilities, Julian was the only one to follow a special profession and even he only became totally committed to naval history later in life. In this practically minded, comfortably off family, none of his relatives was capable of understanding Julian's non-lucrative literary inclinations and preoccupations.

Corbett was educated at Marlborough and Trinity College,

[1] Some factual details of Corbett's life are to be found in the *Dictionary of National Biography* article by G. A. R. Callendar. An informed article on Corbett discussing his work in the Fisher period was published by Peter Marsh Stanford in 1951, and to this article the author is indebted. See Stanford, Peter Marsh, 'The Work of Sir Julian Corbett in the Dreadnought Era', *U.S.N.I. Proceedings* (1951), pp. 60–71. Nevertheless, personal information on Corbett has been obtained from Mr. and Mrs. Brian Tunstall. Mrs. Tunstall is Corbett's daughter. Corbett's papers are in Tunstall's possession, and the author has had complete access to them, both for this chapter and for a full biography of Corbett, now in preparation.

Cambridge. He took an active part in College life at Cambridge and coxed a trial eight for the University. He took a first class in the Law Tripos in 1875 and was called to the Bar at the Middle Temple, but did not pursue the practice of law which he found 'irksome'. On the other hand, his means allowed him to follow his inclination for travel; indeed travel was a family pastime. Corbett visited Canada, the United States and India—the last at a time when casual travel there was not customary. In company with his brothers he spent some time in Algeria, again not a customary tourist Mecca. Also he made almost annual visits to the family fishing lodge in Norway, where on one occasion he met and talked to Ibsen. Of all foreign countries, Italy was his favourite and he generally went there alone, almost annually, and while there he indulged his talent for sketching.

At home he looked after Imber Court,[2] studied local history and wrote a few indifferent novels. In this connexion, it is noteworthy that, with the exception of one novel that was given a Norwegian setting,[3] his literary work, and later his historical production, bore no relation to the places that he visited on his travels. His income allowed him to build up a valuable book collection that was to be of assistance to him later on. Along with the rest of the family he developed an interest in Liberal politics and this interest together with his remarkable liking for and proficiency in social intercourse made this eligible young bachelor a welcome figure in society.

He first turned his attention to serious history in the period 1889–90 during which time he wrote the lives of Monk and Drake for the 'English Men of Action Series'. The *Drake*, in retrospect, is interesting as a preview of his later work on that Elizabethan figure, and the *Monk* book despite its limited scope has never been entirely superseded. This venture into the field of history was given added impetus when Corbett joined the Navy Records Society in July, 1893. This contact led to Laughton requesting him, in 1896, to edit a volume of documents relating to the Spanish War. He accepted. At the same time that he did this and while handling those documentary materials he wrote *Drake and the Tudor Navy*.[4] This was a work of singular power and one that displayed mastery of research techniques surprising in the work of a virtual novice. Even at this stage his future career had not been finally decided upon, but the influence of his cousin, Edith

---

[2] A property afterwards used by the Metropolitan Police.
[3] *The Fall of Asgard* (London, 1886).
[4] J. S. Corbett, *Drake and the Tudor Navy*, 2 vols. (London, 1898).

Alexander[5] whom he married in 1899, was decisive in determining him to continue with naval history writing. Like Mahan at his moment of commitment to history, he was then forty-five years old.

From that time until his appointment as Official Naval Historian of the First World War he wrote books on naval history that illuminated the nature of naval development in the historical period between the age of Drake and that of Nelson. His books taken together covered broad sweeps of historical time after the fashion of Mahan. Mahan's approach had been to link detailed history of the tactics of important naval actions to meaningful but general accounts of diplomatic activity. Corbett, however, traced the growth and use of naval strategy and from the first based his interpretations on extensive documentary research. More detailed than Mahan and less dogmatic than Richmond, Corbett brought to his subject the training of the Bar, the temperament of a novelist and the charm of a cultured mind.

Despite the fact that Corbett was a civilian, the authoritative way that he dealt with his themes communicated itself not only to the public (for this was an age of almost indiscriminate purchasing of military books), but also to the members of the naval service. He became virtually the unofficial historical adviser to the Admiralty in the Dreadnought Age. He lectured to the Naval War College at Greenwich in 1900 and he kept up this association for the remainder of the decade. Also, he wrote articles, especially in the *Monthly Review*, on military questions of the day and especially in support of the educational reforms initiated by Admiral Sir John Fisher.[6] Because of his essentially civilian and intellectual approach to these problems, Corbett never became merely a blind supporter of Fisher but he did appreciate what Fisher was attempting and supported him whenever he could.[7] Corbett was able to provide many of the historical arguments that were used in refuting the claims of the anti-navy conscription advocates. Indeed, the cleverness of Corbett's arguments were a real practical force in postponing the fall of Fisher from 1907 to

[5] Daughter of George Alexander, a Manchester cotton manufacturer.

[6] Corbett wrote a number of articles for the *Monthly Review* between 1901 and 1904. See especially 'Lord Selborne's Critics', pp. 64–75, *Monthly Review* (1903); see also his forceful defence of Lord Fisher in 'Recent attacks on the Admiralty', *The Nineteenth Century* (1907), pp. 195–208.

[7] Commented on by Stanford, 'The Work of Sir Julian Corbett in the Dreadnought Era', p. 68. Testified to by the letters to Corbett from Admiral Fisher in the Corbett Papers. See Brian Tunstall; P. M. Stanford; D. M. Schurman; *Catalogue of the Corbett Papers* (Bedford, 1958), pp. 32–4.

1909. It may help to gauge the impact of Corbett's strategic thought on the naval mind, to realize that in 1916 Lord Sydenham of Coombe saw in Corbett's doctrines, as they had been given to the War College before 1914, one reason for the lack of spectacular British naval success at sea.[8] Whatever the truth of such allegations they do indicate that Corbett's ideas influenced naval officers.

When the First World War broke out Corbett was selected by the Committee of Imperial Defence to write the official naval history. Although the straitjacket of official history did not suit his personality, he nevertheless produced the first three of the official naval histories.[9] Constant interference with his work, however, upset him, undermined his health and contributed to his death by heart attack that occurred on 21 September, 1923.

Corbett's range of activity was great. Aside from being an historian he was a writer of talent and his graceful style almost concealed the informed scholarship that directed it. As a publicist he was formidable. His articles dealing with current defence topics were forceful and clear, demonstrating a considerable knowledge of how to win reader support. He was also a theoretician and any reader who has struggled through Mahan's *Naval Strategy* or Clausewitz's *On War*[10] will find in *Some Principles of Maritime Strategy*[11] a clarity of thought set out in virile prose style that convinces and charms in the same reading. He was also an official lecturer for the Admiralty. In his character as lecturer he managed to bring to a navy that was in dire need of instructional examples the clear knowledge that lessons learned in the age of sail had relevance for the age of steam warfare. He was also an antiquarian.

Although Corbett's historical writing was informed by research and presented in a good prose style, it must be mentioned that he was sometimes obscure. Working up big themes he sometimes lost himself in the involved nature of his own thought patterns. This tendency to transform historical fact into speculative thought was a valuable antidote to the prevailing practical tendencies of writers on naval subjects; it also gave rise to new ways of looking at maritime war. But occasionally this resulted only in a lack of

---

[8] Lord Sydenham's speech was delivered in the House of Lords on 15 November, 1916. A correspondence with Corbett ensued. See Corbett Papers (CP) Box 71.
[9] *Naval Operations*, Vols. I, II, III (London, 1920–21–23).
[10] English edition edited by Col. J. J. Graham.
[11] J. S. Corbett, *Some Principles of Maritime Strategy* (London, 1911).

Sir Julian Corbett

clarity. Corbett was a writer whose work charms while it frustrates its readers. One reason for all of this is probably to be found in the fact that he wrote with an intelligent but ill-defined audience in mind. He was not, like most lecturers, subject to the discipline of questioning by young alert minds.[12]

Drake and the Tudor Navy was a two-volume work published in London in 1898. It undoubtedly had its genesis in the initial preoccupation of the Navy Records Society with the Armada Era. Corbett, working at the Armada documents[13] and having already explored the life of Drake, conceived the idea of using one man as the basic fabric around which he could weave the whole story of the naval history of the Tudor Age. Since other men were then doing research in this period he had the advantage of a favourable scholarly atmosphere to work in. In particular, his research benefited by the publication in 1896 of M. Oppenheim's monumental work *The Administration of the Royal Navy 1509-1660*.[14]

If the general environment was favourable to the execution of such a work as Corbett proposed, the practical problems that he faced were still formidable. Chief among those was Drake's heroic reputation. While Corbett did not quarrel with Drake's historic heroic status, he did feel that the real nature of the Elizabethan's achievement was imperfectly understood. Corbett proposed welding the personality of the man and the peculiar features of the age together. Both Drake and the English nation's developing sea power emerged from the synthesis as more rational and understandable phenomena. Through this approach, the Elizabethans were shown to have formulated a rather sophisticated naval strategy and to have developed both its theorists and its executors together. In this fusion rested the beginning of the strategy that was to create a great Empire and produce the power that was one day to emerge as the arbiter of European development. This concept of a Tudor strategy in depth was too involved for the general reader, but scholars welcomed it, and it has continued to entrance them. As late as 1954, G. R. Elton wrote that this book was 'still a very important work much of which cannot be found elsewhere. Undoubtedly prejudiced in Drake's favour.'[15]

The point that Elton makes about prejudice is an important one. What he is referring to is the running quarrel that has

---

[12] Suggested in conversation by Brian Tunstall.
[13] Julian S. Corbett (ed.), *Papers Relating to the Navy during the Spanish War (1585-87)* (London, 1898).
[14] Published London, 1896.
[15] G. R. Elton, *England under the Tudors* (London, 1954), p. 486.

existed for some time between pro-military historians, like Richmond, who have tended to condemn Queen Elizabeth for her lack of strategic ability, and others, notably Elton himself and R. B. Wernham, who have shown that the Queen was by no means a strategic ignoramus. After Wernham's beautifully clear articles a decade ago the military arguments appear to have less force than formally.[16] However the point is not whether Corbett was prejudiced or not. Every historian is prejudiced. The important thing is that he saw that there was a case to be made for the idea that naval men, by the 1580 period, had built up enough strategic doctrinal claims to determine Elizabethan military and diplomatic policy. Instead of a picture of isolated hit-and-run raids, Corbett revealed a growing maritime self-awareness that had begun to give rise to strategic concepts. That Corbett over-played his hand is arguable; the fact that he invented the game is not.

Indeed the whole book was redolent of a fresh approach. Corbett showed for the first time how Drake regarded naval operations off the Spanish Coast as being the most important Elizabethan form of grand strategy. He developed the basic idea that Spain was most vulnerable to harassment near her heartland, and that a British base in the area would probably render such harassment unbearable. Not only did Corbett open up this early naval strategic conception for historical discussion, but he did it in a way that showed his awareness of the practical difficulties, both material and historical, that rendered Drake's ideas less than perfect. His historical sense made him vividly aware of the especially non-co-operative natures of Elizabethan military *prima donnas*. His historical knowledge, based on close study of contemporary source material, showed him how the kind of equipment and organization of those days set limits to the practical realization of strategic aspirations.

If Drake's biography was used to expose strategic development it was also used to describe tactical evolution. In this field, Corbett was the complete pioneer. The book carefully discussed in general the development of ship design and the growth of improved gunnery. This explained the physical capabilities of the ships that fought one another in the Armada campaign. When Corbett allied such technical knowledge with his discoveries about British and Spanish tactical planning, together with his personal flair for understanding the personalities of the combatant leaders, he was able realistically to reconstruct the Channel fight. Modern

[16] R. B. Wernham, 'Queen Elizabeth and the Portugal Expedition of 1589', *English Historical Review* (1951), pp. 1-26 and 194-218.

writers have upset much of the detail of Corbett's conclusions. Michael Lewis's masterly treatment of Armada guns and gunnery has taken one aspect of Corbett's approach to its logical conclusion.[17] In the same way Garrett Mattingly has used a variety of sources to present a more complete picture of the Spanish point of view.[18] Nevertheless, with the tactical as with the strategic approach it is clear that the need for such investigation in depth originated in Corbett's mind. Furthermore, on certain of the days of the Channel fight of the Armada where direct evidence remains scanty Corbett's reconstructions, informed by his understanding of the whole Tudor period, still hold the field.[19]

Corbett's technique was to make Francis Drake the instrument of fate who understood and attempted to guide naval warfare from its position of unco-ordinated oversea attack and battle, or what Admiral Colomb had called 'cross ravaging', into an arm of statecraft that was somewhat conformable to rules or 'principles of naval war'. The transformation that was effected was the result of deductions made from scholarly investigation rather than of the application of preconceived principles to historical material. Despite the tremendous advance that the book represented, the author's mind was still in a state of development. He was learning as he went along and he allowed his reader to share the explorer's adventure.

At this stage in Corbett's career his mind tended to separate the events in which his hero was intimately involved into military and political compartments. For instance, when explaining the Queen's less than vigorous offensive policy between the autumn of 1587 and the sailing of the Armada, he wrote of Queen Elizabeth's 'fanaticism for peace'.[20] This phrase was perhaps over colourful. Corbett was well aware of the diplomatic and monetary factors that compelled the Queen to restrain Drake's thirst for initiative-keeping offensive action. He was, nevertheless, doubtless impatient that such a decision had to be made. This ambivalent attitude was based on a distinction Corbett made between political and military justification. He wrote, 'Whatever may have been her political reasons for not wishing to deal Philip too crushing a blow, from a military point of view her decision was

[17] Michael Lewis, *The Navy of Britain* (London, 1948). See p. 414–46. Lewis developed this material in more detail in a series of articles entitled 'Armada Guns' in the *Mariner's Mirror* in a series of eight articles beginning in January, 1942, and ending in October, 1943.
[18] Garrett Mattingly, *The Defeat of the Spanish Armada* (London, 1959).
[19] *Ibid.*, See note to Chapter XXV, p. 359.
[20] *Drake and the Tudor Navy*, Vol. II, p. 108.

L

undoubtedly a grave mistake, and even at the time, everyone seemed to see it except herself.'[21] Although that sentence at first glance appears to be a reasoned defence of Drake and a condemnation of the Queen, it is in fact an attempt to make a point by inserting an artificial wall between politics and strategy. In the same fashion Corbett, in speaking of the negotiations Elizabeth carried out with Parma over the winter of 1587-8, condemned her refusal to strike again at the preparing Armada as a grave mistake, but went on to say 'the very reasons which condemn her naval policy are to no small extent a justification of the diplomacy'.[22] This tortuous sentence also indicates a supposed isolation of military from other statecraft.

This tendency to enhance Drake's reputation as a naval strategist and to downgrade that of the Queen was the result partly of hero-worship and partly of an assumption that warfare was better understood by military men than by statesmen. Such preconceived notions produce careless and sometimes unwarranted conclusions. Corbett wrote that most of the blunders and defects of the unhappy Lisbon campaign of 1589 'were directly due either to the express order or to the default of the Government itself, and are in no way attributable either to want of judgement or to neglect on the part of the generals'.[23] He went on to claim the raid as a success. Corbett admitted that Drake disobeyed his orders[24] but he contended that those orders were not based on good strategic thinking.[25] He also blamed the expedition's early delays on the Government authorities.[26] This subject has been discussed more recently by Wernham whose careful investigation has shown that the early delays were a good deal the fault of the military men.[27]

Another questionable strategic approach of Corbett's was his Mahan-like view that commerce destruction was a wasteful and inefficient form of warfare. Diversion of fleet strength for such purposes he was inclined to deplore, and with decreasing emphasis he maintained this approach all the rest of his life. Thus Hawkins was cast in the role of false strategist; as one who advanced the idea 'since so often proved fatal and so often reborn as a new strategical discovery, that a naval war may be conducted on

[21] *Drake and the Tudor Navy*, Vol. II, p. 109.
[22] Ibid., p. 126.
[23] Ibid., p. 332.
[24] Ibid., p. 318.
[25] Ibid., p. 309.
[26] Ibid., pp. 298-9.
[27] Wernham, 'Queen Elizabeth, etc.' *English Historical Review* (1951), pp. 17-21.

economical principles, and a great Power be brought to its knees by preying on its commerce without first getting command of the sea'.[28] Perhaps Corbett had done his homework with Mahan too thoroughly for this view as we have seen was a strong part of Mahan's thinking.

All this is not to suggest, however, that Corbett's strategic appreciations were generally ill-founded. Excepting his views on commerce destruction what one may observe in his work is the contrast between these early views and his later more mature ones. Nothing could be clearer than his views concerning the areas where Spain was most vulnerable to English attack and his consistent advocacy of a policy of attack in Spanish waters.[29]

From the historian's point of view the other faults that the book possessed may be directly attributable to the difficulties that naturally arose from the technique of attempting to relate the history of national naval development through the life of one man. With twin purposes in mind, even treatment was not easy for him to maintain. For instance, referring to naval preparations in the spring of 1588, he stated at one point 'with the new dispositions Drake, if he knew of them, was far from satisfied'.[30] This problem is also apparent in Corbett's treatment of Thomas Doughty who was under Drake's orders during the round-the-world trip. Drake had Doughty executed. A persisting lack of detailed information still shrouds the whole affair in mystery.[31] Corbett used his artistry to support Drake's action. The new historian of Drake, indeed, did not claim to be impartial, and while his book displays the riches of heavy research it was certainly dedicated more to explaining the growth of a naval age in a biography than it was to ascertaining the precise accuracy of each situation as it unfolded. In so doing, he naturally displayed both the prejudices and the search for organic meaning in history that characterized his age.

The strengths of the book, however, are more obvious than the chronicled weaknesses. Not only did Corbett understand the Mahan thesis that navies exist for national purposes, but he also endeavoured to expose that relationship by means of direct

[28] *Drake and the Tudor Navy*, Vol. II, pp. 129, 335. On pp. 368–9 he shows how severe the commerce destruction bore on the Spanish government but, oddly and paradoxically, he states that the very success of this work should have shown the 'vice' of attempting 'to coerce a great power by preying on its commerce'.
[29] *Ibid.*, p. 375; pp. 407–9.
[30] *Ibid.*, p. 139.
[31] J. A. Williamson, *The Age of Drake* (London, 1946), pp. 170–80.

reference to the documentary evidence concerning sea affairs in Elizabethan times. While the modern reader will perhaps cavil at the figure of extravagant genius Drake is made to cut, he yet must acknowledge that by attempting to understand Drake's thought processes through a study and presentation of his times and his writing the author did, in fact, raise his hero from the position of mere dashing pirate to that of naval adviser of national importance. Also, it joins the Mahan sailor-like interest in the true significance of sea war to the historian's understanding of the period. Although facts are important the nature of the mind that filtered them on to the printed page is no less so. It was more than a mere chronicler who pointed out that Drake's greatness was due as much to what he thought and attempted as to what he actually achieved. Indeed, said Corbett, 'no one can measure the greatness of the Elizabethan age who does not know through what a world of shame and disaster it marched to its successes'.[32] He knew.

The purpose of the *Successors of Drake* was to examine and comment on the judgement that the post-Armada period was one 'splendid failure'.[33] In the process, he disclosed himself as an independent thinker of stature for this book struck hard at the extreme naval ideas of the so-called Blue Water School. At a time when some sailors and their romantic academic captives were busy glorifying the virtues of a purely naval as opposed to an army concept of British defence, Corbett told them that what 'the period teaches is the limitation of maritime power'.[34] Speaking to his contemporary audience he went so far as to assert that, since army and naval power were mutually dependent upon one another for national military success, it was wrong to study the histories of British armies and navies in separate watertight compartments. 'The real importance,' he wrote, 'of maritime power is its influence on military operations.'[35] This conclusion was partially the result of studying Mahan; it was also the growing realization as he wrote the book that the explanation of Elizabethan military failures did not rest comfortably on an interpretation that rated the statesmen as incompetent as directors and the sailors as men of strategic genius. If the genius of Drake had made such an interpretation attractive, so his death had removed the occasion for it. Indeed, a good deal of the strength of this book derives from the fact that the period threw up no comparable

[32] J. A. Williamson, *The Age of Drake*, Vol. I, p. 333.
[33] J. S. Corbett, *The Successors of Drake* (London, 1900), Preface, p. vi.
[34] *Ibid.*, Preface, p. vii.
[35] *Ibid.*

Sir Julian Corbett

figures to Drake and Hawkins. In any event, the narrative of this book was not linked to the life of one man.

Thus, although he did not entirely abandon the idea that civilian direction of Elizabethan warfare was somewhat misguided, he came to appreciate that combined operations involved a special, complicated way of making war. Although the Queen's judgements might be incomplete, at the same time he saw that she had, in fact, trusted her men of war, especially at Lisbon in 1589, and that they had failed her.[36] In the course of the book Corbett's praise for the military men became progressively more restrained. That the professional military *dramatis personae* between 1595 and 1601 were not outstanding men is clear. Excessive praise was not, therefore, mandatory. This was certainly true of those involved in the Cadiz raid of 1596. Essex's potential brilliance was capped by his chronic instability; Sir Francis Vere was a good solid army campaign professional but hardly charged with genius; Lord Howard of Effingham had notoriously more presence than presence of mind.[37] Corbett says that Raleigh 'of all Englishmen who have achieved a great reputation as a man of action . . . has most deeply the taint of the man of letters, and to this he owes much of the reputation that men of letters have made of him'.[38] They were easier historical figures to handle than Drake had been since all were possessed of strong qualities, but was none so outstanding as to inhibit the historian's critical faculties. Certainly none of them could stand comparison with Elizabeth Tudor.

Furthermore, a basic change took place in the chemistry of the Spanish War when Drake died. The implacable sense of personal vendetta which he felt towards the Spaniards both provoked and was sustained by a corresponding emotion amongst the nation at large. No other leader's name could produce a similar reaction. Sir Richard Grenville's magnificent but futile death fight[39] was of the age of chivalry and not of Drake, as was the general

---

[36] Corbett, *Successors*, p. 1.
[37] (a) Robert Devereux, 2nd Earl of Essex (1566–1601); soldier, favourite and traitor.
    (b) Sir Francis Vere (1560–1609); soldier and library benefactor.
    (c) Charles Howard, 2nd Baron Howard of Effingham, 1st Earl of Nottingham (1536–1624); statesman and commander against Spanish Armada.
[38] *Ibid.*, p. 149. Sir Walter Raleigh (1552?–1618); poet, historian, military and naval commander.
[39] Sir Richard Grenville (1541?–91); naval commander, died fighting against impossible odds off Flores (Azores).

atmosphere of the military swashbucklers at the court in the fifteen-nineties; most felt that 'active service was the king of field sports'.[40]

Thus it was, with a relatively open mind, that Corbett regarded the most important campaign discussed in the volume: Cadiz 1596. This raid comprised a combination of failure and success, of high conception and miserable result. 'It is probable,' says Corbett, 'that no army more perfectly equipped and disciplined had ever left her shores,'[41] yet it returned months later without having garrisoned its military lodgement on the Iberian Peninsula, with depleted forces and without the consolation of significant quantities of booty. That Cadiz was captured despite the hampering deliberations of too many hesitant councils of war is true. It was not, however, held. This fact had some significance since the Queen, Vere and Essex all seem to have been aware of the strategic value of keeping it.[42] Raleigh, however, was not so persuaded; nor was Howard.[43] Hence the crux of the failure of the expedition can be traced to a lack of command co-operation or co-ordination. Corbett went deeper. His investigations convinced him that the kind of army necessary to keep Cadiz did not exist. He cleverly showed how Sir Francis Vere, while he supported Essex's base-retention plan, was not at all sure that the resources of the army were sufficient to accomplish so desirable an object. He demonstrated that this was clear to Vere long before the sailors and soldiers ever took ship together.[44] In the long view, Corbett felt Vere was proved correct.

Yet a note of caution must be sounded regarding the Corbettian treatment of the Cadiz raid. For contemporaries it is highly possible that the reason it was regarded as a failure was the lack of plunder brought back.[45] Corbett's criticism, however, was that a base was not held owing to the insufficiency of the army for such a custodian's task. This theme of army inadequacy is developed in the narrative of events preparatory to the raid.[46] Again, towards the end of the volume it is allowed to emerge as

[40] Corbett, *Successors*, p. 14.
[41] *Ibid.*, p. 55. This same remark has been applied to the British Expeditionary Force of 1914.
[42] *Ibid.*, pp. 33–5.
[43] *Ibid.*, p. 110.
[44] *Ibid.*, p. 33 and p. 110.
[45] When the expedition returned home the Reports of the leaders of the operation were suppressed and the Queen was angry with her Admirals. See *ibid.*, pp. 129–32.
[46] *Ibid.*, pp. 33, 51.

Sir Julian Corbett

one of the main conclusions of the whole book.[47] However, the vibrant description of the raid itself and the eventual decision to evacuate Cadiz taken on the spot does not emphasize troop shortage. Indeed, Corbett makes it very clear that the actual decision to abandon was forced on the leaders by the homesick indiscipline of the English sailors.[48] That this indiscipline was allowed to develop points both to weak leadership and disunity in the command.[49]

The rest of the book treats of the dreary but successful story of England's attempts to evade invasion after 1596, of the sporadic and unspectacular attacks on New Spain, and of the value of the navy in support operations on the Irish coast where Admiral Leveson[50] showed the advantages of sea command to an army operating miles from its supply depots.[51] Corbett's treatment of these subjects was imaginative and instructive.

Whatever may be thought of the Elizabethan army Corbett admitted that properly deployed and warned in England behind an unvanquished fleet, it was quite sufficient to the task of preventing invasion. In fact, the 'other armada' moves after 1596 were in reality hollow challenges.[52] It speaks volumes for the strategic sagacity of the Elizabethans that the later invasion scares drew such slight responses. The question that disturbed Corbett was whether or not the English should have gone over to the full offensive. His answer was reasonably measured.[53] It was true, he argued, that Elizabeth was a 'little Englander' and that the men of war were expansionists, but it may also have been true that Elizabeth's caution was justified. Her men of war had failed her because the army was too small to enable England to embark on a sea of conquest. One must agree that Elizabethan England was fortunate to have survived so well a struggle with Hapsburg Spain in the sixteenth century. On the other hand, Corbett over-simplified his explanation of the lack of a successful offensive. Elizabethan England had, as he says, established its

---

[47] Corbett, *Successors*, pp. 407–9.
[48] *Ibid.*, p. 111.
[49] This is not to suggest that Corbett was unaware of this weakness. See *ibid.*, p. 134. It is a question of emphasis.
[50] Sir Richard Leveson (1570–1605), Vice-Admiral of England.
[51] Corbett, *Successors*, pp. 323–54. Although the extent of the naval effect on the land campaign has been slightly questioned in Cyril Falls, *Elizabeth's Irish Wars* (London, 1950), p. 300.
[52] Corbett said that, as a defensive operation, the Spanish War was 'a complete triumph', *ibid.*, p. 405.
[53] *Ibid.*, pp. 406–10.

right to exist as a separate Protestant State, it had administered at least a reasonable check to the Counter-Reformation. Whether England had started on her 'mission' to tread underfoot all who would not listen to 'the Brotherhood of Industry',[54] as Corbett called the adoration of the cash box, is another matter.

The Successors of Drake marked an advance in the development of the historians' thought. To have deliberately attacked the excessive adulation accorded the navy in 1900 and suggested a corrective based on a general historical observation of the Elizabethan period was a great achievement. The book showed how Corbett had grown in understanding the necessary relationship between statecraft and warfare, and that he also understood that the ravelling of such a connexion was a complicated process admitting of few useful platitudes. Of the latter, the one to which he was still most addicted was the view that trade war was a relatively useless occupation without having first established sea supremacy.[55] As we have seen he shared this view with Mahan and Laughton. This view was to die hard.

Corbett's next book dealt with the naval expansion of England in the seventeenth century and was entitled *England in the Mediterranean*. The book grew out of lectures to the Senior and Flag Officers' War Course at Greenwich and the Ford lectures delivered at Oxford.[56] The book's main theme is England's entry into the strategic exploitation of the Mediterranean Sea, no attempt being made to include the Anglo-Dutch conflict in home waters. He described administrative progress, proffered pieces of naval lore, investigated obscure campaigns with subtlety and occasionally great detail, and generally probed selected aspects of naval development in the Stuart century. The unity of the book was less than complete; and it was a little thin on sources considering its scope, but as a revealing investigation of the real nature of sea power on the author's own terms it was a triumph. In previous books Corbett had revealed an unrivalled talent for describing the detailed components of strategic movement and the growth of its appreciation among the English. While Laughton had shown this ability he patently had lacked the talent for sustained narrative. Corbett now revealed that naval history involved something more than the success or failure of big fleets in big battles. This influenced his choice of subject for in the time

[54] Corbett, *Successors*, p. 404.
[55] *Ibid.*, p. 385.
[56] Corbett, *England in the Mediterranean*, 2 vols. (London, 1904), Vol. I., Preface.

and area selected for study no big battles excepting Malaga in 1704 took place. First, he showed the importance of introducing the broadside battleship into the Mediterranean Sea and how the English were responsible for it. Then, delving into the obscure history of Venice between 1615 and 1619 for instance, Corbett with the skill of a ballet choreographer set up the dramatic groupings of European power politics around that small state, and then at the crucial moment introduced the child prodigy of England's shipping and allowed it to dance almost inadvertently into the star role, thus giving the whole production new form.[57] This was at the beginning of the book, and, although he never again concocted such a delicate stage setting, he did repeat the theme, showing how Blake's fleet in the Mediterranean changed the structure of power politics *vis-à-vis* the Commonwealth,[58] how the possession of Tangier alarmed Louis XIV and influenced his reaction to the Colbert dream of marine supremacy,[59] and how the use by William III and Marlborough of English sea power in the Mediterranean influenced the land campaigns against Louis XIV.[60] It was a great theme, advanced with imagination and sustained with a restless evocative prose style. For instance, in depicting the influence of Mediterranean Sea strategy on European strategy generally he wrote, 'As always, beneath the apparent failures and disappointments there was still, unseen and almost unnoticed, the silent promise of the chafing fleet that was felt to the farthest borders of the war, even to the far-off Meuse, withering the lilies on the walls of Namur.'[61]

The classic Mediterranean event was the movement by King William of the fleet into the Mediterranean on a year-round basis and Corbett described this important event clearly. This theme was later taken up by John Ehrman who illustrated the move with descriptions of administrative refinements to which Corbett re-

[57] Corbett, *England in the Mediterranean*, Vol. I, pp. 33–65. The comparison with the ballet was chosen deliberately. The whole treatment suffers from a lack of concreteness; yet as an artistic presentation of the subtleties of strategy, these pages leave a remarkable impression on the reader. They do show how an intelligent, if limited, appreciation of sea power to a tender diplomatic situation could produce results out of all proportion to its real physical potential. Undoubtedly this Venetian material reflected Corbett's interest in Italy, and Italian history.
[58] *Ibid.*, pp. 204–25.
[59] *Ibid.*, Vol. II, pp. 2–50 and 63–7.
[60] *Ibid.*, pp. 150–75.
[61] *Ibid.*, p. 182.
[62] John Ehrman, *The Navy in the War of King William III* (London, 1953), pp. 517–53.

mained a stranger.[62] Yet it was Corbett who first perceived and traced the strategic importance of the move and it has been within the framework set out by him that later labourers in this field have worked. The significance of King William's moves lay in that a British fleet 'interposed' itself between 'the two seats of French maritime power'.[63] This policy had been foreshadowed by Blake's stay at Gibraltar in 1650, although the danger to France, implicit in such a move or what Corbett called the 'priceless secret', was only gradually appreciated by the English.[64] Indeed, of the whole Commonwealth naval policy that so firmly had disposed of the menace of Prince Rupert's fleet and brought the European powers to recognize the Commonwealth, Corbett says, 'it must not be supposed, however, that this policy was adopted entirely or quite consciously for political reasons'.[65] Once he had established the idea as a naval tradition Corbett went ahead easily and dealt confidently and authoritatively with Marlborough's attempts to build on Cromwell's and William's beginnings and his attempts to dovetail naval efforts in the Mediterranean with his great European conceptions. He ascribed the reasons for Marlborough's failure to achieve total success in his Grand Strategy to the great Churchill not understanding the limitations of the men and vessels of the Royal Navy, plus the difficulties of the Dutch alliance that he attempted to deploy so intelligently.[66] But Corbett's work revealed for the first time the real strategic importance of Marlborough's policy and its background.[67] 'His [Marborough's] failure went to show that, for the purposes of practical strategy, France was not seriously vulnerable from the south, but it proved that with a dominant sea power well placed within the Straits, her Mediterranean Frontier was useless to her for offence, and that neither for her nor for any other power could the dream of the Roman Empire be revived.'[68] Furthermore, the retention of Gibraltar in 1713 meant that Marlborough's strategy had obtained 'that priceless treasure which has determined the position of England in Europe from that day to this'.[69]

Much of the background for this kind of thinking came from the current historical work of S. R. Gardiner and C. H. Firth whose

[63] Ehrman, *The Navy in the War of King William III*, p. 175.
[64] Corbett, *Mediterranean*, Vol. I, p. 319 ff.
[65] *Ibid.*, p. 225.
[66] *Ibid.*, Vol. II, p. 300.
[67] *Ibid.*, p. 229.
[68] *Ibid.*, p. 314.
[69] *Ibid.*, p. 313.

Sir Julian Corbett

work on the seventeenth century, especially the Cromwellian era, displayed such high standards of documentary accuracy.[70] Also, this research revealed much about the real motivations of English foreign policy. In his book, Corbett's fixed views on the efficacy of commerce protection were brought up hard against the fact that most naval commanders and strategists of the seventeenth century paid attention to the problem. Corbett solved the difficulty by suggesting that to satisfy popular clamour they tended to mask strategic truths in commerce protection garments. He wrote, 'Thus, although strategists, for the purpose of commending their views to the public and the Treasury, naturally wrote in terms of commerce, we must never forget that what they were really aiming at was the command of the sea by the domination of the great trade routes and the acquisition of focal points as naval stations.'[71] He justified this by asserting that commercial lines naturally became the strategic lines. This was true enough but whether seventeenth-century strategists understood this is by no means clear.

As a work producing a new approach to naval history this book was the most important if not the best that Corbett ever wrote. Although it is both diffuse and sometimes excessively selective, yet it served to assist in shifting the minds of serious investigators of naval history away from biography as the chief medium of exposition, and taught them to concentrate on the growth of strategic traditions and the power that navies exert merely through their intelligent disposition. Also in this book if one finds the vivid imagination at play, one also finds the bridling effect of a mind that was beginning to recognize its own responsibilities as an accepted expert. The conclusions are as eminently reasonable as the judgements are careful. Writing in 1904, Corbett's strategic knowledge was still largely a product of his naval and British historical studies. When he next returned to writing naval history, he, as Mahan said, continually allowed it to transpire[72] that he had made contact with the world's most

---

[70] Gardiner died in 1902. His most important works on the era were: *History of England, 1603–42*, 10 vols. (London, 1883–84); *History of the Great Civil War, 1642–49*, 4 vols. (London, 1893); and *History of the Commonwealth and Protectorate*, 4 vols. (London, 1903). Gardiner's work was continued by Firth who wrote, in particular: *The Last Years of the Protectorate, 1656–58*, 2 vols. (London, 1909); *Oliver Cromwell* (London, 1907); and *House of Lords* (London, 1910). Corbett knew Firth, who was producing while Corbett was writing.

[71] Corbett, *Mediterranean*, Vol. I, p. 227.

[72] Mahan, *Naval Strategy*, pp. 16–7. Although Mahan does not mention Clausewitz by name, the inference is clear.

renowned thinker in war, Karl von Clausewitz. As with the mental conjunction of Jomini and Mahan, so with the German and the Englishman the result was felicitous.

In *England in the Seven Years War*,[73] Corbett joined his accumulated experience as a naval historian to the strategic knowledge he had assimilated from deep study of Clausewitz and fused them together with his literary talent to create a great book. In addition he was faced with the problem of dealing with these military problems, taking into account the fact that the war was continental, indeed world-wide in scope, and involved giving due weight to alliance problems. Diplomatically speaking he received much assistance from M. Richard Waddington's *La Guerre de Sept Ans*. By fusing this diplomatic treatment with the Clausewitzian military method, he was able to explain the important part England's sea power enabled her to play in this big broad conflict. Since the book first appeared many authors have made literary assaults on Louisburg and Quebec, refought the Battle of Quiberon Bay and even attempted a panoramic view of the whole war; questions of fact in Corbett's book have been disputed and new information has been published;[74] but his book remains valuable as a unique attempt to write history on the large scale with military principles guiding the selection method. That it is a great book is undoubtedly true, just as it is true that it is a specialist work. In *The Successors of Drake* Corbett had spoken of the need for a maritime policy for Great Britain that would allow army and navy to work together. The Seven Years War supplied the required ingredients for the formulation of such a policy; it was 'radiant with the genius of a maritime state'.[75] Although he did not attempt consciously to explain the naval contribution *at the expense* of army achievement, Corbett did make the essentially maritime nature of the war clear. In this connexion the soldiers were not his main stumbling blocks. He had to do battle with the preoccupation of naval officers and naval historians with historical accounts of acute and dramatic moments of warlike activity. He had taken issue with this big-battle fixation in *England in the Mediterranean*, but this new book was largely devoted to explaining the strategic dangers of assuming

---

[73] J. S. Corbett, *England in the Seven Years War*, 2 vols. (London, 1907).

[74] One example from many is C. P. Stacey, *Quebec, 1759: The Siege and the Battle* (Toronto, 1959). Stacey, for instance, finds Corbett's estimate of the ages of the English commanders at Quebec 'merely silly'. Stacey is right, Corbett was prone to quick conclusions that sometimes were fanciful as we have seen.

[75] *England in the Seven Years War*, Vol. I, p. 9.

Sir Julian Corbett

such conflict to be the only worthy type for a military man. He wrote:

'there may be moments in the most complex war when the destruction of the enemy's main fleet and the securing of the command of a certain sea may be of an importance so great and pressing that naval action may rightly be left free to concern itself with nothing else, and every consideration of diplomatic and military operations must rest subservient to naval strategy. When such rare moments occur, they are invariably so dazzling in their dramatic intensity as to dull our vision of what they really mean and how they were brought about. The imagination comes naturally to concentrate itself upon such supreme catastrophes and to forget that war is not made up of them. Historians, greedy of dramatic effect, encourage such concentrations of attention, and the result is that the current conception of the functions of a fleet is dangerously narrowed, and our best minds cramp their strategical view by assuming unconsciously that the sole function of a fleet is to win battles at sea. That this is the supreme function of a fleet is certain, and it must never be lost sight of; but on the other hand it must not be forgotten that convenient opportunities of winning a battle do not always occur when they are wanted. *The great dramatic moments of naval history have to be worked for and the first preoccupation of the fleet will almost always be to bring them about by interference with the enemy's military and diplomatic arrangements.*'[76]

This approach enabled him to put firm historical underproppings beneath Pitt's traditional accomplishments. For the evidence revealed Pitt to be a strategic genius. As Corbett stated: 'Not only was he able without destroying the enemy's naval force to strike beyond the ocean at the ulterior object, but at home he was able to break down the time-honoured strategy of France, and force her, by goading her into a desperate attempt at invasion, to deliver her main fleets into his hands.'[77] No one can read the history of the Seven Years War as set out in this book and conclude with the impression that its great combats or conquests were the result of military accident. Corbett demonstrated conclusively that they were the result of the 'ordered combination of naval, military, and diplomatic force'.

Corbett used new sources. Especially valuable were the Newcastle and Hardwicke papers, and he applied Clausewitzian techniques to their interpretation. This method produced some surprises by vindicating the Duke of Newcastle's early handling of English pre-war manœuvring which Corbett labelled 'strategic

[76] Corbett, *England in the Seven Years War*, Vol. I, pp. 3–4 (my italics).
[77] *Ibid.*, p. 8.

defensive', stating that the Duke was correct to exploit the situation to any length short of actual war.[78] The British plan was to pursue a policy of pre-war aggression that nevertheless permitted nothing to be done to which the French could conscientiously object by choosing war. The war began in what he called a 'limited' way; being simply a question of involvement because of certain territories in America, and Pitt was shown to be right to keep it that way even as Newcastle had been correct in his general appreciation although wrong in his attempts at execution. Much difficulty was caused by the inability of the Admirals to understand the political significance of their orders, nor did the instructions sent out betray any close familiarity with the 'elementary principles of strategy'.[79]

Corbett regarded Newcastle more highly than had other military writers. He looked on Pitt as superb. The worship of Pitt was excessive, perhaps, but it was also plausible for the strategic genius of Pitt the Elder has never seriously been in doubt. However, the combination of Corbett's veneration and Clausewitz's theory combined to defend Pitt from the more usual consequences of human error. As a result large questions evaporated. Did Pitt, for instance, change his mind on the value of subsidy payments to support an ally in continental war?[80] Pitt's seeming inconsistency was justified by the use of Clausewitzian theory as part of the necessary containing of one foe in one field of endeavour in order to pursue a limited object undisturbed in another.[81] Hence it was that Corbett's respect for Pitt combined neatly with the possibilities of Germanic military theory to produce a picture of events which is much more convincing in retrospect than it must have been at the time of the war. The area of truth probably lies some-

[78] Corbett, *England in the Seven Years War*, Vol. I, p. 27.

[79] *Ibid.*, pp. 58–9. These arguments are advanced by Corbett in connexion with a discussion of Admiral Boscawen's brush with French supply vessels bound for New France, off the Grand Banks. It is likely that Boscawen was not so naïve as Corbett thought him. See Peter Kemp, ed. *Boscawen's Letters to his Wife, 1755–56* (London, 1952), pp. 193–4.

[80] A reference to the fact that in the 1740s and a good part of the 1750s Pitt was a violent opponent to the use of British troops and money in support of King George's Hanoverian or Continental policies. After assuming office and responsibility during the war he abruptly changed, or appeared to change, his mind.

[81] *England in the Seven Years War*, p. 156. Or, as Gipson later put it, 'the validity of the Continental situation ... compelled Pitt to put away sentiment in favour of logic' and to 'eat his own passionate words'. See L. H. Gipson, *The British Empire before the American Revolution*, Vol. VII (New York, 1959), pp. 132 and 128.

where in between Corbett's studied knowledge of Clausewitzian principles and Pitt's apparently instinctive perception of them. It is doubtless this laboured but not unsuccessful attempt to force historical events into a posthumously conceived historical pattern that caused Brian Tunstall to refer to its extremely technical and specialistic nature.[82]

In treating of Pitt's strategy, however, Corbett was able to handle a voluminous mass of primary material and yet allow the essential lines of Pitt's 'system' to stand out clearly. While demonstrating how the larger problems of the Continental alliance were both used and exploited to contribute to the North American goal, he was also able to show how the alliance as a whole was a delicately poised mechanism the efficiency of which was ultimately dependent upon the success of apparently minor undertakings such as diversionary raids.

By describing such a raid, the one on Rochefort in 1757,[83] Corbett showed the strategic value of even the most abortive of supporting actions. He was convinced that the ability to mount such raids and to understand their ultimate strategic possibilities was essential to British success in war.[84] In the case of Rochefort, therefore, the raid served as an illustration of the elements necessary for tactical success in such an undertaking and also to demonstrate that a tactical failure might after all produce a strategic success, since the main purpose of the raid was to draw off French troops from Frederick the Great's front and to show how this was accomplished despite the fact that the port was never captured. This concentration on one seemingly minor aspect of Pitt's strategy was justifiable, since it demonstrated that for a sea power total victory was only as secure as the weakest link in its chain of diplomatic-military cause and effect. In his description of the war, Corbett placed himself in Pitt's place at the centre of the war, and held all the threads in his hand there. It was not an experience conducive to the idea that wars are matters of big conclusive battles standing by themselves.

In discussing the year 1759, Corbett showed not only how the navy was vital to the capture of Quebec in the tactical and army support sense, but he discussed with authority the applications of British maritime force that not only broke down the North American relief system of the King of France but also goaded the

[82] Brian Tunstall, *William Pitt, Earl of Chatham* (London, 1938), p. 5.
[83] *England in the Seven Years War*, Vol. I, pp. 197-222.
[84] Tunstall has shown how Pitt personally had come to an appreciation of the value of containing operations as early as 1743. See Tunstall, *Pitt*, pp. 5, 64-6.

French into disastrous attempts at retaliation against Britain. Again applying the theories of Clausewitz, he showed how Britain's pursuit of a protected 'limited war' in the New World had become so successful that the French could only think it possible to relieve the pressure by turning the war against England into an unlimited war and striking directly at the coils of the British sea stranglehold by invasion of the British heartland. This shows, in a manner that might be instructive to recent rediscoverers of the eighteenth-century theory of limited war, 'the tendency of limited wars to become unlimited in character',[85] now known to strategists as the principle of 'escalation'. After 1759 the war was no longer a limited one.

For Corbett, the British aims were secured by the end of 1760 but the very success of the system raised natural obstacles to peace. Limited objectives are easier to gain militarily than to keep diplomatically. However, although Corbett went on to chronicle the last years of the war it is apparent that for him with the conquest of Canada and the fall of Pitt the sublime aspects had deserted the contest. The concluding narrative chapters are competent but not so dramatic.

Three points stand out in his concluding remarks. First, that incompetent succeeding ministers lost much of Pitt's successes. The second lesson is typically Corbettian. Having built the war up into a vast success story he chose to dilate on Britain's war-time proximity to disaster rather than on their margin of victory at the war's conclusion. As he had defended Newcastle by an appeal to the excellence of French planning during 1755–56, so at the conclusion he defended the French general method of making war according to the principle of the strategic defensive.[86] He claimed that the French nearly spoiled British plans and probably would have produced triumph through an earlier junction of Franco-Spanish forces had it not been that chance intervened and postponed the Spanish succession. That is to say, had 'Ferdinand, the Anglophile King of Spain, died a year or two sooner than he did, Spain would certainly have joined our enemy before we had attained our object in America. . . . Again, if the Czarina Elizabeth had survived one more campaign, it is impossible to see how Frederick could have maintained his position. On all the chances of war we must have been crushed. . . .'[87] It is an example of Corbett's lack of mental rigidity that he should end a book dealing

[85] *England in the Seven Years War*, Vol. II, p. 1.
[86] *Ibid.*, p. 374 especially.
[87] *Ibid.*, p. 373.

Sir Julian Corbett

with the operation of military principles by a partial surrender to the element of chance in history. His third conclusion was a revival of his conviction that commerce destruction was a puerile form of war. The French, he concluded, had captured more British shipping than vice versa, but although these operations 'absorbed in the end almost the whole of her vitality at sea' they could not 'make a sufficient percentage impression to produce any real warlike advantage'.[88] This was an opinion consistent with his previously expressed views.

England in the Seven Years War showed the exasperating complexity of the connexion between military and political policy. Whether it demonstrated firmly the truth of all of the strategic philosophy it introduced is open to doubt. What is incontestable is that in this book for the first time theory of war and *detailed* naval history, on the grand strategy scale and taken from source materials, were made to illuminate one another and that while he did not invariably do so Corbett was quite capable of jettisoning a rounded strategic conclusion in the face of a solid historical fact that stood in the way of its acceptance. His sources were more extensive than those of Mahan. While his less rigidly logical mind was less prone to definite conclusion than that of the American, it was demonstrably more prepared to allow history to dominate rule making. As an attempt to marry strategic philosophy to history the work was a failure; as a common law arrangement it was triumphantly successful. It must have been an exhausting experience and never again did he attempt such a rigorous mixture. In his next book he narrowed his study to a short time span and firmly subordinated theory to historical evidence. In its successor he separated useful theory and illustrated it with considered historical examples. *England in the Seven Years War* was the only one of Corbett's books in which he attempted to fuse military theory and historical evidence and at the same time to give equal weight to each. He came close to accomplishing this impossible task.

In Volume I of *England in the Mediterranean* Corbett had set up, historically, a great symphony of diplomatic cause and effect in order to show how even nominal and unperceptive use of sea power could profoundly affect diplomatic combinations. As an illustration of the real impact of naval movement on grand strategy that description was very good; as a piece of historical investigation, however, it contained too much almost miraculous conjunction of cause and effect to be entirely convincing. He

[88] *England in the Seven Years War*, Vol. II, p. 375.

himself was probably not unaware that his theme was tenuous.[89] Nevertheless, in the *Campaign of Trafalgar*,[90] Corbett returned to this method using for his illustrative purpose the detailed history of the campaign leading up to England's greatest naval victory. At last he felt himself mature enough to move into the 'Holy of Holies' in English naval history. At last he was ready for Nelson. The Battle of Trafalgar is discussed in the book with authority. The battle itself, however, was not central to the book's theme and is not therefore discussed here.

Broadly speaking, it was the younger Pitt's desire to raise up a solid European coalition to defy and crush Napoleon whom Pitt implacably hated and was resolved to destroy.[91] By the use of a judicious supporting action, in conjunction with the Russians in the Mediterranean, it was the British intention not only to bring about an anti-Napoleonic agreement with Russia, but through resolute warlike example, to stimulate the adhesion of Austria as well, and move from alliance to coalition. The key to this design was the island of Malta. On the security of that base and on the regularity of supplies necessary to render its function offensive was based the whole of Pitt's intricate strategy.[92] All through the book, Corbett kept the centrality of this strategic purpose in mind and neither the contemplation of an Emperor at Boulogne threatening invasion of Britain nor of a dying Nelson were able to divert him from his preoccupation with the Mediterranean strategy, the thread that bound the campaign of Trafalgar together. Nor did Corbett shrink from the ultimate reflection that, great as it was, Trafalgar was overshadowed by Austerlitz whereby the great schemes of Pitt had been brought to ruin.[93] Thus the campaign of Trafalgar judged by the canons of statecraft was a failure. The message of this book then is that sea power by itself was an insufficient instrument with which to defeat the great Napoleon. On the other hand, he showed that sea power within its limitations had played an offensive rather than a defensive part in British strategy and had played that part with a competent, professional distinction that implied and produced successes. From under the muzzles of the guns of Trafalgar he thundered again to all who would hear the message previously

---

[89] The implications were 'dimly revealed'. See Corbett, *England in the Mediterranean*, Vol. I, p. 65.
[90] J. S. Corbett, *The Campaign of Trafalgar* (London, 1910).
[91] *Ibid.*, p. 19.
[92] *Ibid.*, pp. 20–6.
[93] *Ibid.*, p. 415.

Sir Julian Corbett

announced in *The Successors of Drake*: without a supporting army, imaginatively led, the navy is not a decisively effective offensive weapon.

Corbett showed that the great foundation of Nelson's success lay in the fact that he understood his naval business. When Nelson returned from the West Indian pursuit of Villeneuve, all sorts of rumours questioning his strategic sense began and they have not ceased. With crushing finality Corbett pointed up the fact that while Nelson was 'missing' the First Lord seemed to distrust him, but when Nelson returned, Barham ordered his journals to be sent up and read them and 'from that moment he [Nelson] was treated frankly as the man of the hour'.[94] Why? Because the First Lord found that this star of the Mediterranean thought and acted in conformity with the same naval traditions that activated his own mind; and that Nelson's and the Admiralty's appreciation were in all important aspects the same. It was this unanimity of purpose and universality of strategic understanding that stamped the English sea moves with success. By this time naval officers worked from an agreed body of common doctrine.

The description of this capable playing of the game of war by the old naval hands was the burden of Corbett's theme. It reached its most exciting and most instructive phase in the last days of July and the beginning of the month of August in 1805. During that period, Napoleon threatening invasion from Boulogne seemed to dominate the strategic patterns of the British and Cornwallis[95] appeared to have nervously succumbed to the strain of the Brest blockade and had, against all the textbook canons of warfare,[96] divided his fleet. Here Corbett was at his best, for he showed carefully how the principle of concentration of force was different on sea than on land, how the British military minds were dominated by other problems than that of simply defeating an enemy fleet, how proper cruiser liaison altered the aspect of naval warfare, and, most important, how the object of the British dispositions was to enable them to act *offensively* in protection of their trade and in sending troops to the Mediterranean rather than merely moving about tamely in response to Napoleon's great threat of invasion. This threat the sailors and Admiralty took seriously, as seriously as it deserved, but they handled it com-

---

[94] Corbett, *The Campaign of Trafalgar*, p. 281.
[95] Sir William Cornwallis (1744–1819), Admiral. Commander-in-Chief Channel Fleet. At that time stationed off Brest.
[96] Mahan had adopted this view and was here opposed by Corbett. See Corbett, *The Campaign of Trafalgar*, pp. 247–54.

petently and never allowed it to disturb their paramount offensive purpose.

The extent and nature of Corbett's sources for this work helped to ensure its comprehensiveness.[97] For French materials on both the diplomatic and the naval side he was fortunate in the fact that in addition to the Napoleon–Tallyrand correspondence, the work of P. Coquelle,[98] Charles Auriol and most importantly Colonel Edouard Desbrière[99] had published much of the French correspondence and official material covering the period. French research had made much Spanish material available. For the English side Corbett used the then recently published diplomatic material edited by J. Holland Rose.[100] Furthermore, he personally consulted the Pitt papers in the Public Record Office. The Papers referring to the blockade of Brest, Nelson material, the *Barham Papers* (then being edited for the N.R.S. by Professor Laughton) and the Cornwallis Papers[101] provided evidence for the unfolding of day-to-day naval strategy. But Corbett went even further than that and checked the detail of ship movements, using Admiralty Records, Ships' Logs and Journals, Admirals' and Captains' letters. This extensive accumulation of evidence concerning a short space of historical time enabled Corbett to study his campaign from political, strategic and tactical angles, and in great detail. The result was a unique production. It was equally instructive to the politician, the professional and the amateur student of war. By relating the detailed inter-relationship of the sailors and politicians against the central, if sometimes shifting objectives of the war, the subtle inter-relationships of seemingly disconnected events was made continually clear.

If the book was intended to appeal to a diverse if select audience, it is none the less clear that it was intended particularly to show naval officers how intensive historical research could reveal the significance of their day-to-day life afloat in war-time. The naval officer who read Mahan intelligently could achieve a general appreciation of how post-naval action had exerted an effect on the carrying out of national policy. In other words, Mahan made the general national importance of naval activity apparent.

This study of Corbett's took the naval officer a step further: it

[97] Corbett, *The Campaign of Trafalgar*, Preface.
[98] *Napoleon et Angleterre, 1803–13* (London, 1904).
[99] *La France, Angleterre et Naples, 1803–6* (Paris, 1904) and E. Desbrière, *La Campagne Maritime de 1805: Trafalgar* (Paris, 1907).
[100] *Select Despatches relating to the Third Coalition against France, 1804–5* (London, 1904).
[101] Published by Historical MSS Commission.

Sir Julian Corbett

enabled him to see how the particular sea-going movements that were a part of his daily routine naval life could assume significance, not only as a minute contribution to some great anticipated naval victory but as a direct particular contribution to the success of national strategy as a whole. It demonstrated the direct connexion between the commander's cabin of a detached frigate, and the Prime Minister and his decision makers in London. The great question earlier asked of the Colombs was, what practical lessons has history to teach the modern professional sailor? Corbett hoped that in his book naval officers would see 'what they looked for in a report on manœuvres today',[102] and that he had demonstrated, once and for all, the need for an historical section at the Admiralty where scholarly erudition and professional know-how might meet to continue this vital education process.

The *Campaign of Trafalgar* seems to have represented a sharp Corbettian reaction to the Clausewitz-dominated methods lavished on his previous book. In his defence of Addington's early conduct of the war, for instance, he remarked 'where a maritime empire is concerned caution is required in applying the simple formulae of continental strategists'.[103] This point was also illustrated in his description of the general military activity of the British during the last weeks of July, 1805. Napoleon was threatening, plans were afoot for Anglo–Russian activity in the Mediterranean, a force in Ireland was preparing to go to the West Indies, and a proposal was in train to capture the Cape. Was this not imbecilic departure from the principle of concentration of aim? By no means said Corbett. To act offensively was all the British could do to encourage a coalition against Napoleon. To act decisively begged the question never discussed, much less answered, by the military castigators of politicians—where, and with what, and with what chance of success? Statecraft and naval ability enabled the English to keep active offensively. They were incapable of doing more and no reference to simple clichés from Clausewitz could alter that fact. Or as Corbett put it, 'the broad combined problems of Imperial defence are not to be solved offhand by the facile application of maxims which are the outcome of narrower and less complex continental conditions'.[104]

The uses of the fleet then were broad and they varied with shifts of strategy. Priorities were not assigned by virtue of a military chart of importances but rather in response to the needs

[102] *The Campaign of Trafalgar*, Preface.
[103] *Ibid.*, p. 4.
[104] *Ibid.*, p. 237.

of shifting conditions. The Royal Navy was not adverse to battle but it did not in those days regard battle as the end purpose of its existence.[105] By the careful and imaginative weaving together of the fibres of day-to-day history in 1805, Corbett was able to point up real national problems and the actual reactions to them. Although history was made to serve instructional purpose, the pedagogy was based on generalities growing out of the carefully sifted detail, nor was the end preconceived in Corbett's mind. The greatness of the work was stamped firmly on the last page when he faced the implications of his investigations squarely and he said of British strategy, 'Against any other man than Napoleon, with any other ally than Prussia as she then was, it might well have done much more. As it was, the sea had done all that the sea could do, and for Europe the end was failure.'[106]

Even as *The Campaign of Trafalgar* set the seal on Corbett's abilities as an historian, so *Some Principles of Maritime Strategy*[107] revealed him as a theoretical thinker on war of the first rank. The English are supposedly a race not given to the study of theory. No doubt this questionable generalization made Corbett eager to explain and like Captain Mahan many years previously he attempted to justify the abstract approach. Yet he was cautious in his claims. Certainly Corbett did not equate the reasoning processes used in the formulation of naval theory with those of 'true scientific analysis'.[108] Not only was naval war theory not scientifically precise but in Corbett's opinion it was 'not . . . a substitute for judgement and experience'.[109] The most that the careful author was prepared to claim was that theorists did have concrete uses. They could 'educate' leaders even if their precepts were best modified on the field of battle in the light of actual experience. He pointed out that a common knowledge of theory opened up channels of communication between leaders and led in the military forces and between leaders in the military forces and

---

[105] The emphasis is on the words 'end purpose'. The point is important since a recent military historian has gone out of his way to accuse Corbett of minimizing the importance of combat. See Cyril Falls, *The Art of War* (London, 1961), p. 44. Corbett goes out of his way to show the difference between Pitt's and Nelson's ideas of how to deal with Villeneuve's fleet in the autumn of 1805. Pitt's idea was to blockade—Nelson's to lure Villeneuve out and destroy him. Corbett naturally agreed with Nelson's appreciation. This question is not one of blood-thirstiness, but of ends and means. See Corbett, *The Campaign of Trafalgar*, pp. 320, 321.

[106] *Ibid.*, p. 424.
[107] J. S. Corbett, *Some Principles of Maritime Strategy* (London, 1911).
[108] *Ibid.*, p. 1.
[109] *Ibid.*, p. 8.

their political masters when all had drunk at the same fountain of knowledge. In the same way a common knowledge of war theory could reduce that intransigent instrument, the Council of War, from a monstrous Tower of Babel to a reasonably potential vehicle for decision. These, of course, were practical values. In the more abstract way, value would result from the tendency for the deduced principle to coincide with 'normal' expectation and although Corbett advanced this point timidly and deferentially he was prepared to say that this measure of normality was demonstrably applicable even to such difficult values as the moral factors. Thus a study of theory could prepare one for *normal* contingences and although no substitute for either judgement or experience it was 'a means of fertilizing both'.[110] This defence was considerably less emphatic than that of Mahan. Certainly Corbett refrained from claiming that theory produced immutably valid rules but at the same time he was a strong advocate of the value of such principles for the serving practical military man. It may be doubted whether such disarming modesty or perhaps accuracy would have served to make the book a success were it not for the open claim advanced by Corbett that while military and naval theory complement one another they are not by any means the same thing.[111] Thus while the justification of the value of theory to the practical officer are interesting to the student of military theory, it was to the convincing manner in which he presented a case for the study of naval theory as a specialized discipline that his success in this book was undoubtedly due.

Corbett did not attempt the demolition of the Clausewitzian strategic structure: he was too much indebted to it for that. Furthermore, Clausewitz possessed the great merit in Corbett's eyes that he 'was no mere professor' but rather an experienced campaigner.[112] However, Corbett did show that due to a general lack of complete comprehension of the great German's strategical work, people were inclined to rest content with early aspects of that thought which further investigation showed had become considerably modified as he investigated war more deeply.[113] Thus, due to his being incompletely understood, Clausewitz had unwittingly assisted in enshrining the two, supposedly most important, master Napoleonic lessons in the collective mind of military Europe: that the offensive must be preferred at almost

[110] Corbett, *Some Principles of Maritime Strategy*, p. 8.
[111] *Ibid.*, pp. 8–9.
[112] *Ibid.*, p. 21.
[113] *Ibid.*, pp. 42–3, 45.

any risk, and that the enemy main forces must always be the main military objective.[114] This preoccupation tended to direct men's thoughts away from the basic precept that national warfare must always be the servant of national policy, and tended to cause strategic war plans to be based on the activities of the last immediate war rather than the imminent requirements of the new war. Reasoning on these lines thus caused a rigid codification of types of war under the main categories of 'offensive' and 'defensive'. Corbett was impelled to show that this sort of definition was only valuable as a broad classification, that the idea of attack was as implicit in the defensive concept as in that of the offensive and indeed that defence was meaningless without the idea of attack supporting it.

More fruitful categories, Corbett held, were the classification of war as limited and unlimited, which idea Clausewitz came to when his thought was more mature and which unfortunately came to be less well known than the earlier offensive-defensive classification.[115] Whether a war was limited or unlimited depended upon the nature of the political object involved in the conflict. A 'limited war' implied a limited object and in such a war the objective was not always, indeed seldom, the armed forces of the foe and was often simply a piece of territory. Corbett said that Clausewitz at this point did not understand the deep implications of his own theory. The German stated that the military justification for limited war was dependent upon the geographical position of the object.[116] This was a true view in Corbett's eyes but because Clausewitz did all of his thinking in terms of battlefields on the European *land mass* he found no reasonable examples with which to fortify and expand his highly intelligent conclusion. A shifting of the analytic eye from Rossbach to Quebec during a consideration of the Seven Years War might have been sufficient to explain the principle but Clausewitz never discarded his Continental blinkers.

Corbett stepped into this gap and building on Germanic foundations stated roundly that limited war was possible to an island sea-separated power 'when the Power desiring limited war is able to command the sea to such a degree as to be able not only to isolate the distant object, but also to render impossible the invasion of the home territory.'[117] In this bold sentence was sum-

[114] Corbett, *Some Principles of Maritime Strategy*, pp. 20–22.
[115] *Ibid.*, pp. 38–43.
[116] *Ibid.*, pp. 51–2.
[117] *Ibid.*, pp. 54–5.

marized the result of Corbett's thinking on the historical evidence of the Seven Years War. Naval island kingdom empires represent a strategic special case. On this foundation he rested all the new and original developments of his thought. From the limited war concept was drawn his strong advocacy of raiding activity which while it seemed to violate the 'principle' of concentration was certainly an acceptable half-way house between all and nothing in the way of attacking an enemy too strong to be hit a mortal military blow on the battlefield. Warfare, he claimed, must be sometimes a creature of makeshift rather than an example of classic art. In the same line of thought he showed that the big battle was not always possible. 'We say,' he wrote, 'that the whole available force should be developed for the vital period of the struggle. No one can be found to dispute it nowadays. It is too obviously true when it is a question of a conflict between organized forces, but in the absence of all proof we are entitled to doubt whether it is true for that exhausting and demoralizing period which lies beyond the shock of armies.'[118] In this intelligent but somewhat obscure sentence Corbett was not maintaining that wars could be won without fighting, but simply that successful side operations in conjunction with long-term strategic plans were much to be preferred to sacrificial offerings of thousands of men on an enemy's selected battlefield where he was preponderant. This conclusion had a real and vivid relevance to the First World War.[119] The only real problem was that it was not a simple thing to keep a limited war from becoming unlimited. Corbett cleverly used the usually despised Crimean War as an example of how this difficult task could sometimes be accomplished.[120] All of this was a refreshing and original look at problems and possible solutions confronting a maritime nation at war.

He next turned his attention to that over-worked concept 'the command of the sea'. Such command was, supposedly, the necessary prelude to the isolation of the object in limited war. What did the term 'command of the sea' really mean? Although Corbett was careful to note the fact that 'command' need not be held by any one power, but could be in dispute, his definition of what it really was came direct and unacknowledged from the brain of Sir John Colomb. As Sir John had argued, sea command did not

[118] *Some Principles of Maritime Strategy*, p. 147.
[119] In the First World War the lack or seeming lack of a useful alternative caused Great Britain to spend torrents of blood in a war of attrition. The cost was so severe that victory and defeat were almost meaningless terms in 1918.
[120] *Some Principles of Maritime Strategy*, p. 77.

involve conquest of sea area but rather control of maritime communicatons. Such command does 'not mean that the enemy can do nothing, but that he cannot interfere with our maritime trade and oversea operations so seriously as to affect the operations of the war, and that he cannot carry on his own trade and operations except at such risk and hazard as to remove them from the field of practical strategy.'[121] When he came to work the problem of trade defence into his general theory of warfare, Corbett was somewhat less inclined to discount its validity than he had been in previous works. Indeed, he was prepared to admit that 'there is no part of strategy where historical deduction is more difficult or more liable to error'.[122] Nevertheless, he launched an attack on the increasingly believed modern idea that steam trade was both more important and more difficult to defend than the old sail trade. J. C. R. Colomb was mainly responsible for this modern strategic notion, a notion with which Corbett disagreed. He felt that this preoccupation with trade was based on two questionable assumptions: that trade vulnerability was in proportion to trade volume; and that the more trade that moved the harder would it be for an enemy to make an 'effective percentage impression' and history had shown that trade defence was customarily in proportion not to the value and size of home trade but rather in reaction and proportion to the enemy force attacking that trade.[123] In short, what knowledge we possess regarding the defence of trade and particularly of bases shows that 'modern material make them tell in favour of defence rather than attack'.[124] Hence in this book he does not say that commerce warfare is unprofitable or that defence against such attack is of no importance but rather that *for military reasons* the probability of such attacks succeeding in their object was not great.

The conclusions drawn about the uses of the cruiser force so patiently researched for the Trafalgar book were again set out in this volume. Their permanent function was to exercise the sea supremacy won by the doughty 'line' ships. Misapprehension of the basic needs behind Nelson's oft-quoted plaintive cry for more cruisers[125] had led Corbett's contemporaries to over-value the 'eyes of the fleet' function for cruisers to the point where they were being increased in size and up-graded in function to rival battle-

[121] *Some Principles of Maritime Strategy*, p. 103.
[122] *Ibid.*, p. 269.
[123] *Ibid.*, p. 278.
[124] *Ibid.*, p. 182.
[125] *Ibid.*, p. 111.

Sir Julian Corbett

ships themselves and hence their main purposes, the functional tasks of convoy, commercial blockade and search were much neglected. This is an important point for if Corbett misunderstood the nature of commerce attack in the coming war or at least minimized its probable intensity, it is also true that he here registered his protest against the over-concentration on the building of ships whose only function was to fight big battles. In this protest, he clearly pinpointed the main idiocy of the First World War at sea—the persistent view that the Royal Navy's *main* purpose was to fight the Germans in a great battle in the North Sea.

This fixation with the big battle which Corbett foresaw with such clear eyes made the other activities of the Royal Navy in the First World War reflect their low priority in naval planning. To be sure, it was 'logical' to suggest that a big battle was an essential preliminary to 'command of the sea' but, said Corbett, war is not logical. It is 'a complex sum of naval, military, political, financial, and moral factors'. It cannot be understood by a mere mental jousting with 'well-turned syllogisms'.[126] For instance, the phrase 'to seek out and destroy', that banner of the apostles of cutlasses on the quarterdeck of the *Dreadnought*, is after all a relative term. The ocean is wide—suppose your foe is not located at once—what then? Do you play his game and search blindly? This was the legitimate question in Queen Elizabeth's mind (or at least one of them) when she prevented Drake's sailing for the Spanish coast in the spring of 1588. He might have been lucky; he might not. In the same way, in this day of fortified harbours, how was one to seek out and destroy an enemy who is unwilling to gratify that desire for an all-out battle surging in the patriotic brain of a British or Allied commander?[127] If the enemy is superior, is one justified in supposing that British courage will sustain an unequal contest and engage at *all* hazards? Again, if the margin of superiority is in doubt, is it not legitimate to determine in what way a fleet may best serve? His points were and are strong, and they are made stronger by his patent appreciation that there are times when morale is best served by the offensive move against hopeless odds; not, however, when the gallant gesture ignored some great strategic object.

Another general maxim at which he levelled his cannon was the so-called principle of 'concentration of force'.[128] He did not

[126] *Some Principles of Marine Strategy*, p. 236.
[127] *Ibid.*, pp. 158–9.
[128] *Ibid.*, p. 130 ff.

assert that such a condition was of no value; rather he suggested that real concentration was not a huddling together of ships in close proximity to one another. Intelligent concentration of force involved a loose formation with power to join at the crucial moment. 'We must,' he said, 'regard every detached force as a trap to lure the enemy to destruction. The ideal concentration, in short, is an appearance of weakness that covers a reality of strength'.[129] This was almost exactly, if inadvertently, achieved by the Grand Fleet at Jutland in 1916.[130]

What Corbett had to say about invasion was said in the shadow of an army–navy quarrel that had done much to force the resignation of Lord Fisher from the Admiralty as the soldiers challenged the navy's ability to defend against invasion.[131] Corbett had been involved in that quarrel as a Fisher supporter, but the information he had to offer about defence against invasion was not merely composed to meet a transitory propaganda need but rather stemmed from a deep knowledge of British practice extending back in historical time over three or more centuries.[132] With proper dispositions and a reasonable fleet the thing was impossible. Indeed, looking at historical results he was able to show that a serious move towards invasion by a foe almost invariably involved him in a naval disaster, as the years 1588, 1759 and 1805 bear witness.[133] However, an invasion of England was an almost impossible operation due partly to the peculiar geography of the British and French Channel coast lines that gave treacherous shoals to the French and snug harbours to the English; partly to the prevailing westerly wind that enabled a British fleet holding off to the westward to be an abiding and unbearable threat to an invading force that had not brought it to action; and partly to the cool eyes of the Admiralty, the Admirals and the Captains on the spot who never lost sight of the fact that in a serious Channel crisis the Royal Navy must go for the transports of the invading force rather than the enemy battle fleet and that even a superior escorting force did not render those transports invulnerable. Such

[129] *Some Principles of Maritime Strategy*, p. 153.
[130] He also referred to Cornwallis's concentration potential off Brest in 1805, a subject he had discussed in *The Campaign of Trafalgar*.
[131] Fisher resigned in 1910, partly as a result of disagreements with the War Office.
[132] Corbett wrote material for Fisher's and the Admiralty's use in controverting the views of Lord Roberts and the National Service League. See Tunstall, et al., *Catalogue of Corbett Papers*, especially letters in Box 12, pp. 32–34.
[133] The reader will recall that this was also a special field of interest for Admiral Colomb.

Sir Julian Corbett

was the logic of the past that Corbett re-deployed to lay once again the invasion bogey.[134]

It was fitting that the final chapter in the book should be one on combined operations for it is on this conception of the joint function of army and navy that his reputation ought chiefly to rest. From the moment in the eighteen-nineties that he realized that Elizabethan warlike effectiveness was hampered by too little rather than too much army, he had made the special nature of British military requirements his particular field for investigation and elucidation. The purpose and usefulness of such operations were implicit in his earlier discussion of limited war with its necessary handmaids of the diversionary raid and the eccentric attack. Here he confined himself to a description of technical problems involved. The naval role was not only to provide protection for troops in transit but actively to assist at the scene of the fighting as well.[135] To do this, the army group required transport, a transport squadron (for immediate defence of the transports) and a covering squadron for the whole force which must be always used *except* where the operations were to take place using a friendly country as the army base. Furthermore, the covering force should never be so strongly committed to tactical army support that it could not be detached to meet the threat from the sea. Obviously, said Corbett, such an operation required careful planning and close consultation between the army and navy leaders. Hence, if sea opposition to the invading force was likely, the Admiral must choose the army landing place; in the same way, if the sea was free from interruption, the decision should be left to the General; and in any event a close consultation was mandatory to ensure success. These principles were all in accord with the historical practice of such men as Drake and Wolfe, and with the highly successful sea arrangements of the Crimean War.[136]

The book had its flaws. There was, for example, his cheerful description of the ease with which combined operation's 'feints' could be carried out.[137] This was a strange aspect of his thought, since he was certainly in no doubt that an invasion, for instance, would advertise itself early to the British by its own logistic movement; in the same way he ought to have been aware that 'feints', if they are to disturb, must have a logistic background that is not provided by merely talking about it. Sometimes, also, Corbett

[134] *Some Principles of Maritime Strategy*, pp. 236–60.
[135] *Ibid.*, p. 285.
[136] Generally discussed, *ibid.*, pp. 285–310.
[137] *Ibid.*, p. 308.

lays himself open to the charge of violating his own teaching. Admittedly, strategy has thousands of teeth with which to bite the unwary acolyte, but it surely begs questions for Corbett to write of an enemy holding a line of passage in force 'until his hold is broken by purely naval action, combined work remains beyond all legitimate risk of war'.[138] The truth of this assertion would depend upon relative fleet dispositions. It would, no doubt, be true of invasions but whether it would be true of all diversions is another matter. In the same way, when referring to limited war in an earlier passage, he says that isolation of the limited object 'can never be established until we have entirely overthrown the enemy's naval forces'.[139] What does entirely overthrow mean, big battle or neutralization? The answer does not deserve to be left in the air where Corbett leaves it.

Having said this, however, it is worth noting that this subject of strategy that so lends itself to urbane obscurantism, a vice to which Corbett had not previously been an entire stranger, was treated here with a careful practical realism that commands respect. Whatever its general merits, *Some Principles of Maritime Strategy* did two things very competently: it adapted Clausewitzian thought to fit the needs of a sea power and to conform to the special idiosyncracies of sea warfare; and it took past practice and codified it. Corbett wrote this strategy book as a result of rather than as a key to historical study. That is why the careful historian must prefer him, with all his misty outlook, to the downright plain-speaking Mahan who learned his principles first and then went to history for his examples.

If *Some Principles of Maritime Strategy* was somewhat of a *tour de force* it met with a mixed reception. Since, in a way, it represented Corbett's strategic ideas codified, its origins and the naval atmosphere in which it was written have a bearing on one's understanding of it.

Since *Drake and the Tudor Navy* was written, Corbett had become the weightiest naval historian in England. This was not due so much to his views being completely accepted as it was to the visibly solid nature of his publishing achievement, and also undoubtedly to the patronage of Admiral Fisher until the latter's fall from power in early 1910. During this period he was a sort of semi-official naval personality and his views held weight with both naval officers and the general public because of this situation. For instance, he gave his occupation on the title page of his books

[138] *Some Principles of Maritime Strategy*, p. 310.
[139] *Ibid.*, p. 83.

as 'Lecturer to the Naval War College'. The degree of acceptance accorded his views in the naval service is not easy to determine. It is probably safe to say that as a lecturer on naval war he was not always completely understood by his naval audience. Furthermore, it is clear that his doctrines bred opposition. However, so long as his lectures to the War College were restricted material, then any opposition could only come from his classes themselves, even though rumours of discontent might sometimes become audible.

Thus *Some Principles of Maritime Strategy* posed come difficult problems. It was, for instance, possible to lecture service audiences and tell them that in past wars Britain had triumphed through the artful use of naval forces since those audiences were always prepared to hear that there was more to naval success then they had imagined when they were midshipmen. To be told that their predecessors were often so clever that big battles were sometimes unnecessary was palatable. But for their lecturer to write and publish a book that said it was not always a good thing to go for the enemy in any and every situation—that was to suggest a non-Nelsonic approach to naval war. That was heresy. The worst fears of naval officers about their too clever civilian lecturer must have been then realized.

It was this kind of background and thinking that caused this book which drew on all Corbett's reading over a fifteen-year period to be less than sympathetically received in some naval and military quarters. Men like Admiral Custance and Spencer Wilkinson who belonged to the hearty or offensive-at-all-costs school were displeased.[140] Years later, Lord Sydenham of Combe inferred that Corbettian ideas had infected the fleet with semi-defeatism.

Corbett was not accustomed to opposition. Indeed one of the reasons for the sometimes ethereal nature of his thought probably stems from his lack of combative contact with the working world and especially with students in an academic situation. Not having to mark examinations or papers he never had his lectures played back at him and he had no practical way of testing his theories except for reviewers comment. Certainly this isolation must have contributed to Corbett's independence of mind for his work made no concessions even to people who were enthusiastic supporters, expecting his readers to follow all his subtleties faithfully.

Some Principles of Maritime Strategy as well as *The Campaign*

[140] It was attacked especially by Spencer Wilkinson. See *Morning Post*, 19 February, 1912.

of Trafalgar were both indebted to Corbett's editing work for the Navy Records Society which he carried on as he wrote his books. Especially the volumes exploring the evolution of British naval tactics, *Fighting Instructions, 1530–1816* and *Signals and Instructions, 1776–94*,[141] made him an expert in the sort of description that is generally only handled well by professional sailors. It would be hard to over-value this editing work for its own sake but for Corbett the historian the confidence it engendered is evident in his later books.

Corbett also edited a volume on the Dutch Wars[142] and the first two volumes of the Private Papers of Earl Spencer—all for the Navy Records Society.[143]

Treatment of the development of Corbett the historian stops here with his publication of *Some Principles of Maritime Strategy*. After this period he did contribute to *Naval and Military Essays*[144] which he edited for the Cambridge University Press in 1913. He also, of course, wrote a good deal of the naval history of the First World War. Official history is a specialized occupation and its consideration would not add to our knowledge of Corbett's development as an historian. His great aim, fully revealed in his pre-war books, was to attempt a marriage between principles and history while not ignoring the canons of historical accuracy nor the requirements of research in depth.

From the scholar's viewpoint he came very close to achieving that aim: from a practical viewpoint he was certainly triumphantly successful. That such independent work could come from the pen of a man who enjoyed high naval patronage and at a time when subservience to the needs of military men in high places was both common and respectable is a measure of both his character and his accomplishment.

---

[141] Published in 1905 and 1908, respectively.
[142] J. S. Corbett, *Views of the Battles of the Third Dutch War* (London, 1907).
[143] J. S. Corbett, *The Spencer Papers* (London, Vol. I, 1913; Vol. II, 1914).
[144] He wrote one chapter, entitled 'Staff Histories'.

EPILOGUE

WHEN the grey ships of the Grand Fleet moved obediently into the positions prepared for them by the confident hand of Winston S. Churchill in 1914, the innovating work of the historians whose ideas are described in this book was completed. As has been shown, Richmond still had to show by more writing how the politico-strategic ideas that emerged from his study of one particular war could be applied to wider historical surveys. But there can be little doubt that the main lines on which even he approached historical problems in naval warfare had also been already determined.

Although these writers had exhibited differences on the question of whether history ought to serve a utilitarian purpose or not, they all, in fact, did their writing in response to a need engendered by the fierce international naval rivalry that was a feature of their time. That being the case, how much influence did they have on the conduct of the First World War, or on its natural successor, the Second?

Indirectly they may have exerted influence that is hard to trace, but it must be reported that their obvious influence was not overwhelming. This is clearly true regarding 1914-18, for this was a war in which most of the operations appear to have been predetermined by the material available to the combatants. Yet if there was one thing that the writers described in this book had in common, it was their aversion to the idea that success in war is determined more by equipment than by human moral factors.

A number of examples of this lack of contact between the literary and the practical men could be given. One is the Battle of the Falkland Islands. After the war, Winston Churchill who had a direct hand in the human chain of events that had helped to make the battle possible described it. Of the poignant moment when the

German armoured cruiser *Gneisenau* came within sight of Stanley harbour in the early morning of 8 December, 1914, he wrote, 'A few minutes later a terrible apparition broke upon German eyes. Rising from behind the promontory, sharply visible in the clear air, were a pair of tripod masts. One glance was enough. They meant certain death.'[1] Tripods, of course, were only carried by Dreadnoughts; vessels that represented a material superiority that the Germans could neither contend with nor escape from. Lord Fisher, the father of the Dreadnoughts, reacted with pardonable pride to the results obtained by the superior metal he had sent out when he wrote 'it may have been like shooting pheasants'.[2] His material views had been justified. Churchill verified this by his comment, 'I made haste to ascribe to him all the credit that was due'.[3] It was a grand confirmation of the Fisher building policy. This illustration of the way in which the victory at the Falkland Islands was supposed to be directly due to the physical superiority of the British ships—to material— is even more striking when it is realized that Churchill, the narrator, was not merely a material man, but one who had a great respect for the importance of human factors and strategic appreciation in war. Yet what Churchill's account lacked, in common with that of most other writers on this subject, was an appreciation of the part that the facilities at the Falkland Islands themselves had played in bringing about the action.

The Germans knew that, over all, the Royal Navy quantitatively and in weight of metal was stronger than they were. The whole purpose of their detached squadron at the beginning of the war had been to cause damage out of proportion to their real strength by using the cover of vast ocean spaces to strike down ships without being brought to battle by superior forces. Although the dispatch of the two Dreadnoughts to the South Atlantic did not make this task easier for Von Spee's squadron, it did not by itself ensure British success. There had to be a lure to make the junction and hence the battle possible. To understand how this came about it is necessary to bear in mind that when that contact was made the British ships were *coaling* at their naval base. It had been John and Philip Colomb's idea that success in war at sea was largely determined by the security of communications and that the security of communications depended upon the main-

---

[1] W. S. Churchill, *The World Crisis, 1911–1914* (London, 1923), p. 436.
[2] Fisher to Churchill, 10 December, 1914. See Arthur J. Marder, *Fear God and Dread Nought, 1914–20*, Vol. III (London, 1959), p. 91.
[3] W. S. Churchill, *The World Crisis, 1911–1914*, p. 452.

Epilogue

tenance of naval bases located at useful points around the world. Furthermore, a battleship's radius of action depended upon her coal supply and this again depended upon the availability of fuel at set places along the communications lines. Thus it was a strategic situation set up as a result of Colomb-type thinking that had occasioned the battle and caused it to take place when and where it did.

If such a communications and supply centre was vital to the proper exercise of British sea power in the area, then it was natural that the German Admiral should wish to destroy it although he has since been criticized for attempting to do so.[4] It was due to Admiralty foresight energetically translated into action that the odds were against the Germans when they paid their call—and luck was involved in the timing; but strategically speaking the base was the logical meeting place for opposing sea forces in the South Atlantic in 1914. The battle justified the strategic theory of Imperial Defence of which the Colombs were the founding fathers. In the same way it was the desire to destroy base facilities at the Cocos Islands that had led the *Emden* to her doom on 9 November, 1914. Although it was fortuitous that HMAS *Sydney* was passing with a convoy when Captain Muller made his visit the communications facilities there presented a natural target. In war-time great ships are at sea for a purpose, and barring accident, particularly in the days before radar and long-range aircraft, could only be discovered by protecting what they were bound to wish to destroy.

These points, set out to demonstrate the impact of naval writers' thought on the First World War, take on even more significance when one realizes that the Battle of the Falkland Islands was really *the* decisive naval battle of that conflict. At the beginning of the war Britain set out to keep and the Germans to disrupt British overseas communications. This battle allowed the British to move shipping safely in the waters of the southern hemisphere. Jutland, in comparison, was a battle that merely maintained an existing strategic situation. Both were important, but whereas Jutland did not alter the strategic outlook, the Falkland Islands did.

The other real problem of the First World War at sea was posed by the gradually revealed destructive power of the submarine. The solution for the Royal Navy proved to be the introduction of the convoy system. None of the naval writers discussed in this

[4] Barrie Pitt, *Coronel and Falkland* (London, 1960), p. 95. See also Geoffrey Bennett, *Coronel and the Falklands* (London, 1962), p. 130.

book foresaw the deadly nature of the submarine; much less did they propose a means of dealing with it. However, it is possible to argue that convoy might have been introduced before 1917 if the Royal Navy had not been so wedded to the concept that its whole aim was to fight a large-scale fleet action in the North Sea. The services were held captive by the view that big ships meant big fights. This attitude, when allied to the natural apprehension felt by Admirals towards risking their expensive chariots at a time when torpedo attacks were terribly feared, led to a policy of jealously guarding the number of ships comprising the Grand Fleet and its auxiliary vessels. This rigid exclusiveness of outlook hampered the naval planning of the Dardanelles expedition, it invited the initial defeat at Coronel and it prevented the early growth of more effective methods of dealing with submarines. All these things were caused indirectly by an obsession with material and the idea of the big battle. Richmond and Corbett had both taught that the true purpose of sea power is to control and regulate the movement of ships at sea. They did not deny that it was useful to win battles but they did persist in regarding them as means rather than ends. The difference between the two methods of thinking about sea warfare appears to be small but they engender enormous differences in practical result. Therefore, the fact that the naval historians were neglected by most sailors and politicians does not necessarily mean that they were wrong.

When the Second World War broke out the Royal Navy had not only not learned from what pre-First World War historians had argued but the service had not even learned as much as it might from its own mistakes of 1914–8. When the time came for naval rearmament it was size rather than versatility that was the main objective of the building programme. Men were slow to re-admit the extent of the convoy successes in the First World War, and when they did so found themselves so short of escort vessels that, had it not been for the destroyer-base agreement with the United States, the problem of trade defence might have been not only difficult but insuperable.

The same kind of reasoning was also observable in the controversies between exponents of air power and those who supported traditional sea power, both prior to and during the war. Emphasis on the big-battle ideas had concentrated men's minds on the idea that the value of weapons lay in the amount of distinctive power they possessed (the size of the bang) which led in turn to arguments turning on whether weapons were, or would be, decisive or not. It is one of the tragedies of the Second World

War that this argument turned on absolute rather than comparative value—for this left the door open to final judgements depending on what appeared to be the revealed destructive power of explosives. Hence it was by photographs of German cities detailing destruction that Air Marshal Harris bolstered his confidence, inspired his bomber crews and maintained the support of the most powerful man in England.

Both Philip Colomb and Julian Colomb had made the historical investigation of combined operations their special interest. Official attitudes to this kind of war, however, altered considerably between the First and Second World Wars. The Dardanelles was an attempt to utilize the advantages that such a method made available, but as Captain Roskill has clearly shown[5] the result of that failure was to discredit combined operations between 1915 and 1918. Many critics of 'side-shows' as they were ungenerously called were convinced that the war could only finally have been 'won' by a direct concentrated attack on a selected front aimed at the enemy's heartland. If one accepts that American support rather than simply relentless purpose of the Allied Forces finally forced the Germans to surrender, it is possible to argue that greater results might have been obtained with less loss of life elsewhere than on the Western Front, and this argument even leaves out of account the possibilities that might have opened up as a result of successes away from the Franco-German trench line.

In the Second World War combined operations again became fashionable, although Roskill argues that the adoption of this technique owed more to the success of Hitler's Continental operations than to British strategic brilliance.[6] Virtually the British had no other choice if they did not wish entirely to surrender initiative to the Germans. As a result the Norwegians, North African and Italian operations took place, together with a number of more modest short-run attacks on the coasts of Nazi-controlled Europe.

Whether or not this kind of operation was forced upon Churchill there can be no doubt that he found it congenial. Opinions at the time, and since, have varied as to whether or not the method was, on balance, successful and whether these operations were necessary preludes to the invasion that took place in 1944. It seems reasonable to assert, however, that Churchill cheerfully accepted the method forced upon him by circumstances, kept

[5] Captain S. W. Roskill, *The Strategy of Sea Power* (London, 1962), p. 126.
[6] *Ibid.*, p. 240.

First World War casualties firmly in mind despite American pressure for precipitate action and fought his invasion after a series of successful combined operations and consequently at a more modest cost. This important achievement was directly related to the work of Corbett. In 1915, Lord Esher wrote to the Secretary of the Committee of Imperial Defence, Sir Maurice Hankey, '. . . do we worry about history? Julian Corbett writes one of the best books in our language upon political and military strategy. All sorts of lessons, some of inestimable value, may be gleaned from it. No one, except perhaps Winston, who matters just now has ever read it. Yet you and I are fussing about the strategical history of the war. Obviously history is written for schoolmasters and arm-chair strategists. Statesmen and warriors pick their way through the dusk.'[7] That Churchill was the exception turned out to be important. He reinforced his Corbett study by his Marlborough studies in the nineteen-thirties, and brought a new dimension of understanding to the conception and control of 'conjunct operations' as they were known in the eighteenth century. Since Corbett's thought capped that of his fellow writers, it can be seen that the ultimate effect of the work of these men was not slight, even when judged by the shifting criteria of the 'practical' world.

Some of the ideas put forward by these writers have appeared and become fashionable in the nuclear age. The most prominent of these is the notion that 'limited war' may be a useful strategic conception for modern strategists. This idea has been put forward particularly by Henry Kissinger[8] and R. E. Osgood.[9] Although both of these men exhibit some feeling for the historical precedents behind the strategic ideas they advance, it seems fair to add that their approach has not been primarily historical. Clausewitz, of course, is mentioned by them but Corbett's ideas on the subject do not seem to have illuminated their thinking. This is a pity, for Clausewitz's thought despite its breadth was geographically tied to the Continent of Europe and perhaps overly fixed on Napoleon's example: an approach natural enough for a German writing after 1800. Corbett, however, approached the question of limited war from a more global point of view and hence it is possible that he has more to say to moderns. Corbett noted that Clausewitz, towards

[7] 15 March, 1915. See Viscount Esher (Oliver), *Journals and Letters of Reginald, Viscount Esher, 1910–15*, Vol. III (London, 1938), p. 221.
[8] Henry A. Kissinger, *Nuclear Weapons and Foreign Policy* (New York, 1957).
[9] R. E. Osgood, *Limited War: the Challenge to American Strategy* (Chicago, 1957).

the end of his life, recognized that limited warfare was only practicable if it could be carried on by a power fortunate enough to be able to isolate the attacked territory from the heartland of an opponent. Otherwise ties fostered by interest, proximity and kinship would be so engaged that a war that began with a limited purpose would tend as we say today to 'escalate'. As an Englishman, Corbett was able to argue that the feature that made it possible to wage limited war with success was sea power, an activity over which Great Britain exercised almost monopolistic control in the eighteenth and nineteenth centuries. It was possible for her, as in the Seven Years War, to keep the intervention on the Continent limited to small numbers of regular troops plus subsidies to Frederick the Great while the French Empire was dealt with overseas. British objections were limited in that it was not the intention of the British Government to fight a mortal conflict with France and this was possible because French overseas possessions could be dealt with after first being cut off by sea power. Since the problem of isolating a battlefield and the avoidance of isolation are two of the factors that prevent a more wholehearted acceptance of the ideas of the limited war thinkers, Corbett's insight might have something to teach the planners of the nineteen-sixties.

Naval history has advanced in technique since 1914, but it would be arrogant to attempt to discuss cursorily more modern naval historians and their works. Two significant developments, however, demand mention. One is the adding of a new dimension to naval history writing, and the other the raising of official naval history writing in Britain to a high level of independence of control from the active admirals and their hesitant successors. This latter achievement has been wrought by Captain Roskill. The other very important development took place when John Ehrman wrote *The Navy in the War of William III* (Cambridge, 1953). This original work clearly pointed up the manning, maintenance, material and administrative problems that lay behind the tactical and strategic naval events of King William's reign. The connexion between shore and ship sailors and their civilian masters and supplies is set out with revealing clarity. What Oppenheim tried to do for the Tudor navy, Ehrman did do for that of the great Dutch King of England. He showed how the navy was part of the nation in a new way, and, to use his analogy, he showed how, if the nation could be likened to a layer cake, then the navy represented a cross section rather than a layer of the cake. Merely to read his work indicates the sort of integration that still remains to be done before we begin to understand the naval history of the more recent wars. He has made certain that naval history is not a diminishing field.

Yet the revived ideas of the real nature of sea power which the earlier historians had done so much to adapt to the steam age have made their impact. It would be hard to argue that the more difficult works of Mahan, Richmond and Corbett are favourite bedtime reading for either Admirals or politicians but a great change has taken place. Not too long ago a British First Sea Lord was asked whether it was proper to teach young officers the complete truth about history and military problems or whether to use historical propaganda to engender the idea that they were invincible. The answer was that the young men of the twentieth century had to be told the truth, so far as that was possible. Historians renowned for their romantically patriotic approach to history he denigrated. Romance is not fashionable in the teaching of history at Greenwich and has not been since Brian Tunstall wrote *The Realities of Naval History*[10] before the Second World War. If the naval officers in positions of power in the Second World War were not all naval historians by instinct, they had at least more interest in it than Jellicoe, who was almost illiterate in that sense. Indeed, Richmond's career was a tragedy in the sense that he was blocked by the anti-intellectuals, but it was a smashing triumph in that the ideas that he stood for penetrated the service by 1939 and clichés culled from his and his fellow writers' work in naval history were common currency of expression by 1960. What more tribute to the ideas of these men finally gaining the day could there be but the first volume of Captain S. W. Roskill's *The War at Sea*?[11] The official historian of the Second World War was a naval officer who understood the work of the pioneers, indeed it had become a part of his intellectual fibre. Times have changed and these six men have succeeded in their Education of a Navy.

[10] London, 1936.
[11] London, 1954.

BIBLIOGRAPHICAL NOTE

THIS book is mainly based on a study of the published work of six naval writers. The books that each of them wrote or edited are placed in separate lists, and the order in each list is determined by the date of publication. Their publications in article form were extensive. Only those that have been referred to in the text or footnotes are included here. Such restriction was necessary. Laughton, for instance, wrote about eighty articles and in addition wrote some nine hundred 'lives' for the *Dictionary of National Biography*. Mahan's article production was also extensive, but much of it had to do with subjects not immediately germane to this topic. No effort has been made to refer to Richmond's extensive periodical writings on matters of naval policy between the two great wars. Corbett's historical ideas are set out clearly in his books. The work of the two Colombs is more exhaustively represented.

Biographical information about the writers themselves comes from both published and unpublished sources, and varies considerably in scope. In the case of John Colomb and Corbett private manuscript sources were available. The bulk of information about Richmond has come from the extracts from his *Diary* as published in book form by Arthur Marder, together with some earlier *Diary* material not yet published. Much scholarly work has been published about Mahan and therefore his private papers, although consulted for special points, have not been extensively used. Not much biographical source material was available concerning Philip Colomb and Laughton.

The general bibliography, with one or two exceptions, refers to sources in the footnotes. Important and extensive biographical or interpretive material bearing on this study is starred.

MANUSCRIPT MATERIAL
Carnarvon Papers
J. C. R. Colomb Papers
Corbett Papers
Mahan Papers
Richmond Papers

WRITINGS OF THE SIX AUTHORS DISCUSSED
Books: Written or Edited

JOHN CHARLES READY COLOMB
   The Protection of Our Commerce and Distribution of Our Naval Forces

Considered (London, 1867)
Colonial Defence (London, 1873)
The Defence of Great and Greater Britain (London, 1880)

PHILIP HOWARD COLOMB
Slave Catching in the Indian Ocean (London, 1873)
Naval Warfare (London, 1891)
Essays on Naval Defence (London, 1896)
Memoirs of Sir Astley Cooper-Key (London, 1898)

JULIAN STAFFORD CORBETT
Monk (London, 1889)
Sir Francis Drake (London, 1890)
Drake and the Tudor Navy, 2 vols. (London, 1898)
(ed.) *The Spanish War, 1585–1587*, N.R.S. (London, 1898)
The Successors of Drake (London, 1900)
England in the Mediterranean, 2 vols. (London, 1904)
(ed.) *Fighting Instructions, 1530–1816*, N.R.S. (London, 1905)
England in the Seven Years War, 2 vols. (London, 1907)
(ed.) *Signals and Instructions, 1776–1794, N.R.S.* (London, 1908)
A Note on the Drawings in the Possession of the Earl of Dartmouth Illustrating the Battle of Salebay, N.R.S. (London, 1908)
The Campaign of Trafalgar (London, 1910)
Some Principles of Maritime Strategy (London, 1911)
(ed.) *The Spencer Papers*, N.R.S., 2 vols. (London, 1913 and 1914)
(ed.) *Naval and Military Essays* (Cambridge, 1913)
Official History of the Great War: Naval Operations, 3 vols. (London, 1920, 1921 and 1923)

JOHN KNOX LAUGHTON
(ed.) *Nelson's Letters and Despatches* (London, 1886)
Studies in Naval History (London, 1887)
Memoirs Relating to Lord Torrington (London, 1889)
(ed.) *State Papers Relating to the Defeat of the Spanish Armada*, N.R.S., 2 vols. (London, 1894)
Nelson (London, 1895)
The Nelson Memorial (London, 1896)
(ed. with Sullivan, J.Y.F.) *Journal of Rear Admiral Bartholomew James*, N.R.S. (London, 1896)
Memoirs of the Life and Correspondence of Henry Reeve, 2 vols. (London, 1898)
From Howard to Nelson (London, 1900)
(ed.) *The Naval Miscellany*, N.R.S., 2 vols. (London, 1902 and 1912)
(ed.) *Letters and Papers of Charles, Lord Barham, 1758–1813*, N.R.S., 3 vols. (London, 1907, 1910 and 1911)

ALFRED THAYER MAHAN
The Gulf and Inland Waters (New York, 1883)
The Influence of Sea Power upon the French Revolution and Empire, 2 vols. (London, 1892)
The Life of Nelson, 2 vols. (London, 1897)
Types of Naval Officers (London, 1902)

Sea Power in its Relations to the War of 1812, 2 vols. (London, 1905)
From Sail to Steam (New York, 1907)
(ed.) *Naval Administration and Warfare* (London, 1908)
Naval Strategy (London, 1911)

HERBERT WILLIAM RICHMOND
Papers Relating to the Loss of Minorca, N.R.S. (London, 1913)
The Navy in the War of 1739-48, 3 vols. (Cambridge, 1923)
Command and Discipline (London, 1927)
National Policy and Naval Strength (London, 1928)
The Navy in India (London, 1931)
Economy and Naval Security (London, 1931)
Imperial Defence and Capture at Sea in War (London, 1932)
Sea Power in the Modern World (London, 1932)
The Navy (London, 1937)
The Invasion of England (London, 1941)
British Strategy, Military and Economic (Cambridge, 1944)
Statesmen and Sea Power (Oxford, 1946)
(ed.) by E. A. Hughes, *The Navy as an Instrument of Policy* (Cambridge, 1953)

ARTICLES AND PAMPHLETS

COLOMB, J. C. R.
'On Colonial Defence', Royal Colonial Institute *Proceedings*, 1873.
'Naval Intelligence and Protection of Commerce in War', R.U.S.I. *Journal*, 1881.
'Imperial Federation—Naval and Military', R.U.S.I. *Journal*, 1886.
'British Defence its Popular and its Real Aspects', *The New Century Review*, 1897.
'British Defence, 1880-1900', Royal Colonial Institute *Proceedings*, 1900.
British Dangers (London, 1902)

COLOMB, P. H.
'Naval and Military Signals', R.U.S.I. *Journal*, 1863.
'Ship Lights at Sea', R.U.S.I. *Journal*, 1866.
'The Attack and Defence of Fleets', R.U.S.I. *Journal*, 1872.
'Great Britain's Maritime Power', R.U.S.I. *Journal*, 1878.
'Naval Mobilization', R.U.S.I. *Journal*, 1888.
'The Relations between Local Fortifications and a Moving Navy', R.U.S.I. *Journal*, 1889.

CORBETT
'Education in the Navy', *Monthly Review*, 1902 (2 articles).
'Education in the Navy', *Monthly Review*, 1902.
'Lord Selborne's Critics', *Monthly Review*, 1903.
'Recent attacks on the Admiralty', *The Nineteenth Century*, 1907.

LAUGHTON
'The Scientific Study of Naval History', R.U.S.I. *Journal*, 1874.
'Sir Thomas Brassey on the British Navy', *Edinburgh Review*, 1882.
'Review Article VIII', *Edinburgh Review*, 1883.
'Notes on the Last Great Naval War', R.U.S.I. *Journal*, 1885.

'Forts and Fleets', *Quarterly Review*, 1891.
'Rodney and the Navy of the Eighteenth Century', *Edinburgh Review*, 1892.
'Captain Mahan on Maritime Power', *Edinburgh Review*, 1893.
'The Battle of La Hogue and Maritime War', *Quarterly Review*, 1893.
'Naval Armaments', *Edinburgh Review*, 1894.
'The Study of Naval History', R.U.S.I. *Journal*, 1896.
'Emma, Lady Hamilton', *Edinburgh Review*, 1896.
'Captain Mahan's Life of Nelson', *Edinburgh Review*, 1897.
'The National Study of Naval History', Royal Historical Society *Transactions, 1909.*
'Mr. Corbett's Drake and his Successors', *Edinburgh Review*, 1901.
'The Centenary of Trafalgar', *Edinburgh Review*, 1905.
'La Campagne Maritime de 1805', *Edinburgh Review*, 1907.
'Hardman's History of Malta', *Edinburgh Review*, 1910.

MAHAN, A. T.
'Naval Education for Officers and Men', U.S.N.I. *Proceedings*, 1879.
'Presidential Address at the Opening of the 4th Annual Session of the Naval War College', U.S.N.I. *Proceedings*, 1888.
'The Practical Character of the Naval War College', U.S.N.I. *Proceedings*, 1893.

RICHMOND,
'The Navy and its Record from the Armada to Trafalgar', *The Mariner's Mirror*, 1938.

OTHER PRINTED SOURCES
Books

ALBION, R. G., *Forests and Sea Power* (Cambridge, Mass., 1926).
BAKER-BROWN, W., *History of the Corps of Royal Engineers*, Vol. 4 (Chatham, 1952).
BAXTER, J. P., *The Introduction of the Ironclad Warship* (Cambridge, Mass., 1933).
*BENNETT, FRANK M., *The Steam Navy of the United States* (Pittsburg, 1896).
BENNETT, GEOFFREY, *Coronel and the Falklands* (London, 1962).
BRIGGS, SIR JOHN H., *Naval Administration, 1827–1892* (London, 1897).
BRASSEY, T. A., *The British Navy*, 5 vols. (London, 1882).
CHURCHILL, W. S., *Lord Randolph Churchill*, 2 vols. (London, 1906).
———, *The World Crisis, 1911–1914* (London, 1923).
*CLARKE, G. S., *Fortifications* (London, 1890).
*CLARKE, G. S., & THURSFIELD, J., *The Navy and the Nation* (London, 1897).
CLAUSEWITZ, KARL VON (Col. J. J. Graham, ed.) *On War* (London, 1949).
CLOWES, SIR W. L., *The Royal Navy*, 7 vols. (London, 1897–1903).
COLE, D. H., *Imperial Military Geography* (London, 1953).
COQUELLE, P., *Napoleon et Angleterre* (Paris, 1904).
CUSTANCE, R., *The Ship of the Line in Battle* (London, 1912).
——— under pen, name 'Barfleur'—*Naval Policy* (London, 1912).
———, *A Study of War* (London, 1924).
*D'EGVILLE, HOWARD, *Imperial Defence and Closer Union* (London, 1913).
DESBRIÈRE, E., *La France, Angleterre et Naples* (Paris, 1904).
———, *La Campagne Maritime de 1805 : Trafalgar* (Paris, 1907).
*EARLE, EDWARD MEAD (ed.), *Makers of Modern Strategy* (Princeton, 1952).
*EHRMAN, JOHN, *The Navy in the War of William III, 1689–97* (Cambridge, 1953).
ELTON, G. R., *England under the Tudors* (London, 1954).

Bibliographical Note

ESHER, VISCOUNT OLIVER, *Journals and Letters of Reginald Viscount Esher, 1910–15*, Vol. 3 (London, 1938).
FALLS, CYRIL, *Elizabeth's Irish Wars* (London, 1950).
———, *The Art of War* (London, 1961).
*FOLSOM, A., *The Royal Empire Society* (London, 1933).
GIBBS, NORMAN H., *The Origins of Imperial Defence* (Oxford, 1955).
GIPSON, L. H., *The British Empire before the American Revolution*, Vol. 7 (New York, 1959).
*GOOCH, G. P., *History and Historians in the Nineteenth Century* (London, 1913).
*GRAHAM, G. S., *Empire of the North Atlantic* (Toronto, 1950).
HANNAY, DAVID, *A Short History of the Royal Navy*, 2 vols. (London, 1898 and 1909).
JAMES, ADMIRAL SIR WILLIAM, *Old Oak* (London, 1950).
———, *A Great Seaman* (London, 1956).
JAMES, WILLIAM, *A Naval History of Great Britain*, 6 vols. (London, 1860).
JOHNSON, F. A., *Defence by Committee* (Oxford, 1960).
KEMP, PETER (ed.), *Boscawen's Letters to His Wife, 1755–56* (London, 1952).
KISSINGER, HENRY A., *Nuclear Weapons and Foreign Policy* (New York, 1957).
*LEWIS, MICHAEL, *The Navy of Britain* (London, 1948).
*LIVEZEY, W. E., *Mahan on Sea Power* (Norman, Okla., 1947).
LLOYD, C. C., *The Navy and the Slave Trade* (London, 1949).
MACKESY, PIERS, *The War in the Mediterranean, 1803–10* (London, 1957).
*MARDER, ARTHUR J., *The Anatomy of British Sea Power* (New York, 1940).
*———, *British Naval Policy* (London, 1941).
  (The above titles refer to the same book published in two different countries.)
*———, *Portrait of an Admiral* (London, 1952).
*———, *Fear God and Dread Nought*, 3 vols. (London, 1952, 1956 and 1959).
MATTINGLY, GARRETT, *The Defeat of the Spanish Armada* (London, 1959).
OLLIVIER, M. (ed.), *The Colonial and Imperial Conferences*, 3 vols. (Ottawa, 1954).
OPPENHEIM, M., *The Administration of the Royal Navy, 1509–1660* (London, 1896).
OSGOOD, R. E., *Limited War: The Challenge to American Strategy* (Chicago, 1957).
*PARES, RICHARD, *War and Trade in the West Indies* (Oxford, 1936).
*PARKES, OSCAR, *British Battleships* (London, 1957).
PATTERSON, A. TEMPLE, *The Other Armada* (Manchester, 1960).
PITT, BARRIE, *Coronel and Falkland* (London, 1960).
*PULESTON, W. D., *Mahan* (London, 1939).
Register of West Point Graduates and Former Cadets (U.S.M.A., 1953).
ROSE, J. HOLLAND, 'The Struggle with Napoleon', *The Cambridge History of the British Empire*, Vol. 2 (Cambridge, 1940).
*ROSKILL, CAPTAIN S. W., *The War At Sea*, Vol. 1 (London, 1954).
*———, *The Strategy of Sea Power* (London, 1962).
*SCHURMAN, D. M., *Imperial Defence, 1868–1887* (Unpublished Ph.D. Thesis, Cambridge, 1955).
STACEY, C. P., *Quebec, 1759: The Siege and the Battle* (Toronto, 1959).
TANNER, J. R., *Samuel Pepys and the Royal Navy* (Cambridge, 1920).
*TAYLOR, CHARLES CARLISLE, *The Life of Admiral Mahan* (London, 1920).
*TUNSTALL, W. C. BRIAN, *The Realities of Naval History* (London, 1936).
———, *William Pitt, Earl of Chatham* (London, 1938).
*———, 'Imperial Defence, 1815–70' *The Cambridge History of the British Empire*, Vol. 2 (Cambridge, 1940).

*TUNSTALL, W. C. B., TUNSTALL, P. M., SCHURMAN, D. M., *Catalogue of the Corbett Papers* (Bedford, 1958).
*TYLER, J. E., *The Struggle for Imperial Unity* (London, 1938).
WALKER, E. A., *The Study of British Imperial History* (Cambridge, 1937).
WEBSTER, SIR CHARLES, and FRANKLAND, NOBLE, *The Strategic Air Offensive Against Germany*, 3 vols. (London, 1961).
*WILLIAMSON, J. A., *The Age of Drake* (London, 1946).
WROTTESLEY, GEORGE, *Life and Correspondence of Sir John Burgoyne*, 2 vols. (London, 1873).

Articles and Pamphlets

CRUTCHLEY, LT. W. C., 'On the Condition of the Mercantile Marine Personnel and Material, with a view to its more complete utilization as a Reserve for the Royal Navy', R.U.S.I. *Journal*, 1888.
DEWAR, CAPTAIN ALFRED, 'The Necessity for the Compilation of a Naval Staff History', R.U.S.I. *Journal*, 1921.
DUNCAN, FRANCIS, 'Mahan—Historian with a Purpose', U.S.N.I. *Proceedings*, 1957.
ELLICOTT, J. M., 'Sidelights on Mahan', U.S.N.I. *Proceedings*, 1948.
——, 'Three Naval Cranks and what they Turned', U.S.N.I. *Proceedings*, 1924.
FREEMANTLE, R. A., HON. EDMUND R., 'Naval Tactics', R.U.S.I. *Journal*, 1886.
——, 'Speed as a Factor in Naval Warfare', R.U.S.I. *Journal*, 1888.
HOWARD, MICHAEL, 'Bombing and the Bomb', *Encounter*, 1962.
JAMES, R. R., 'Lord Randolph Resigns', *History To-day* (November and December, 1958).
LEPAWSKI, ALBERT, 'A Tribute to Mahan, as a Social Scientist', U.S.N.I. *Proceedings*, 1940.
NEUMANN, W. L., 'Franklin Delano Roosevelt: A Disciple of Admiral Mahan', U.S.N.I. *Proceedings*, 1952.
STEAD, W. T., 'What is the Truth about the Navy', *Pall Mall Gazette*, 15 September, 1884.
——, 'The Truth about Our Coaling Stations', *Pall Mall Gazette*, 16 October, 1884.
*TREVELYAN, GEORGE MACAULAY, 'Admiral Sir Herbert Richmond', British Academy, *Proceedings*, 1946.
WALKER, MAJOR G. R., 'Fortifications and Fleets', R.U.S.I. *Journal*, 1889.
*WERNHAM, R. B., 'Queen Elizabeth and the Portugal Expedition of 1589', *English Historical Review*, January and April, 1951.

INDEX

Principal references are in **bold type**
e.g. **83–109**; *bis* or *ter* after a page number means that the subject indexed is mentioned *twice* or *thrice* in separate paragraphs on the page indicated.

Acton, Lord (John Dalberg, 1834–1902): 74 *bis*, 74 *n*, 85 & *nn*
Addington, Henry (Viscount Sidmouth, 1757–1844): 173
Administration of the Royal Navy 1509–1660, The (Oppenheim): 151
Admiralty, Board of: 4–8 *passim*, 11, 19 *bis*, 20, 25, 26, 29, 30 *bis*, 34, 37–45 *passim*, 51, 58, 59, 95, 103 *bis*, 112, 114, 115, 123, 124 *bis*, 129, 132, 136 & *n*, 150, 171 *bis*, 187; planning at, 103 *bis*, 113, 118, 119, 122 *bis*, 124, 125–6, 145; Records, 88, 89; Richmond's criticisms of, 123–4
Age of Drake, The (Williamson): 155 *n*, 156 *n*
Air power: 130, 188–9
Albemarle, HMS: 121
Albion, R. G.: 140 *n*
Algiers, HMS: 83 & *n*
American Civil War (1861–65): 89 & *n*
American Historical Association: 71 & *n*
American Revolutionary War (1775–83): 142–3
Anatomy of British Sea Power, The (Marder): 36 *n*, 60 *n*, 90 *n*
Anglo-Dutch Wars (xvii century): 53, 55, 77, 160, 184

Annapolis, U.S. Naval Academy at: 63, 64, 68, 121
Antarctica: 121
Application of doctrines (1914–18 & 1939–45): **185–92**
Area demands, conflicting: 140–1
Armada campaign (1588) and era: 84, 93, 100, 151, 152–3
'Armada Guns' (Lewis): 153 *n*
Armour-plating: 42
Army, British: 5, 50 *n*; and defence of Britain (1850s), 18, 47; and defence of bases, 24, 26 (*see also* Bases); primacy of, 44, 171; and navy, 106, 171: and Cadiz (1596), 158; Elizabethan, 159
Army Council: 122
Arnold-Forster, Hugh O.: 120 *n*
Art of War, The (Falls): 174 *n*
Artillery, naval: 4–5, 27
Ashford, Cyril: 120 *n*
Atlantic, Battle of the (1939–43): 129
'Attack and Defence of Fleets, The' (Colomb, P.): 39 *n*
Auriol, Charles: 172
Austerlitz, Battle of (1805): 170
Author, the: 16 *n*, 26 *n*, 30 *n*

'Baillie de Suffren, Le' (Laughton): 85 *n*, 87 *n*
Baker-Brown, W.: 51 *n*
Balaclava, Battle of (1854): 39
'Balance of Power': 141
Balfour, Arthur James (*later* Earl Balfour, 1848–1930): 32
Baltic nations, influence of: 145

INDEX

'Barfleur' (Sir Reginald Custance, q.v.): 14 n
Barham, Admiral: 171
Barham Papers (ed. Laughton): 172
Barry, Captain Henry D., R.N.: 119 nn
Barton, Edmund: 30 n
Bases, naval and military: importance of, 23, 24, 144 bis, 163, 186–7; Britain secures, 23–4, 43, 80, 163; defence of, 24, 26, 27 n, 30, 144, 178; command of, 26; financing of, 27; 'grabbing', 80
Battenburg, Captain Prince Louis of, R.N.: 91
'Battle of La Hogue and Maritime War, The' (Laughton): 100 n
Battleships, broadside: 161
Beatty, Admiral Sir David (*later* Earl Beatty): 113, 114, 115 & n
Bell, Sir Hugh: 112 n
Bell, M. H.: 111 n; *quoted*, 111
Bennett, Frank M.: 64 nn, 66 n
'Big battle' concept: 142, 164; 188; Richmond on, 142; Corbett on, 164, 165 (*quoted*), 179 bis
Biography, Mahan on: 66 n, 76–7
Blake, Admiral Robert: 161, 162
Blockade: 45, 79; and trade war, 138–40, 154–5, 160, 179
'Blockade under existing conditions of Warfare' (Colomb, P.): 45 n
'Blue Water School': 22, 46, 57, 141, 156
Board of Trade: 39
Boer (South African) War (1899–1902): 29
'Bombing and the Bomb' (Howard, Michael): 80 n
Boscawen, Admiral: 166 n
Boscawen's Letters to his Wife, 1755–56 (ed. Kemp): 166 n
Bowden-Smith, Captain Sir Nathaniel, R.N.: 47 & n
Brackenbury, Colonel (*later* General) Sir Henry: 47 & n
Bradford, Rear-Admiral Sir Edward: 113
'Brassey on the British Navy, Sir Thomas' (Laughton): 102 n
Brassey, Sir Thomas A. (*later* Earl Brassey): 20 n, 40 n, 94 & n
Brest (1805): 180
Bridge, Admiral Sir Cyprian: 91 & n, 93 bis, 96
Briggs, Sir John H.: 2 n
Britannia, HMS (training ship): 111
British Army: *see* Army, British
British Battleships (Parkes): 3 n, 20 24 n, 40 nn
British Dangers (Colomb, J.): 31 n
'British Defence, 1800–1900, (Colomb, J.): 30 n, 34 n
'British Defence: its Popular and Real Aspects' (Colomb, J.): 29 n
British Empire, the: 10, 102
British Empire before the American Revolution, The (Gipson): 166 n
British Expeditionary Force (1914): 158 n
British Naval Policy (Marder): 1 n
British Navy: *see* Royal Navy
British Navy, The (Brassey): 20 n, 40 n
'Brotherhood of Industry': 160
Browning, Robert (1812–89): 111
Burgoyne, General Sir John: 18 n; *Life and Correspondence of* . . . , 18 n
Burmese War (1852): 37
Burrows, Montague: 97 n

Cadiz raid (1596): 157, 158–9
Calcutta, HMS: 83 & n, 91
Callendar, Sir Geoffrey: 83 n, 91 n, 147 n; *quoted*, 83, 84
Cambridge, Duke of: 8, 33
Campagne Maritime, 1805, La (Desbrière): 106, 172 n
'Campagne Maritime de 1805, La' (Laughton): 106 nn
Campaign of Trafalgar, The (Corbett): 170–4 & nn, 180 n, 183–4
Canada and the Battle of the Atlantic (1939–43): 129
Canopus, HMS: 112 & n
Cape Colony (1780–81): 143
Cape St. Vincent, Battle of (1797): 101
Captain, HMS: 40 & n
'Captain Mahan on Maritime Power' (Laughton): 66 n
'Captain Mahan's Life of Nelson' (Laughton): 100 n
Caribbean Sea, island invasions in the: 56
Carnarvon Commission (1879–82): 27 n, 30–3 passim, 49 & nn; *its full title*, 30, 49; *Report of* . . . , 49 & nn

Index

Carnarvon, Earl of: 30 & n, 48–9 & nn
Carson, Sir Edward: 114
Cartagena (1740): 138
'Centenary of Trafalgar, The' (Laughton): 105 n
Chance in warfare: 142, 168–9
'Chap-book, mendacious' (Laughton's phrase): 98
Chicago, USS: 66 bis, 68
China Station (1874–77): 37
Churchill, Lord Randolph (1849–94): 33, 43
Churchill, (*later* Sir) Winston S.: 33 n, 57, 125, 185 bis, 186 & nn, 189–90, 190
Civil Service, the: 124
Clarke, Sir George Sydenham (*later* Lord Sydenham, *q.v.*): 99 & n, 124 n
Clausewitz, Karl von (Prussian strategist): 78, 105, 150, 163 n, 164, 166, 173, 175, 176, 182, 190–1
Clowes, Sir William Laird (*The Times* naval correspondent): 13 & n, 14, 67 n, 91 & n
Coaling stations overseas: 24, 33, 43, 186, 187
Coast defence (*see also* Fortifications): 24, 40, 48, 50
Cocos Islands (1914): 187
Colbert, Jean Baptiste (1619–83): 100, 161
Cole, D. H.: 24 n
Colomb, Captain Sir John Charles Ready, R.N.: 1, 3, 7 ter, 8 bis & n, 10–11, 11 & n, 12, 14, 15, **16–35**, 36, 39 n, 43 & n, 44 & n, 46 & n, 47, 50, 59, 62, 85, 96, 135, 141, 186, 187 bis, 189; his methods and influence, 11; personal details of, **16–17, 32–5**; *Memorandum Relative to his Work*, 17 n, 25 n, 27 n; and inter-service co-operation, 20; and world-wide strategy, 20–1; his Papers (1867), 20 *ff.*; on Imperial Defence, 20–35, 129; and bases, 23–4, 26, 27; and India, 26; his rigidity of thought, 27–8, 33; and publicity, 28–9; in Parliament, 28–9, 29 n, 31 bis; as 'Imperial Federationist', 25, 28; and naval efficiency, 29–32; and departmentalism, 30–1; and statistics, 32, 33; and colonials, 32; and party politics, 33; his influence, 34–5; and 'command of the sea', 177–8; and trade protection, 178
Colomb Papers, The: 17 n, 25 n, 27 n
Colomb, Vice-Admiral Philip Howard: 7 bis, 8 bis, 11 bis, 12 ter, 14, 17, 27, 34 bis, **36–59**, 62 bis, 78 bis, 90 n, 93, 95, 97, 104, 106, 141, 153, 180 n, 186, 187 bis, 189; his methods and influence, 11–12, 40, 44; personal details of, **36–8**; and R.U.S.I., 38, 44, 51, 54, 58; his Papers, 38–42, 45; and J. Colomb, 39 & n; his historical approach, 40, 44, 45, 50, 54, 55–8, 71; his 'moderation', 41; his 'broadside' on naval defences of U.K., 46–8; refutes Walker at R.U.S.I., 51; and Mahan, 52–3, 66 & n; 'a real historian', 58
Colomb's Flashing Signals: 17, 37
Colonial and Imperial Conferences, 1887–1937, The (Ollivier): 29 n
Colonial Conference (1887): 29, 34, 43, 49 n; *Proceedings of the . . .* , 43 n, 49 n
'Colonial Defence': 25, 29, 33
Colonial Defence Committee (1885): 43 & n
Colonial Defence, On (Colomb, J.): 29 n
Colonial Naval Defence Agreement (1884–87): 25 n
Colonies, British: their share of defence costs, 25
Combined ('Conjunct') Operations: 138, 144 & n, 157, 181, 189–90
'Command of the Sea' (naval supremacy): 53 *ff*, 55, 138, 155, 159, 165 (*quotation*); definition of, 177–8; and the 'big battle', 179
Commerce: *see* Trade
Committee of Imperial Defence: 34, 49–50, 103, 114, 122, 124 n, 150, 190
Commonwealth, the British: 129
Commonwealth, HMS: 113 & n
Communications, maritime: bottlenecks in, 23; protection of, 21, 22–3, 27, 45, 186–7, 187
Complacency, dangers of: 145
'Concentration of aim': 173

o

'Concentration of force': 179–80
Conqueror, HMS: 113 & *n*
Construction, naval: *see* Ship-building
Continental system, Napoleon's: 105–6
Convoy system: 11 *n*, 14, 45, 179, 187–8, 188
Co-operation, inter-service: 19, 20, 22, 26, 30–1, 144 *bis*, 156, 164, 181
Cooper-Key, Admiral Sir Astley: 8, 38, 58 & *n*, 87, 88 *bis*; *Memoirs of* ..., 38 *n*, 58–9, 58 *n*
Coote, Sir Eyre: 144 & *n*
Coquelle, P.: 172 & *n*
Corbett, Edith (*nee* Alexander): 148–9
Corbett, Sir Julian Stafford: 6, 9, **13**, 14, 15, 18 *n*, 50 *n*, 72, 78, 94 *n*, 96–101 *passim*, 107, 108, 113 *n*, 114, 117 & *n*, 126, 132 *bis*, 134, 145, **147–84**, 188, 190 *bis*, 191, 192; personal and family details of, **147–50**; as historian, 148–52; his influence, 150; official naval historian, 149, 150; as writer and publicist, 150; his *Drake and the Tudor Navy*, 151–6 & *nn*; his *Successors of Drake*, 156–60 & *nn*; his *England in the Mediterranean*, 160–4 & *nn*, 169; his *England in the Seven Years War*, 164–9 & *nn*; and Clausewitz, 164 *bis*, 175–6, 182; on 'the supreme function of a fleet', 165; on Pitt the Elder, 165, 166–7; his sources, 165–7, 169, 172; on historical evidence and military theory, 169; his *Campaign of Trafalgar*, 170–4 & *nn*; and Nelson, 170–1; and 'concentration of aim', 173; his *Some Principles of Maritime Strategy*, 174–82 & *nn*; on theory and practice in naval warfare, 174–5; on limited war and 'side-shows', 176–7; on 'command of the sea', 177–8, 179; on trade protection, 178; on cruiser forces, 178–9; on the 'big battle' fixation, 179; on 'concentration of force', 179–80; on invasion, 180–1, 181; and Fisher, 180, 182; on combined operations, 181; his publishing achievement, 182–3; non-Nelsonic, 183; and opposition, 183; and British naval tactics (1530–1794), 184; his other works, 184; his great aim, 184
Corbett Papers, The, 115 *n*, 122 *n*, 123 *n*, 149 *n*, 150 *n*, 180 *n*
'Corbett's Drake and his Successors', Mr. (Laughton): 100 *n*
Cornwallis, Admiral Sir William: 171 & *n*, 180 *n*
Cornwallis Papers, The: 172
Coronel, Battle of (1914): 113 *n*, 187 *nn*, 188
Coronel and Falkland (Pitt): 187 *n*
Coronel and the Falklands (Bennett): 187 *n*
'Council of War' the: 175
Cowper, Earl: 47–8, 47 *n*
Cradock, Rear-Admiral Sir Christopher: 113 *n*
Creighton, Mandell (*History of the Papacy*): 74
Crescent, HMS: 112, 121
Crimean War (1854–56): 17–18, 18 *n*, 19, 83, 177, 181
Cruiser forces: 178–9
Crutchley, W. C.: 45 *n*
Cullum, Major-General G. W.: 63 *n*
Custance, Admiral Sir Reginald: 14 & *n*, 42 & *n*, 55–6, 183

D.N.B.: *see Dictionary of National Biography*
Dardanelles expedition (1915): 188, 189
Darwin, Charles (1809–82): 111
Defeat of the Spanish Armada, The (Mattingly): 153 *n*
Defence and offence: 175–6
Defence by Committee (Johnson): 124 *n*
Defence, Minister *and* Ministry of: 49, 50 *n*
Defence of British Possessions and Commerce Abroad, Royal Commission on: *see* Carnarvon Commission
'Defence of the Empire' (Colomb, J., speech): 31 *n*
Defence of the United Kingdom: principles of, 18–20, 21; Royal Commission *and* Select Committee on (1859), 18, 46, 47
D'Anville, Duc de: 139 & *n*
D'Egville, Howard: 11 *n*, 16 *n*, 31 *n*
Departmentalism: 30–1

Index 203

Desbrière, Colonel Edouard: 106, 172 & n
Design (of ships): 2 bis, 3, 4, 19; Admiralty Committee on, 20, 24 n, 40 n
Devastation, HMS: 20, 24 n, 38 n, 40 & n; ... Class, 20 n, 24 n, 40 n
Devereux, Robert: see Essex, Earl of
Dewar, Captain Alfred, R.N.: 126 & n
Dewar, Commander, K. G. B.: 114 n, 127
Diary (Richmond's): 113 n, 114 n, 116 n, 117 nn, 118 nn, 119 nn, 120 nn, 121 nn, 123 n, 125 n, 126 nn, 127 nn, 128 nn, 131 n
Dictionary of National Biography (D.N.B.): 9, 83 n, 84, 87 n, 91 n, 93 n, 97, 110 n, 111 n, 147 n
Diplomacy and war: 78, 105, 141, 145, 149, 152, 153–4, 160, 167, 169, 176
Distractions or diversions, strategic: 143, 167, 181
Documents, publication of: 13
Dogma and war: 86
Doubleday, Abner: 89 n
Doughty, Thomas: 155
Drake (Corbett): 148
Drake and the Tudor Navy (Corbett): 100, 101, 148 & n, **151–6** & nn, 182
Drake, Sir Francis (c. 1540–96): 100, 101, 148, 149, 151–7 passim, 179, 181
Dreadnought Age (era): 134, 142, 147 n, 149
Dreadnought, HMS: 112 & n; Class, 142, 186
Dreadnought to Scapa Flow, From the (Marder): 1 n, 118 n, 120 n
Dryad, HMS: 37
Duke of Wellington, HMS (naval shore establishment): 38, 119 n, 121
Duncan, Francis: 75 & n, 81 n
Durnford, Rear-Admiral John: 120 n
Durston, Eng. Rear-Admiral Sir John: 120 n
Dutch, the (mid-xviii century): 137

East India Company, the Hon. (1600–1858): 143, 144
Edinburgh Review: 9, 61 n, 66 & nn, 84, 85 & nn, 89 n, 90 & n, 96, 99, 100 nn, 101 n, 104 n, 105 n, 106 n

'Education in the Navy' (Corbett): 117 nn
Education, naval: 117, 123 n
Ehrman, John: 140 n, 161 & n, 162 n, 191–2
Elizabeth I, Queen (1558–1603): 152, 153–4, 157, 158 & n, 159, 179
Elizabethan military failures: 156
Elizabethan strategy and tactics (naval): 151, 152–3, 156, 159–60
Elizabethan warfare: 157
Elizabeth's Irish Wars (Falls): 159 n
Ellicott, Captain J. M., U.S.N.: 66 n, 68 nn
Elliot, Admiral Sir George: 47 & n
Elton, G. R.: 151–2, 151 n; quoted, 151
Emden (German cruiser): 187
'Emma, Lady Hamilton' (Laughton): 101 n
'Emma', Nelson's (Lady Hamilton): 101–2
Empire of the North Atlantic (Graham): 141 n
Empress of India, HMS: 111–12, 111 n, 119 n
Encounter (magazine): 80 n
Encyclopaedia Britannica: 9
Engineers, naval: promotion to command, 120
England in the Mediterranean (Corbett) **160–4** & nn, 169, 170 n
England in the Seven Years War (Corbett): 132, **164–9**
England under the Tudors (Elton): 151 n
English Historical Review: 13 & n, 76 n, 152 n
Erben, Rear-Admiral Henry, U.S.N.: 66 & n
Erin, HMS: 114 & n
'Escalation': 168, 191
Esher, Viscount: 190 n; quoted, 190
Esquimalt: 24
Essays on Naval Defence (Colomb, P.): 38 & n, 45 n
Essex, Earl of (1566–1601): 157 & n, 158
Evolutions, ship and fleet: 39
Ewing, James A: 120 n
Excellent, HMS (naval gunnery school) 37
Expenditure: on defence, 9–10; on navy, 2, 103

204 INDEX

Falkland Islands, Battle of the (1914): 14, 185–7, 187
Fall of Asgard, The (Corbett): 148 *n*
Falls, Cyril: 159 *n*, 174 *n*
Falsom, A: 7 *n*
Fanshawe, Admiral Sir Edward: 91 & *n*
Fear God and Dread Nought (Marder): 118 *n*, 186 *n*
Fighting Instructions, 1530–1816 (Corbett): 184
Firth, Sir Charles: 93 & *n*, 96, 162–3
Fisher, Admiral of the Fleet Sir John ('Jackie', *later* Lord Fisher, 1841–1920): 36, 37 *n*, 39, 57, 59, 79, 95, 111, 112 & *n*, 118 bis, 119 bis, 120 bis & *n*, 121 ter & *n*, 123 quat, 124 *n*, 125 & *n*, 132, 142, 149 & *nn*, 180 & *n*, 182, 186 & *n*
Fisher, Commander Thomas: 127
'Fishpond', the: 122
Fitzalan-Howard, Henry (15th Duke of Norfolk): 92 *n*
Fitzgerald, Captain Penrose, R.N.: 47 & *n*
'Fleet-in-being' (concept): 90
Ford Lectures (Oxford, 1943): 145, 160
Foreign policy and sea power: 145
Forests and Sea Power . . . (Albion): 140 *n*
Fortifications (Clarke): 99 & *n*
'Fortifications and Fleets' (Walker): 51 *n*
Fortifications (fixed) *versus* ships (moving), (*see also* Coast defence): 54–5, 56, 78, 90 *n*, 99 & *n*,106,1 79
Fortnightly Review: 48 *n*, 131
'Forts and Fleets' (Laughton): 99 *n*
'Fortress England': 18
Fremantle, Admiral Sir Edward: 44 & *n*, 45 & *nn*
Froude, J. A. (historian): 9, 101
Functions of warships: 2, 4
Furious, HMS: 112 & *n*
Furnivall, Frederick J.: 92–3, 92 *n*

Gallantry, justified and unjustified: 179
'Geddes Axe': 115 & *n*
Gardiner, Samuel R. (historian): 9, 92 bis & *n*, 96, 162–3, 163 *n*; his works on xvii century, 163 *n*

Germany (*see also* Prussia): 28
Gibbs, Professor Norman H.: 43 *n*
Gibraltar (1658 & 1713): 162
Gipson, L. H.: 166 *n*
Gladstone, William Ewart (1809–98): 9, 111
'Glorious First of June' (1794): 101
Gneisenau (German cruiser): 186
Gooch, G. P.: 74 *n*, 76 & *n*
Gordon, General Charles George (1833–85): 44
Graham, G. S.: 141 *n*
Graham, Colonel J. J.: 150 *n*
Grand Fleet, the: 113, 180, 185, 188
'Great Britain's Maritime Power' (Colomb, P., *prize essay*): 36 *n*, 39–42, 39 *n*
Great Seaman, A (James): 119 *nn*
Greene, Francis: 89 *n*
Greenwich: *see* Royal Naval College
Grenville, Sir Richard (*c.* 1541–91): 157 & *n*
Guerre de Sept Ans, La (Waddington): 164
Gulf and Inland Waters, The (Mahan): 62 & *n*, 65 *n*, 68, 89 *n*
Gunnery, naval: *see* Artillery
Guns: 20, 42

Haddock, Admiral Nicholas: his Mediterranean Force (1741), 133 *n*
Hamilton, Lady (Emma): 101–2
Hamilton, Admiral Sir Richard Vesey: 42 & *n*, 46–7, 91 & *n*, 96
Hannay, David: 14 & *n*, 91 & *n*, 94, 99
Hankey, Sir Maurice (*later* Lord Hankey): 114, 190
Hannibal (247–*c.* 182 B.C.): 72
Hansard: *see* Parliamentary Debates
Harding, Captain Edward D., R.M.A.: 127
'Hardman's History of Malta' (Laughton): 102 *n*
Harris, Air Chief Marshal Sir Arthur: 189
Hastings, HMS: 37
Hawkins, Sir John (1532–95): 154, 157
Hayes-Sadler, Commander Arthur: 119 *n*, 120 *n*
Herbert, Arthur (Earl of Torrington): 59 & *n*, 90
Herbert, Henry Howard Molyneux (4th Earl of Carnarvon): 30 & *n*,

Index

48 & *n*, 49 *n*
High Seas Fleet (German): blockaded (1914–15), 14
History, academic: 1, 6, 12, 40, 55, 95, 96; and prophecy, 55
History and Historians in the Nineteenth Century (Gooch): 74 *n*, 76 *n*
History, French: Mahan's use of, 70
History, naval (*see also* Navy Records Society): 1–15, 27, 55, 67, 84, 85–7, 89, 90, 95, 96, 98–9, 108; interest in, 57; and principles of war, 86–7; sources for, 87–9, 98; and naval cadets, 117; scope and uses of, 126, 160, 163, 172–3; and military theory, 169; its influence on the two World Wars, 185, 190; since 1914, 191–2; and Roskill, 191
History To-day: 33 *n*
Hong Kong: 24
Hood, Captain the Hon. Horace L. A., R.N.: 120 *n*
Hornby, Admiral Sir Geoffrey Phipps: 38
Hoskins, Admiral Sir Anthony: 91 & *n*
Howard, Michael: 80 *n*
Howard of Effingham, Lord (1536–1624): 157 & *n*, 158
Howard to Nelson, From (ed. Laughton): 97 & *n*
Howe, Admiral Sir Richard (*later* Lord Howe): 46, 101
Hughes, Admiral Sir Edward (xviii century): 142, 143 & *n*, 144 & *n*
Hughes-Suffren naval duel *and* period: 131, 142
Human factor in war: 144, 185–7
Hyacinth, HMS: 120 *n*

Imperial Conference (1887), (*see also* Colonial Conference): 43
Imperial Defence (*see also* Bases): 7, 8, 10, 16, 43, 129 *bis*; John Colomb on, 20–35, 129, 187; India and, 26; cost of, 29; Dominions and, 29 *n*; Philip Colomb on, 36–59, 187; Corbett on, 173
'Imperial Defence, 1815–70' (Tunstall) 18 *n*, 21 *n*, 22 *n*
Imperial Defence, 1868–87 (Schurman) 16 *n*, 26 *n*, 30 *n*
Imperial Defence and Capture at Sea in War (Richmond): 129 *n*, 130 *n*, 132
Imperial Defence and Closer Union (D'Egville): 11 *n*, 16 *n*, 31 *n*
Imperial Defence College: 115, 129
Imperial Federation: 33, League, 25 *n*, 28, 34, 42–3, 43 *n*
'Imperial Federation—Naval and Military' (Colomb, J.): 8 *n*, 33 *n*, 44 *n*
Imperial Military Geography (Cole): 24 *n*
Imperialism, Age of: 2, 3, 10
India: 26
Influence of Sea Power Upon History, The (Mahan): 52–3, 52 *n*, 60, 62 *n*, 65, 66, 71 *bis* & *n*, 72 & *n*, 73, 77 *n*, 81; Philip Colomb on, 52–3
Influence of Sea Power Upon the French Revolution and Empire, The (Mahan): 62 *n*, 66, 79 & *nn*, 81
Influences: **1–15**
Intelligence Department of Admiralty, Naval (1882): 31, 46 *n*
Interchangeability of specialist naval officers: 120 & *n*
Invasion: 180–1
Invasions: of British Isles, 53–4, 90; overseas, 54–5, 56, 57
Iris, HMS: 121 & *n*
Iron ships: 20, 24, 34

James, R. R.: 33 *n*
James, Admiral Sir William: 54 *n*, 60 *n*, 119 *nn*
Jellicoe, Admiral Sir John (*later* Earl Jellicoe): 113, 114 *bis* & *n*, 192
Jervis, Admiral Sir John ('Old Jarvie', *later* Earl of St. Vincent, *q.v.*): 101
Jingoism in Britain: 44
Johnson, F. A.: 124 *n*
Jomini (writer on warfare): 63, 69–70, 70 *n*, 164
Journal, Admiral Hughes's: 143 *n*
Journals and Letters of Reginald, Viscount Esher, 1910–15: 190 *n*
Jutland, Battle of (1916): 113, 180, 187

Kemp, Peter: 166 *n*
Kerr, Henry S. (9th Marquess of Lothian): 92 *n*
Key, Admiral Sir Astley Cooper: *see* Cooper-Key

INDEX

King Edward VII, HMS, Class (the 'Wobbly Eight'): 113
Kissinger, Henry A.: 190 & *n*

La France, Angleterre et Naples, 1803-6 (Auriol): 172 *n*
La Gloire (French warship): 20
Laughton, Sir John Knox: 6, 7, 8 & *n*, 9, **12–13**, 14, 34–5, 40 & *n*, 42, 50, 57, 61 *n*, 62 & *n*, 66 & *n*, 78, **83– 109**, 134, 135, 148, 160 *bis*; personal details of, **83–4, 89, 90– 1, 107–8**; and Navy Records Society (*q.v.*), 91–6; his abilities and limitations, 96–7, 101–9; and biography, 96–7, 96 *n*; and naval history, 98–9; and historical fact, 99–101; and Mahan, 99–100; and Corbett, 100–1; his conservatism, 101–2; and contemporary international situation, 102; and nationalism, 102; and democracy, 102, 104; and Maltese, 102; and education of naval officers and civilians, 103; and naval planners, 104; and 'concentration of force', 105; his tactical and strategic thought, 105–7; and Trafalgar, 105–6; final assessment of, 108–9; and trade protection in war, 136
Lee, Sir Sidney: 93 & *n*
Lepawsky, Albert: 63 *n*
Leveson, Admiral Sir Richard: 159 & *n*
Lewis, Michael: 118 *n*, 153 & *n*
Life of Admiral Farragut, The (Mahan): 62 & *n*, 66
Life of Admiral Mahan, The (Taylor): 61 & *n*, 63 *n*, 65 *n*, 67 *n*, 79 *n*, 80 *nn*, 81 *n*
Life of Nelson, The (Mahan): 62 & *n*, 66 & *n*, 74–5, 76 & *nn*
Limited war: 168, 190–1
Limited War: The Challenge to American Strategy (Osgood): 190 *n*
Lisbon Campaign (1589): 154, 157
Livezey, William E.: 60 *n*, 62 *n*, 80 *n*
Lloyd, C. C.: 37 *n*
Lloyd George, David (*later* Earl Lloyd George): 114
London, City of: 21
Lord Randolph Churchill (W.S.C.): 33 *n* (James): 33 *n*

'Lord Selborne's Critics' (Corbett): 149 *n*
Louis XIV, King of France (1643–1715): 100, 161
Lothian, Marquess of: 92
Louisburg (1745): 138
Luce, Commodore (*later* Rear-Admiral) Stephen Bleecker, U.S.N.: 65 & *n*, 68
Luck in warfare: 142, 168–9
Lyall, Sir Alfred Comyn: 93 & *n*

MacGregor, Sir Evan: 120 *n*
Mackesy, Piers: 105 & *n*
Mahan (Puleston): 61 & *n*, 63 *n*, 65 *nn*, 67 *n*, 68 *nn*, 69 *n*
Mahan, Captain (*later* Admiral) Alfred Thayer (1840–1914): 1, 9, 12, 13, 14, 34, 35, 52 *nn*, 53, 57, **60–82**, 89 *n*, 96–100 *passim*, 104, 107, 108, 131 *bis*, 135, 140, 141, 145 *bis*, 149 *bis*, 150, 155 *bis*, 156 *bis*, 160, 163 *n*, 164, 169, 172, 174, 175, 192; and War College, *see* U.S. Naval War College; his influence 60–1, 79–80; his 'Influence' books, 62 & *n*; as historian, 62, 68–77; his three careers, 62–3; personal details of, **63–8, 81**; on the British soldier, 64 *n*; his Prize Essay (1878), 64–5, 68; as biographer, 66 *n*, 76–7; as naval schoolmaster, 67; and Theodore Roosevelt, 67; and technology, 68–9; his sources, 69, 70, 74; and definition and use of word, 'principles', 71–3; on Lord Acton, 74–5, 76, 76–7; and original research, 75; and God's plan, 75; historical merit of his works, 75–6; and Neapolitan Revolution, 76–7; as strategist, 77–9; his influence on naval warfare, 79–80; and Britain's naval predominance, 80; as prose writer, 80–1, 81; as a ship commander, 81; and naval history, 82; and the principles of war, 87; and Laughton, 87; on trade protection in war, 136 & *n*; quoted, 69
Mahan, Professor Dennis Hart (A.T.M.'s father): 63, 68, 69; 'Biographical Sketch of . . .'

Index

(Cullum), 63 *n*
'Mahan: Evangelist of Sea Power' (Sprout): 61 *n*
'Mahan—Historian with a Purpose' (Duncan): 75 *n*, 81 *n*
Mahan on Sea Power (Livezey): 60 *n*, 68 *n*
Mahan Papers: 62 *n*, 66 *n*
Majestic, HMS: 112 & *n*, 118, 119 *n*
Makers of Modern Strategy (ed. Earle, E. M.): 61 *n*
Malaga, Battle of (1704): 161
Malta and the Maltese: 102, 170
Man in the Iron Mask, The: 85 *n*
Manchester Guardian (now *The Guardian*): 68
Manpower in Britain: 21
'Manual of Fleet Evolutions' (Colomb, P.): 37 *n*
Mariner's Mirror: 153 *n*
Marder, Professor Arthur J.: 1 *n*, 36 *n*, 60 *n*, 90 *n*, 110 *n*, 113 *nn*, 114 *nn*, 115 *n*, 116 *n*, 118 *n*, 120 *n*, 123 *n*, 125 *n*, 126 *n*, 127 *nn*, 128 & *nn*, 130 & *n*, 131 *n*, 186 *n*; quoted, 123
Maritime Strategy, Some Principles of (Corbett): see *Some Principles of* . . .
Markham, Sir Clements: 94
Marlborough, Duke of (John Churchill, 1650–1722): 104, 161, 162, 190
Mathematics: and fleet operations, 88; for naval cadets, 116–17
Mathews, Admiral Thomas: 133 & *n*, 135, 142
Mattingly, Garrett; 153 & *n*
May, Vice-Admiral W. H.: 122 *n*
Mediterranean Sea: 160, 161 *bis*, 162, 170, 173
Memoirs of Sir Astley Cooper-Key (Colomb, P.): 38 *n*
Memoirs of the Life and Correspondence of Henry Reeve (Laughton): 96 *n*
Memoirs Relating to Lord Torrington (Laughton): 90 *n*
Memorandum Relative to Sir John Colomb's Work . . . (Colomb Papers): 17 *n*, 25 *n*, 27 *n*
'Mercantile Marine Personnel and Material, On the Conditions of' (Crutchley): 45 *n*
Merchant (trade) navy: 10, 11
Mercury, HMS: 119 *n*

'Military Policy' (Colomb, J., speech): 31 *n*
Miller, Commander Francis S.: 119 *n*
Milne, Admiral Sir Alexander: 30 *n*, 49 & *n*
Minorca: 113 *n*
Mobilization, naval: 45–6
Monk (Corbett): 148
Monk, Admiral George (Duke of Albemarle): 148
Monthly Review: 9, 117 & *n*, 149 & *nn*
Moore, Sir John: 69
Morning Post (since incorporated in *Daily Telegraph*): 183 *n*
Morse Code: 37
Mountbatten, Admiral of the Fleet Louis Alexander (1st Marquess of Milford Haven): 91 *n*
Muller, Captain (German): 187

N.M.M.: see National Maritime Museum
Napoleon Bonaparte (1769–1821): 24, 45, 77 *n*, 105, 106, 170, 171, 173, 191; his two main principles, 175–6
Napoleon et Angleterre, 1803–13 (Coquelle): 172 *n*
Napoleon III (President and Emperor of France, 1848–70): 18
National Maritime Museum (N.M.M.): 114 *n*, 121 *nn*, 123 *n*, 126 *nn*, 127 *nn*
National Policy and Naval Strength (Richmond): 131 & *n*
National Service League: 96 & *n*, 180 *n*
'National Study of Naval History, The' (Laughton): 99 *n*, 103 *nn*
Nationalism: and the British, 44; colonial, 129 *n*
Naval Administration, 1827–92 (Briggs): 2 *n*
Naval Administration and Warfare: 71 *n*, 74 *n*, 75 *nn*
Naval and Military Essays: 184
Naval and Military Magazine, Illustrated: 38, 52
'Naval and Military Signals' (Colomb, P.): 38 *n*
'Naval Armaments' (Laughton): 104 *nn*
Naval Defence Act (1889): 1, 103
'Naval Defences of the United Kingdom, The' (Colomb, P.): 46–8

Naval Essay Prize (R.U.S.I.): Philip Colomb's, 39–42
Naval History of Great Britain (William James, 6 vols.): 60 *n*
'Naval Intelligence and Protection of Commerce in War' (Colomb, P.): 31 *n*
'Naval Mobilization' (Colomb, P.): 46 *n*
Naval officers of xix century, British: 107
Naval Operations (Corbett): 113 *n*, 150 *n*
Naval Policy ('Barfleur'): 14
Naval power: *see* Sea power
Naval Review: 127–8 & *nn*
'Naval Staff History, Necessity for Compilation of a' (Dewar): 126 *n*
Naval Strategy (Mahan): 65 *n*, 71, 72 & *nn*, 73 & *n*, 77 *n*, 78 *nn*, 80 *n*, 150, 163 *n*
Naval supremacy: *see* Command of the sea
'Naval Tactics' (Fremantle): 45 *n*
Naval War College (American): *see* United States Naval War College
Naval War Colleges (British), Greenwich and Portsmouth: 113, 124, 127, 149, 160, 183
Naval War Staff: 103, 122–4, 125 *bis*, 126
Naval Warfare (Colomb, P.): 38 & *n*, 52 *bis*, 53 *nn*, 53–9, 54 *nn*
Navies, relative strengths of: 2
Navigation Committee: 119, 120; members (*named*), 119–20 *nn*
Navigation School of R.N.: 119, 121
Navy and the Nation, The (Thursfield & Sydenham): 13 *n*
Navy and the Slave Trade, The (Lloyd): 37 *n*
Navy as an Instrument of Sea Power, The (Richmond, ed. Hughes): 144–6 & *nn*
Navy in India, The (Richmond): 131, 142–4 & *nn*; sources for, 143 *n*
Navy in the War of William III, 1689–1697, The (Ehrman): 140 *n*, 161, 162 *n*, 191
Navy in the War of 1739–48, The (Richmond): 12 *n*, 112 *n*, 131, 132–42 & *nn*
Navy League: 99

Navy in Britain, The (Lewis): 118 *n*, 153 *n*
Navy Records Society: 9, 84 *bis*, 113, 148, 151, 172, 184 *bis*; formation and achievements of, **91–6**
Navy, Royal: *see* Royal Navy
'Neapolitan Republicans and Nelson's Accusers' (Mahan): 76
Nelson, Admiral Lord (Horatio) (1758–1805): 19, 27, 40, 75, 76 *bis*, 86, 90, 96, 100, 105, 107, 140, 142, 149, 170 *bis*, 174 *n*, 183; and 'Emma', 101–2; his strategic sense, 171; and cruisers, 178
Nelson, HMS: 111 & *n*
Nelson Memorial, The (Laughton) 96–7
Nelson's Letters and Despatches (Laughton): 89 *n*, 90 *n*
Neumann, W. L.: 61 *n*
New Century Review: 29 *n*
Newbolt, Sir Henry: 9
Newcastle, Duke of: 132, 165–6, 168
Nicholas, Sir Harry: 97
Nicholson, General Sir Lothian: 48 & *n*, 50
Nile, Battle of the (1798): 72
Nineteenth Century (and After): 48 *n*, 149 *n*
Norfolk, Duke of: 92
Norris, Admiral Sir John: 133, 135 & *n*
'Notes on the Last Great Naval War' (Laughton): 101 *n*
Nuclear Weapons and Foreign Policy (Kissinger): 190 *n*
Nugent, Colonel Sir Charles, R. E.: 47 & *n*

Offence and defence: 175–6
Old Oak (James): 54 *n*
Oliver, Commander (*later* Admiral) Sir Henry: 118, 119 & *n*, 120–1
Ollivier, M.: 29 *n*
On War (Clausewitz, *q.v.*): 150
Oppenheim, M.: 151 & *n*, 191
'Organization Man': 103
Origins of Imperial Defence, The (Gibbs): 43 *n*
Osborne, Royal Naval College (Isle of Wight): 120 *n*
Osgood, R. E.: 190 & *n*
Other Armada, The (Patterson): 143 *n*
Ottley, Captain Sir Charles, R. N.: 124 & *n*

Index

Pall Mall Gazette: 43 & *nn*
Papers (Richmond): 114 *n*
Papers Relating to the Loss of Minorca (Richmond): 113 *n*
Papers Relating to the Navy during the Spanish War (1585–87), (*ed.* Corbett): 151 *n*
Pares, Richard: 135 & *n*
Parkes, O.: 3 *n*, 20 *n*, 24 *n*, 40 *nn*
Parliament: 2, 8, 28–9, 29 *n*, 30, 32
Parliamentary Debates (Hansard): 31 *nn*, 32 *n*
Parliamentary Papers: 43 *n*, 49 *n*
Patterson, A. Temple: 143 *n*
Pax Britannica: 10, 80
Peninsular War (Napier): 69
Pentagon, the: 76
Phipps-Hornby, Admiral Sir Geoffrey T.: 91 & *n*
Pitt, Barrie: 187 *n*
Pitt, William, the Elder (Earl of Chatham), (1708–78): 104, 132, **165**, 166 & *nn*
Pitt, William, the Younger (1759–1806): 79, 170, 174 *n*
Planning for naval warfare (*see also* Admiralty: planning): 125–6, 145
Plunkett, Commander the Hon. R. A. R.: 127
Policy, naval (British): 1 *n*, 10–11
Political control of the services, 26, 27, 28, 33, 34, 41, 50, 75–6, 103–5, 141, 145, 153–4, 191
Portrait of an Admiral (Marder): 110 *n*, 113 *nn*, 114 *nn*, 115 *n*, 123 *n*, 126 *n*, 127 *nn*, 128 *nn*, 130 *n*, 131 *n*
'Practical Character of the Naval War College, The' (Mahan): 60 *n*, 69 *n*
Presidential Address . . . American Historical Association (Mahan, 1902): 71 & *n*, 73
Presidential Address . . . Naval War College, U.S.A. (Mahan, 1888): 65 *n*, 67 *n*
Presidential Address . . . U.S.N.I. (Mahan, 1892): 60 *n*, 69 *n*
Press, the: 2, 8, 28, 34
Primacy of the navy: 26, 27, 28, 34
Prince George, HMS: 121 & *n*
Principles of war (from history): 86–7, 105 *bis*
Proceedings of the Royal Colonial Institute: 7, 30 *n*, 34 *n*
Projectiles: 5
Protection of our Commerce and Distribution of our Naval Forces . . ., Th (Colomb, J., anon.): 16, 17 *n* 20–4 *nn*, 26 *n*, 27 *nn*
Prussia: 18, 20
Public interest in the navy: 3, 10, 41, 90, 103
Public Records Office: 88, 89
Puleston, W. D.: 61 & *n*, 63 *n*, 65 *nn*, 67 *n*, 68 *nn*, 69 *n*, 81 *n*

Quarterly Review: 99 *n*, 100 *n*
Quebec, capture of (1759): 167–8, 176
'Queen Elizabeth and the Portugal Expedition of 1589' (Wernham): 13 *n*, 152 *n*, 154 *n*

R.C.I.: *see* Royal Colonial Institute
R.M.A.: *see* Royal Marine Artillery
R.U.S.I.: *see* Royal United Service Institution
Racer, HMS (R. M. C. Osborne): 120 *nn*
Raleigh, Sir Walter (*c.* 1552–1618): 157 & *n*, 158
Ramillies, HMS: 112 & *n*, 120 *n*
Realities of Naval History (Tunstall): 192
'Recent Attacks on the Admiralty' (Corbett): 149 *n*
Reeve, Henry (editor): 9, 96
'Relations between Local Fortifications and a Moving Navy, The' (Colomb, P.): 48 & *nn*, 90 *n*
Revenge, HMS: 119 *n*
Revival, naval (1889–): 2, 10
Richmond, Elsa (*née* Bell): 112 *n*
Richmond, Admiral Sir Herbert William: 12 & *n*, 14, 94, 97, 108, **110–46**, 120 *nn*, 149, 152, 185, 188, 192; his methods, 12; personal details of, **110–11, 121–2**; afloat and ashore, 111–15; at Cambridge, 115–16; his early naval career, 116–17; and training of young officers, 117, 123 *n*; at Admiralty, 118 *ff.*; and navigation, 118–19; and Fisher, 117–24; appointments refused and missed, 121, 127; and Admiralty organization, 124; and Naval War Staff, 122–5; and Naval War Course College,

127; and *Naval Review*, 127–8; and Imperial Defence, 129; and air power, 130; his extra-service propaganda, 130–1; as historian, 131–46; his *Navy in the War of 1739–48* (*q.v.*), 132–42 & *nn*; and Admiral Mathews (1744), 133; and defence of trade, 135–8; and combined operations, 138, 144; and trade war and blockade, 138–40; and the 'big battle', 142; his *Navy in India* (*q.v.*), 142–4 & *nn*; and bases, 144; and human factor in war, 144; his *Statesmen and Sea Power* (*q.v.*), 144–6 & *nn*; his *Navy as Instrument of Sea Power* (*q.v.*), 144–6 & *nn*; and complacency, 145; and Baltic nations, 145; final appreciation of, 145–6

Richmond, Sir William Blake, R.A.: 110–11, 111 *n*, 116

Roberts, Field-Marshal Earl, V.C. (1832–1914): 7, 96 & *n*, 180 *n*

Robinson, Admiral Sir R. Spencer: 47 & *n*

Rochefort raid (1757): 167

Rodney, Admiral Sir George Brydges: 105

'Rodney and the Navy of the Eighteenth Century' (Laughton): 99 *nn*

Roosevelt, Franklin Delano (President, U.S.A., 1933–45): 61 *n*

Roosevelt, Theodore (President, U.S.A., 1901–09): 62, **67** & *nn*

Rose, Professor J. Holland: 115, 135 & *n*, 172 & *n*

Roskill, Captain S. W., R.N. (official naval historian): 189 *bis*, 189 *nn*, 191, 192

Royal Academy, The: 111; *Proceedings of* . . . , 1946, 110 *n*

Royal Colonial Institute (*later* Royal Empire Society, *q.v.*; *now* Royal Commonwealth Society, *q.v.*): 7 *bis*, 7 *n*, 9, 28, 29 *n*; *Proceedings of* . . . , 7, 30 *n*, 34 *n*

Royal Commonwealth Society (*formerly* Royal Empire Society, *q.v.*; *and* Royal Colonial Institute, *q.v*): 7

Royal Empire Society (*formerly* Royal Colonial Institute, *q.v.*; *now* Royal Commonwealth Society, *q.v.*): 7 *n*

Royal Engineers: 37; *History of the Corps of* . . . (Baker-Brown), 51 *n*

Royal Historical Society: 84; *Transactions of* . . . , 99 *n*

Royal Institution: 84

Royal Marine Artillery: 16 *bis*, 24

Royal Marines: 17

Royal Military College of Canada: 84 *n*

Royal Naval College, Greenwich (*formerly at* Portsmouth): 38, 42, 83, 84, 87, 97, 98, 149, 160, 192

Royal Naval College, Osborne (Isle of Wight): 120 *n*

Royal Navy: 10, 12, 13, 50 *n*, 98; public interest in, 3, 10, 41, 90, 103; and army, 106, 171; and defence of U.K., 18–20; and *La Gloire*, 20; primacy of, 26, 27, 28, 34, 59; and City brokers, 45; historians of, 70; Hannay's history of, 99; function of (Laughton), 104; after Trafalgar, 106; of xviii century, 107; and mercantile prosperity, 137; overstretched (1778–83), 143; not a decisive offensive weapon, 171; its purpose in 1805, 174; in First World War, 179, 185–8; in Second World War, 188; 'a part of the nation', 191

Royal Navy, History of the (Clowes): 13 *n*, 67 *n*

Royal Navy 1217–1815, Short History of the (Hannay, 2 vols.): 14 *n*, 99

Royal Sovereign, HMS: Class, 3 *n*

Royal United Service Institution (R.U.S.I.): 4 *n*, 7, **7–9**, 28, 34, 38 *ter*, 39, 44, 51 & *n*, 54, 58, 84, 85, 87 & *n*, 90, 126; *Proceedings of* . . . , 90 *n*

R.U.S.I. *Journal*: 8 *nn*, 31 *n*, 33 *n*, 36 *n*, 39 *nn*, 40 *n*, 44 *n*, 45 *nn*, 46 *nn*, 48 *nn*, 50 *nn*, 51 *nn*, 62 & *n*, 86 *n*, 87 *nn*, 90 *n*, 101 *nn*

Ruck-Keene, Commander William C. E.: 120 *n*

Runciman, Walter (*later* Viscount Runciman): 126 & *n*

Rupert, Prince: 162

Ruskin, John (1819–1900): 111

Russell, P. Dale: 120 *n*

Index

Russia: 44, 77, 170, 173
Ryder, Vice-Admiral Sir A.: 37

Sadowa, Battle of (Königgrätz, 1866): 18, 20
Sail, age of: 1-5
Sail to Steam, From (Mahan): 60 *n*, 62-6 *nn*, 68 *n*, 69 *n*, 79 *n*, 80 *n*
St. Vincent, Admiral of the Fleet the Earl of (John Jervis): 46, 54 & *n*, 101
Salisbury, Marquess of (1830-1903): 43 & *n*, 50
Samuel Pepys and the Royal Navy (Tanner): 140 *n*
Saxe-Coburg and Gotha, Duke of: 93 & *n*
Scares, naval: 103
Schurman, D. M.: 16 *n*, 26 *n*, 30 *n*
Science in fleet operations: 86
'Scientific Study of Naval History, The' (Laughton): 8 *n*, 40 *n*, 85, 86 *n*, 87 *n*, 98 *n*, 105 *n*
Scientists: 4
Scribner's Magazine (U.S.A.): 9
Sea power: American, 102; British, 80, 85-6, 106, 145, 151, 161, 164, 170, 191; Japanese, 102
Sea power: basis and true nature of, 56, 140 *n*, 156, 160, 188, 192; and foreign policy, 145; limitation of (Corbett), 156; and land campaigns, 161; and air power, 188; and limited war, 191
Sea Power in its Relation to the War of 1812 (Mahan): 62 *n*, 67, 70 *n*, 81, 'Seek out and destroy!' . . . How?: 179
Seeley, Sir John R. (historian): 74, 92 *bis*, 92 *n*
Selborne, Earl of: 120
Selborne Education Scheme for R.N. (1902): 118, 119-20; Committee for (members *named*), 120 *n*
Select Documents relating to the Third Coalition against France, 1804-5 (Rose): 172 *n*
Seven Years War (1756-63): 164, 165, 176, 177, 191
Seymour, Rear-Admiral Sir Michael: 83 *n*
Ship-building, naval: 2, 3, 79-80, 103, 129, 188
'Ship Lights at Sea' (Colomb, P.): 39 *n*

Ship of the Line in Battle, The (Custance): 14 *n*
'Ships *versus* forts' controversy: *see* Fortifications (fixed)
Short History of the Royal Navy, 1217-1815 (Hannay, 2 vols.): 14 *n*
'Side-operations' (in conjunction with grand strategy): 177, 189
'Sidelights on Mahan' (Ellicott): 68 *n*
Signalling, fleet, 37, 38-9
Signals and Instructions, 1776-94 (Corbett): 184
Simmons, General Sir John Lintorn: 48 & *n*, 49 & *nn*, 50 *n*
Singapore: 24
Slade, Captain Edmond J. W., R.N.: 124 & *n*, 125
Slave Catching in the Indian Ocean (Colomb, P.): 37 *n*
Slave-trade: 37
Small vessels in xviii century, lack of: 140
'Smaller Navies' (Richmond): 115 *n*
Snagge, Geoffrey: 17 *n*
Societies *before* Navy Records Society: 92, 93
Society for the Propagation of Sea Military Knowledge: 127
Some Principles of Maritime Strategy (Corbett): 18 *n*, 50 *n*, 150 & *n*, 174-82 & *nn*, 183, 183-4; appreciation of, 181-2; its reception, 183; and Navy Records Society, 184
South African (Boer) War (1899-1902): 29
Specialization: 4, 5; and interchangeability in R.N., 120 & *n*
Spee, Admiral von: 113 *n*, 186, 187
'Speed as a Factor in Naval Warfare' (Fremantle): 45 *n*
Spencer, Earl: 92, 93, 94, 184
Spencer, John Poyntz (5th Earl Spencer): 92 *n* (*See also next above*.)
Spencer Papers, The (ed. Corbett): 94 & *n*, 184 *n*
Sprout, Margaret Tuttle: 61 *n*
'Staff Histories' (Corbett): 184 *n*
Stanford, Peter Marsh: 147 *n*, 149 *n*
State Papers Relating to the Defeat of the Spanish Armada (Laughton): 93, 94 *n*

INDEX

Statesmen and Sea Power (Richmond): 130 *n*, 137 *n*, 144–6 & *nn*
Stead, W. T.: 43 & *n*
Steam, age of: 5 *ff.*
Steam propulsion: 20, 24, 34
Steam Navy of the United States, The (Bennett): 64 *nn*, 66 *n*
Stone, Captain (*later* Brigadier-General) Francis G., R.A.: 48 & *n*, 50 & *n*
Strategic Air Offensive Against Germany, The (Webster and Frankland): 130 *n*
Strategy (general) and national policy: 176
Strategy, naval: 3, 4, 6, 8, 10–13 *passim*, 71, 72, 124, 143, 149; in xviii and xix centuries, 19–20, 143; and the army, 19, 20, 22, 26, 30–1, 144 *bis*; and national policy, 75–6, 142, 143; and duty of commanders, 142; Elizabethan, 151, 152; in Mediterranean (xvii century), 161–2; of Trafalgar campaign, 171–2, 174
Strategy of Sea Power, The (Roskill): 189 *nn*
Struggle for Imperial Unity, The (Tyler): 34 *n*
'Struggle with Napoleon, The' (Rose): 135 *n*
Studies in Naval History (Laughton): 85 *n*, 87 *n*, 90 *n*
Study of British Imperial History, The (Walker): 115 *n*
'Study of Naval History, The' (Laughton): 62 *n*, 87 *n*, 93 *n*
Study of War, A (Custance): 14 *n*
Submarine warfare: 11 *n*, 187–8
'Subordination in Historical Treatment' (Mahan): 71 *n*, 74 & *n*, 75 *nn*
Successors of Drake, The (Corbett): 100 *n*, **156–60** & *nn*, 164, 171
Suffren, Admiral le Bailli de (French): 85, 105, 131, 142, 143, 144
Sydenham of Combe, Lord: 13, 14, 99 *n*, 124 *n*, 132, 183; and Corbett, 150 & *n*
Sydney, HMAS: 187

Tactics, naval: 3, 4, 8, 38, 45 *n*, 71, 72, 86, 143, 149, 184; Nelson's, 27; Elizabethan, 152–3

Tanner, Joseph Robson (historian): 96 & *n*, 140 *nn*
Taylor, Charles Carlisle: 61 & *n*, 63 *n*, 65 *n*, 67 *n*, 79 *n*, 80 *nn*, 81 *n*
Technology and fleet operations: 88
Theory and practice in military (and naval) operations: 174–5
Three-deckers (men-of-war): 3
'Three Naval Cranks . . .' (Ellicott): 66 *n*, 68 *n*
Thunderer, HMS: 24 *n*, 38, 40
Thursfield, Lieut.-Commander (*later* Captain) H. G., R.N.: 110 *n*, 127
Thursfield, J. R. (*The Times* correspondent): 13, 14, 93
Times, The: 13, 36, 43, 48, 70 *n*, 83 *n*, 91, 108, 115 & *n*
Torrington, Admiral the Earl of: 56 & *n*, 90
Toulon, Battle of: 133, 142
Trade, Imperial (overseas): 21; defence of, 23, 27
Trade protection in war: 135–8, 163, 178, 188
Trade war and blockade: 138–40, 154–5, 160, 179
Traditions: British attitude to, 28 *bis*, 39; dangers and value of, 86
Trafalgar, Battle of (1805): 105–6, 170
Treasury control (of expenditure): 3, 104
Trevelyan, Charles P.: 126 & *n*
Trevelyan, George Macaulay: 85 & *n*, 110 *n*, 112 *n*, 116; *quoted*, 85 *n*
'Tribute to Mahan as a Social Scientist, A' (Lepawsky): 63 *n*
'Truth about the Coaling Stations, The' (Stead): 43 & *n*
'Truth about the Navy, What is the?' (Stead): 43 & *n*
Tryon, Rear-Admiral Sir George: 25 *n*
Tudor Strategy and tactics (naval): 151, 152–3
Tunstall, Brian: 167 & *nn*, 180 *n*, 192
Tunstall, W. C. B.: 18 *n*, 21 *n*, 22 *n*, 147 *n*, 151 *n*; Mrs., 147 *n*
Turner, Frederick Jackson (historian): 74
'Two-power (naval) Standard': 3, 30 *n*
Tyler, J. E.: 34 *n*
Types of Naval Officers . . . (Mahan): 67 & *n*

Index

U.S.N.I.: see United States Naval Institution
United Services Magazine: 85
United States Naval Institution: 60 *n*, 65
United States Naval War College (Newport, R.I.): 64, 65 & *nn*, 66, 67 & *n*, 68, 69, 70; Mahan's address on, 60 *n*
United States Navy: 61, 63

Venice (1615–19): 161
Vere, Sir Francis (1560–1609): 157 & *n*, 158
Vere Harmsworth Chair of Imperial and Naval History at Cambridge: 115
Vernon, Admiral Edward: 138 & *n*, 141
Vernon, HMS: 111 *n*
Vesey-Hamilton, Admiral R.: *quoted*, 34
Views of the Battles of the Third Dutch War (ed. Corbett): 184 *n*
Vigo (1718): 56
Villeneuve, Admiral (French): 171, 174 *n*
Vindictive, HMS: 112 *n*
Volunteers, the (late 1850s): 18

Waddington, Richard: 164
Walker, E. A.: 115 *n*
Walker, Major G. R., R.E.: 51 *bis*, 51 *nn*
War and diplomacy: see Diplomacy
War at Sea, The (Roskill): 192
War Cabinet, Imperial: 114
War College, American: see United States Naval War College
War Course College, British: see Naval War Colleges
War in the Mediterranean, The (Mackesy): 105 *n*
War, limited and unlimited: 168, 176, 190–1
War not logical (Corbett): 179
War Office: 6, 26, 29, 30 *bis*, 31, 34, 45, 46, 47, 49 *n*, 76
Warfare, economic: 79
Warfare in xviii and xix centuries: 19–20

Warfare, military (on land): traditional principles of, 17
Warfare, modern (technical): 11, 28
Warfare, naval: its effect on politics, 95; principles of, 5–6, 11, 18, 23, 45, 54, 55
Warren, Vice-Admiral Sir Peter: 138 & *n*, 139
Warrior, HMS: 20
Warships, functions of: 2, 4
Webster, Sir Charles *and* Noble Frankland: 130 *n*
Wellington, Duke of (1769–1852): 18 *n*
Wemyss, Admiral Sir Rosslyn Erskine (*later* Lord Wester Wemyss): 114 & *n*, 120 *n*
Wernham, R. B.: 13 *n*, 152 & *n*, 154 & *n*
West Point (U.S.A.): 63, 68, 69
Westminster, Statute of (1931): 34
'What is the Truth about the Navy?' (Stead): 43 & *n*
Wilkinson, Spencer: 183 & *n*
William III, King (1688–1702): 104, 161 *bis*, 162, 191
William Pitt, Earl of Chatham (Tunstall): 167 *nn*
Williamson, J. A.: 155 *n*, 156 *n*
Wilson, Woodrow (President, U.S.A., 1913–21): 61 *n*
'Wobbly Eight' the: 113
Wolfe, General James: 181
Wolseley, Viscount (Garnet J.), (1833–1913): 51
'Work of Sir Julian Corbett in the Dreadnought Era, The' (Stanford) 147 *n*, 149 *n*
World Crisis, 1914–1918, The (Churchill): 186 *nn*
World War, First (1914–18): 12, 76, 78, 95, 125 *bis*, 128, 134, 142, 144, 149, 150, 177 & *n*, 179 *bis*, 185, 187–90 *passim*; naval history of, 184
World War, Second (1939–45): 76, 78, 144, 185, 188–9, 189, 192
Writers on naval topics: 1–15

York, Duke of (*later* King George V): 93
Yorke, Sir Henry F. R.: 93 & *n*